Cyber Warfare

Its Implications on National Security

Cyber Warfare

Its Implications on National Security

by

Col Sanjeev Relia

(Established 1870)

United Service Institution of India

New Delhi

Vij Books India Pvt Ltd

New Delhi (India)

Published by

Vij Books India Pvt Ltd
(Publishers, Distributors & Importers)
2/19, Ansari Road
Delhi – 110 002
Phones: 91-11-43596460, 91-11-47340674
Fax: 91-11-47340674
e-mail: vijbooks@rediffmail.com

ISBN (PB) : 9789385563096 (2016)

Contents

List of Tables, Figures and Maps

Figures

Tables

Maps

Foreword

Cyberspace has become an integral part of our daily lives and our dependence on its underlying infrastructure is ever increasing. Unfortunately as our dependence has grown, so have hostile cyberattacks on the critical information infrastructure by network predators. The lack of cyber security as a core element in the initial design stages of such infrastructure makes them vulnerable to different types of attacks. Convergence within the computer and telecom technology sectors is also challenging underlying concepts of traditional infrastructures.

In today's global environment, national security is not only measured in economic and military terms, but also a nation's social advancement and reliance upon efficient, robust and secure information, electrical power, transportation and other such critical infrastructures. Such high dependence on ICT has resulted in the cyberspace becoming the fifth domain of warfare. It is a domain, where a war can be waged through the virtual medium, without the two nations being actually at war. In cyberspace warfare domain, traditional and conventional national security measures in term of doctrine and security services force structure will not work as effectively as they do in the physical world. Hence, there would be a need to evolve new doctrines and create organisations which can handle such form of warfare. A number of nations have already done this. The United States Armed Forces Cyber Command is an example of how a nation has tasked its armed forces in defending the country against cyberattacks, and of how Department of Defence will integrate cyber capabilities into military operations. India too needs to create such structures which can defend her against both war time as well as peace time cyberattacks.

The book, "Cyber Warfare – It's Implications on National Security" by Colonel Sanjeev Relia is an in-depth analysis of such critical aspects. It gives a detailed account of how India's critical Info-infrastructure is threatened from the cyberspace and what actions need to be taken to protect it. The book also ventures into the realms of strategic and operational cyber warfare and describes each of them in detail. It makes recommendations about policy and strategy framework along with organisational structures required at the national level to counter the threat of cyberwar. Colonel Sanjeev Relia has also delved into the aspect of cyber warfare and the Indian Armed Forces and has made practical recommendations on the kind of organisational structure which the armed forces need to create to counter the threat of cyber warfare.

The book is an important resource in terms of its exhaustiveness and analytical insight on a contemporary subject of national and military importance. It will prove to be an indispensable compendium for every student of Cyber Warfare in the times to come

August 2015

Lt Gen S P Kochhar
AVSM**, SM, VSM (Retired)

Acknowledgements

Land, sea and air warfare has been on for a number of years now. All three have gone through an evolution process which has been studied in great detail. Lessons drawn from various campaigns fought in the past have been imbibed to augment the war waging potential of powerful nations. Even space warfare has been on for some time now and therefore has been studied in good amount of detail by scholars. Growth of cyberspace and its invasion into every aspect of life is a relatively new phenomenon. Being a technology intensive domain, most research work has been done on technical aspects of cyber security and forensics of cyber crime. Not many studies have been conducted on how a war can be waged through the cyberspace. I therefore feel privileged to have been given this opportunity by the Indian Army to study various nuances of cyber warfare and its impact on India's national security. I place on record my gratitude to United Service Institution of India (USI of India), New Delhi for accepting my research proposal and providing me with a stimulating and thought provoking research environment.

I would like to place on record my sincere thanks and gratitude to Lieutenant General PK Singh, PVSM, AVSM (Retired), Director, USI for encouraging me and providing all the support for my research. But for his timely help, I would have never got the opportunity of interacting with renowned scholars in the field of cyber warfare at the Centre for Strategic and International Studies (CSIS), Washington and East West Institute (EWI), New York. Besides the research work, he also encouraged me to attain additional qualifications in this field, such as Post Graduate Diploma in Cyber Law and Certification in Ethical Hacking (CEH). Both these topics helped me enormously in understanding the finer aspects of cyber warfare. I would also like to thank Major General YK Gera (Retired), former Consultant & Head (Research) and Major General BK Sharma, AVSM, SM** (Retired), Deputy Director (Research) and Head of

Centre for Strategic Studies and Simulation, USI for providing a conducive research environment in the faculty. Special thanks to General Sharma for having started the USI blog and encouraging us to write for the Strategic Perspective and USI Journal. Writing for these journals helped us hone our creative skills especially for first time authors like me.

Two people, without whose guidance and constant course correction, this study would not have been possible are Lieutenant General SP Kochhar, AVSM**, SM, VSM (Retired) and Major General (Dr) GS Lamba, VSM (Retired), my guides for the research work. Their advice and suggestions helped me tremendously is shaping the book. I also wish to thank Lieutenant General Davinder Kumar, PVSM, VSM** (Retired) for sparing his valuable time for me whenever I requested for it and helping me understand the subject. I also greatly benefited from numerous talks delivered by him at various cyber forums in New Delhi.

I wish to express my gratitude to three key individuals associated with this book. The first is Brigadier MU Nair, DACIDA (DIARA) who reviewed my work and gave me a large number of valuable suggestions. Second is Major Sonali Gupta (Retired) who helped me in editing this book. Without her support, this book would have never been submitted on time for publication. Lastly is Tishya Relia, my daughter who designed the cover for the book. Together we deliberated on a large number of covers designed by her before finally selecting this one.

My job would be incomplete if I did not thank all my fellow research scholars at USI of India. The thought provoking discussions everyday in the morning over a cup of tea have been very useful in understanding a large number of issues associated with the topic of my research. My special thanks to Doctor Roshan Khanijo, Brigadier Saif Ul Islam Khan and Colonel Rohit Mehrotra for all the suggestions, comments and recommendations which were of great help. I also wish to thank all my friends who constantly encouraged me to go on and do a good job.

Lastly, I must accept that nothing would have been possible without the support and help of my wife Sonia Relia, an author herself. Her belief in me constantly motivated me to go on with the research work.

New Delhi
Aug 2015

Sanjeev Relia

Abbreviations

3G	Third Generation
AFCC	Armed Forces Cyber Command
AMI	Advanced Metering Infrastructure
BSNL	Bharat Sanchar Nigam Limited
C4ISR	Command, Control, Communications, Computers, Intelligence, Surveillance and Reconnaissance
CCD COE	Cooperative Cyber Defence Centre of Excellence
CCS	Cabinet Committee on Security
CERT	Computer Emergency Response Team
CII	Critical Information Infrastructure
CIIP	Critical Information Infrastructure Protection
CISO	Chief Information Security Officer
CNP	Comprehensive National Power
CVE	Common Vulnerabilities Exposures
DDoS	Distributed Denial of Service
DHS	Department of Homeland Security
DoD	Department of Defence
DoS	Denial of Service
DSCI	Data Security Council of India

DTRA	Defense Threat Reduction Agency
EM spectrum	Electro Magnetic Spectrum
EMP	Electro Magnetic Pulse
GPS	Global Positioning System
HTTP	Hypertext Transfer Protocol
ICS	Industrial Control System
ICT	Information and Communication Technologies
IED	Improvised Explosive Device
IIS	Internet Information Server
IoT	Internet of Things
IP	Internet Protocol
ISIS	Islamic State in Iraq and Syria
ISO	International Organisation for Standardisation
IT	Information Technology
ITAA 2008	Information Technology Act Amendment 2008
LERF	Large Early Release Frequency
NATO	North Atlantic Treaty Organisation
NCCC	National Cyber Coordination Centre
NCIIPC	National Critical Information Infrastructure Protection Centre
NCSP 2013	National Cyber Security Policy 2013
NCW	Network Centric Warfare
NTRO	National Technical Research Organisation
OS	Operating System

PLA GSD	People's Liberation Army General Staff Department
R&D	Research and Development
RMA	Revolution in Military Affairs
SCADA	Supervisory Control and Data Acquisition
SIGINT	Signal Intelligence
SMTP	Simple Mail Transfer Protocol
TBA	Tactical Battle Area
TCP	Transmission Control Protocol
UAV	Unmanned Aerial Vehicle
UDP	User Datagram Protocol
UNICRI	United Nations Integrated Crime and Justice Research Institute
US CYBERCOM	United States Cyber Command
VoIP	Voice over IP
WANK	Worms Against Nuclear Killers
WEP	Wired Equivalent Privacy
WPA	Wi-Fi Protected Access

Introduction

"I know not with what weapons World War III will be fought, but World War IV will be fought with sticks and stones."

— *Albert Einstein*

"We worried for decades about WMDs - Weapons of Mass Destruction. Now it is time to worry about a new kind of WMDs - Weapons of Mass Disruption."

— *John Mariotti*

The last two decades have seen a revolution of a new kind - information revolution. It is a revolution where awesome computing power of computers and other mobile devices is networked over global telecom highways. This has lead to the use of Information Technology in every sector of human activity be it communication, banking, trading, learning and teaching, entertainment, socializing, government and management. Cyberspace has invaded all spheres of our lives. Today a car has more computing and data handling components than the space vehicle that landed the first men on the moon and brought them back. By the beginning of 2015, 39% of the world's population or 2.8 billion people were connected to the Internet. In India, by March 2015, there were 99.20 million broadband Internet users. This figure is estimated to have crossed 100 million in June 2015. While it took 10 years for India to get her first 10 million users, in the very next decade we had hit the 100 million mark. Today, we are adding five million new users every month which should take the user base in India to 500 million by 2018-19. This implies that by the end of 2018 -19, over forty five percent of population of our country would be online. Every second person in the country would either be shopping, trading or gaming online. With the launch of Digital India which aims to digitally empower all citizens; which talks about provisioning of digital infrastructure as a utility to every citizen and promises to provide governance and services on demand to the citizens of India, the reach of Internet is going to increase manifold and will cover the rural framework of the country too.

While the rapid spread of network services in the country is going to fuel growth and development of India in a big manner, there is one challenge associated with such services which needs to be taken care of as we reach out to more and more people. The challenge is to ensure the security of cyberspace. Unless we ensure safe and secure passage of data across millions of users in the country, along with the growth of cyberspace, we will also see an exponential growth in cases of cybercrime, cyber espionage, cyber sabotage and attack on our infrastructure dependent on cyberspace. In short, while we move towards being digital, we will also have to prepare ourselves for a new form of warfare — cyber warfare.

When internet was created and network protocols were being developed, no one had imagined that a new domain for warfare was being created. A battle space where attacks would be executed using digital bit streams and pings, cyber espionage would be the order of the day and not only people but systems could be subverted. Cyberspace was largely designed to function on trust. Its relative simplicity enabled its seamless scaling up over the last three decades to support millions of users for virtually every aspect of life. But because of its simple design, not only individuals but even nation states have taken advantage and used it for destructive activities.

Cyberspace has some very unique characteristics. The more networked you become as a nation, the more vulnerable you become to cyberattacks. Also, the might of powerful nations can be challenged by a small unheard of country or even a handful of individuals. For example the June 2015 CIA hack which saw one of the biggest cyber espionage cases ever reported. As accused by the US Government, Chinese hackers reportedly broke into the Office of Personnel Management network which holds the personal data of the agents working for the CIA. If the media reports are to be believed, CIA systems containing information related to the background investigations of over four million "current, former and prospective" federal employees, and others for whom background checks were conducted was breached. What the hackers blatantly exhibited to the world was that the big and the mighty are just as vulnerable in the cyberspace and that a group of motivated men or a nation state, all are equally capable of waging a cyberwar.

Cyber security and cyber warfare are often talked of in the same breath by a large number of people. While cyber security is about securing a medium that is today vital for our existence, cyber warfare is much more than that. Cyber warfare is about state sponsored actors exploiting the vulnerabilities of the cyberspace for a number of reasons, thereby destabilising the very fabric of cyberspace. What makes it even more complex is that till day there is no universally accepted definition of the term 'cyber warfare'. That is the reason that the debate on the very existence of cyberwar is split down the middle between those who are convinced about the inevitability of cyberwar and those who are of the opinion that the dangers of cyberspace are unnecessarily magnified. This study is therefore trying to establish what cyber warfare is and does it pose any threat to India's national security?

The very concept of national security seems to have undergone a change in the last two decades. Today national security does not mean just the security of our land borders, skies and territorial waters. National security today encompasses military security, political security, economic security, environmental security, security of energy and natural resources and cyber security. The research work on the topic of "*Cyber Warfare: It's Implications on National Security*" was undertaken with this as a background. The challenges posed by the cyberspace to our national security need to be identified and action needs to be initiated to ensure that it does not pose any threat not only to our sovereignty and territorial integrity but also the economic and political growth as well as overall environment of the country. At the end of the research work, it must clearly emerge what kind of cyber strategy does India need to evolve. The organisation that we need to put in place not only to guard against cyber threats but also undertake offensive cyber operations if the need arises must also clearly emerge at the end of the research work. Accordingly, the book has been divided into six chapters. The First Chapter defines what cyberspace is and how cyberattacks are undertaken. In Chapter Two the global and regional cyber scenario has been discussed along with some well know cyberattacks. Chapter Three and Four discuss the threat to national critical info-infrastructure and how the CII is being protected in India presently. Chapter Five describes a cyber war model both at strategic level as well as operational level. Finally Chapter Six gives certain recommendations for preparing India to counter the cyber threat which looms over the country.

1 Cyber Space – What does it Mean?

"This world – cyberspace - is a world that we depend on every single day... [it] has made us more interconnected than at any time in human history."

— President Barack Obama, May 29, 2009

Historical Perspective

Human race through a long process of cultural development over thousands of years has evolved into what it is today. Warfare has been an integral part of this long evolutionary journey. Historical records indicate that nations have engaged in armed conflicts since the prehistoric times and will perhaps continue to live in a state of conflict in the times to come too. Only the nature of warfare changes and evolves. Conflicts that have been extremely destructive in nature, have wiped out dynasties and resulted in a holocaust, have all been a part of our history.

The last century has seen rapid advancement in the field of science and technology. Each new technology has not only impacted the nature of peace but also war and has eventually changed the outcome of battles. Inventions and innovations like stirrup, stream propulsion, explosives, basic telephony, air transport, space and nuclear fission have transformed the art of warfare. Every time a new technology came about, it resulted in introduction of new and superior ways of war fighting. Invariably the nation states that had better technological war fighting tools available on their inventory came out as victors thereby, strengthening the faith in technology. The two gulf wars perhaps proved this point beyond doubt and a number of nations sat up and took note of how a sudden Revolution in Military Affairs had taken place.

Information and Communication Technologies (ICT) too have impacted warfare to a great extent. When the first Morse code was sent in 1836 to a distance of 500 yards over a wire, it set the foundation for a revolution that was to follow. A number of milestones thereafter were added to this path leading to ICT revolution. Each of these technologies was meant to ensure that commanders at various levels kept themselves abreast with the latest information on the battlefield and their orders conveyed to the troops engaged in a battle in the quickest possible manner. In other words, information was being transported from one place to another using technology. As technology advanced, the odds that the information has been delivered at the correct destination, went up. Today, when warfare has entered a Network Centric era and war waging does not merely constitute the troops in contact but also the critical national infrastructures; a combination of a number of such technologies is now required to ensure information assurance and information dominance at all times.

Cyberspace: A New Domain

For centuries, mankind had only two physical domains to operate in – the land and the sea. While man was able to conquer the land with relative ease, oceans could be accessed by humans only with the aid of technology—the galley, sailing ship, steam ship, nuclear submarine etc. A little over a century ago, we added a third physical domain—Air space. Once again, technology played a very vital role in gaining control of this new dimension. It was only when humans were able to fly with some degree of freedom, was the use of air as a physical domain mastered. In 1957 we added a fourth physical domain – Space or the Outer Space. Although outer space is not yet as militarily or commercially pervasive as the air, it has deep and essential links to operations and activities in all other environments.

Each of these four physical domains is fundamentally different from each other as each one of them has unique physical characteristics. Similarly, war fighting in each of these domains is unique with little or no resemblance to the other. But one thing that stands out distinctively is that each of these four domains is usable only through the use of technology to exploit its characteristics. This includes military exploits for waging a war.

To these domains we have now added a fifth domain, the Cyber Domain or the Cyberspace. The word Cyber and Cyberspace originally appeared in a number of science fiction literature. It was actually through the work of William Gibson, a science fiction author, that the word became prominently identified with online computer networks; beginning with the 1982 story "Burning Chrome" and popularised by his 1984 novel "Neuromancer". Today Cyberspace is a household name and has been recognised as the fifth domain of warfare. Ever since the term Cyberspace was coined, a large number of definitions of this term too have appeared. It is therefore essential that some of these definitions are analysed to understand what Cyberspace truly means.

Margaret Rouse defines Cyberspace as, "*A domain characterised by the use of electronics and the electromagnetic spectrum to store, modify, and exchange data via networked systems and associated physical infrastructures. In effect, cyberspace can be thought of as the interconnection of human beings through computers and telecommunication, without regard to physical geography*".[1]

Princeton University defines cyberspace as "*a computer network consisting of a worldwide network of computer networks that use the TCP/IP network protocols to facilitate data transmission and exchange*"[2]

According to the US Department of Defense: "*Cyberspace is a domain characterised by the use of computers and other electronic devices to store, modify and exchange data via networked systems and associated physical infrastructures.*"[3] This definition was coined way back in 2001.

Perhaps one of the most exhaustive definitions of Cyberspace has been given by Dr Dan Kuehl of the National Defence University, United States Department of Defence. He says, "*Cyberspace is an operational domain whose distinctive and unique character is framed by the use of electronics and the electromagnetic spectrum to create, store, modify, exchange and exploit information via interconnected ICT based systems and their associated infrastructures.*"[4]

1 Margaret Rouse, January 2008 as available at http://searchsoa.techtarget.com/definition/cyberspace

2 Princeton, 2006.

3 Joint Chiefs of Staff, Joint Publication 1-02, Washington D.C., US Department of Defense, 12 April 2001.

4 From Cyberspace to Cyberpower, Defining the Problem, Dr Dan Kuehl, available at http://www.carlisle.army.mil/DIME/documents/Cyber%20Chapter%20Kuehl%20Final.doc

In the Indian context, the Data Security Council of India (DSCI), Cyber Security advisory report defines Cyberspace, *"As a domain that comprises IT networks, computer resources, and all the fixed and mobile devices connected to the global Internet."*[5] The National Cyber Security Policy 2013 also defines cyberspace in a very similar manner.

All the above definitions contain some common elements, namely; computer networks, information space and resources available on the internet. If one analyses these definitions and many more that have been coined, what clearly emerges from them is:

(a) Cyberspace is a domain where individuals and organisations using technologies, act and create effects. This implies that in a way, cyberspace is no different from any of the other four physical domains—air, land, sea and outer space. Today we live in an era where cyberspace is the place where we create and use the digital information that fuels the global economy.

(b) Use of the energies and properties of the EM spectrum that sets cyberspace apart from the other environments. What makes cyberspace different from the Air and Space domains is the use of the EM spectrum as the means of "movement" within cyberspace. This clear distinction from other physical environments is a critical factor within the national security domains. This aspect will be dealt with in detail in Chapter 3.

(c) Cyberspace is used to "create, store, modify, exchange and exploit" information via electronic means. Information is power. The different ways in which we can create, store, modify, exchange and exploit information has made this aspect of the cyberspace into an instrument of national power.

(d) Another common factor which perhaps is also the most important is the networking of interconnected ICT based systems and infrastructures. These systems are the ones which have brought cyberspace to the forefront of debates over its impact on and importance to national security and international affairs.

---

5 NASSCOM-DSCI CYBER SECURITY ADVISORY GROUP REPORT 30 April 2012 available at http://www.dsci.in/node/1092.

Characteristics of Cyberspace

Over the past 20 years, the Internet has become integral to our lives. As per a news report published in the Economic Times on the 01 Jan 2014, the number of users accessing the web on their mobile handsets in India would cross over 155 million by March 2014 and was further expected to grow to 185 million by June 2014. But is Cyberspace only about computer networks and the Internet? Or is it something more than this? To understand clearly what cyberspace might be, it is essential to identify its salient characteristics. David Clark in his paper "Characterising Cyberspace: Past, Present and Future" has suggested a four layered model to understand the characteristics of Cyberspace.[6] From the top down, these layers are:

- **The people** who participate in the cyber-experience – who communicate, work with information, make decisions and carry out plans, and who themselves transform the nature of cyberspace by working with its component services and capabilities.
- **The information** that is stored, transmitted, and transformed in cyberspace.
- **The logical building blocks** those constitute the services and support the platform nature of cyberspace.
- **The physical foundations** that support the logical elements.

The above clearly indicates that it is not only the computer, the interconnecting networks or the internet that creates the phenomenon we call cyberspace; it is much beyond this. Cyberspace is a subset of the global information environment. David Clark's explanation of cyberspace can be represented lucidly in diagrammatic form as under:

6 David Clark Characterizing cyberspace: past, present and future. Version 1.2 of March 12, 2010 available at http://web.mit.edu/ecir/pdf/clark-cyberspace

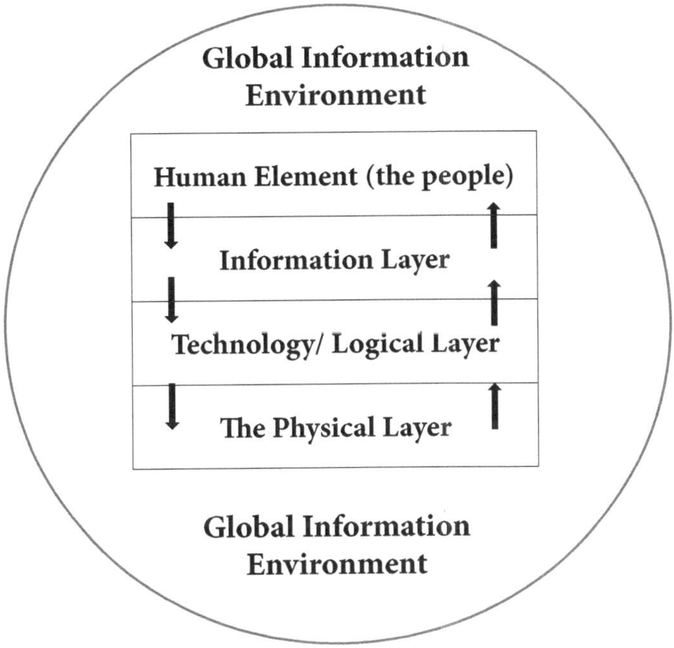

Figure 1: Four Layered Representation of Cyberspace

Let us now analyse what constitutes each of these layers.

The Physical Layer

The physical layer is the foundation block of cyberspace; the physical devices out of which the cyberspace is built. What constitutes this foundation? Millions of PCs and servers, supercomputers and grids, sensors and transducers, the network and the communications channels based on varied media, like fiber optic cable, satellite terminal or radiating media. The physical layer is perhaps the easiest to grasp; since it is tangible, its physicality gives it a sense of location and hence the jurisdiction of the physical layer can be established.

While the physical layer is being discussed, it is essential to understand how the Internet Works. The Internet is a global system of interconnected computer networks. When two or more electronic devices like computers, tablets or modern mobile devices are connected so that they can communicate, they become part of a network. The Internet consists of a world-wide interconnection of such networks, belonging to companies, governments and individuals, allowing all of the devices connected to these networks to communicate with each other.

All computers connected to the network, to effectively communicate, need to understand each other. On the Internet, all devices use the same "language" or protocol, called the Internet Protocol (IP). IP forms the basis for all communication on the Internet. Sending Data over the Internet using the IP is akin to sending the pages of a book by post broken up in lots of different envelopes. All of the envelopes use the same sender address and the same destination address. Even if some envelopes are transported by road, air or ship, the envelopes all eventually arrive at their intended destination and the book can be reassembled. The order in which the pages arrive eventually does not matter. Figure below depicts the transportation of packets of Data between two computers with the packets travelling through different nodes.

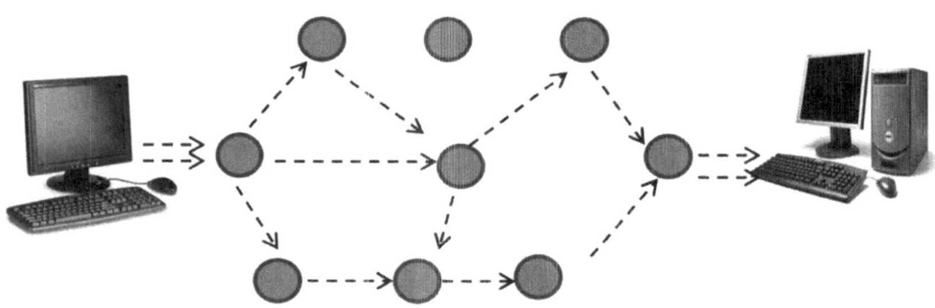

Internet Node (Traffic controller/ISP)

Figure 2: TCP IP Network

On the Internet, the contents of the envelope are also based on conventions/ protocols, one for each type of communication. Examples of such conventions on top of IP are:

- Simple Mail Transfer Protocol (SMTP) for sending emails.
- Hypertext Transfer Protocol (HTTP) for accessing web sites.
- BitTorrent for peer-to-peer (P2P) file sharing, a way to exchange data files, media files such as books, music, movies, and games with large groups of people

The above protocols are used universally. Universal use of a single protocol for all communications has a number of advantages. These are:

(a) The devices (called routers) that transport Internet data do not need to be programmed differently to deal with different types of data. Imagine having a different kind of postal system for different types of letters.

(b) Routers don't need to know anything about the data they are transporting as long as it is all using the Internet Protocol. Like the postman delivering traditional mail, only has to look at the outside of the envelopes to be able to deliver the message. It doesn't matter what the envelope contains.

All that a router needs is the correct address of the destination at which the data is to be delivered. Hence, the Digital Address of each device connected on the internet has to be unique. This unique address which is a numerical address is called the IP Address. IPv4, the existing version of IP addresses consists of 32 bits which limits the address space to 4294967296 (2^{32}) or approximately 4.3 billion possible unique addresses. According to an estimate (June 2013), there are over 2.4 billion internet users connected to the web and the number of people who form part of this unique domain called the cyberspace is constantly growing.

The Logical Layer

The strengths and limitations of the cyberspace derive more from the decisions made at the logical level than the physical level. While the network itself may form part of the physical layer; how the network is built, what are its capabilities and vulnerabilities and how it acts and reacts forms part of the logical layer. The design of the Internet leads to a cyberspace that is build out of components that provide services, and these services are designed so that they can be composed and combined to form more complex services. Low level services include program execution environments, mechanisms for data transport and standards for data formats. Out of these are built applications, such as a word processor, a database or the Web. By combining these, more complex services emerge. For example, by combining a database with the Web, we get dynamic content generation and active Web objects. On top of the Web, we now see services such as Facebook that are themselves platforms for further application development. Cyberspace, at the logical level, is thus a series of platforms on each of which new capabilities are constructed; which in turn become a platform for the next innovation. Cyberspace is very plastic, and it can be described as recursive; platforms upon platforms upon platforms. The platforms may differ in detail, but they share the common feature that they are the foundation for the next platform above them.[7]

The Information layer

As noted above, there are many aspects to cyberspace, including the technology-mediated interconnection of people. But clearly the creation, capture, storage and processing of information is central to the experience. Information in cyberspace takes many forms – it is the music and videos we share, the stored records of businesses, all of the pages in the world wide web, online books and photographs, information about information (meta-data). It is information created and retrieved as we search for other information (as is returned by Google). Putting in one sentence, information is the currency of cyberspace. Without information or data there would be no cyberspace.

The Top layer - People

People are not just the passive users of cyberspace; they define and shape its character by the ways they choose to use it. The people and their character, which may vary from region to region, is an important part of the character of cyberspace. If people contribute to Wikipedia, then Wikipedia exists. If people tweet, then Twitter exists. So we must recognise people as an important component of cyberspace, just as we must recognise wires and protocols.

Based on the consideration that the cyberspace is formed by four distinct layers, a more comprehensive definition of cyberspace would be: *Cyberspace is that human created digital medium used to collect, store and transmit data and information between humans using electronic devices through the EM spectrum enabling nearly instant, boundless, global connectivity without respect to organisational, cultural, national or political borders.*

---

7 Ibid

Uniqueness of Cyberspace

When compared to land, sea, air and space, the cyberspace has very unique properties. Some of them are :[8]

(a) Cyberspace relies on the Electromagnetic Spectrum (EMS). Cyberspace cannot exist without being able to exploit the naturally existing EMS. Without the EMS, not only would millions of information and communications technologies (ICT) be unable to communicate with each other, but the ICTs themselves would be unable to function.

(b) Cyberspace requires man-made objects such as computer chips, fiber-optic cable and other ICTs to exist. Without technology, there would be no cyberspace. This makes cyberspace unique when compared to the land, sea, air, and space domains. Space would still exist if humankind were not able to place satellites in Earth orbit; the sea would still exist if humans had been unable to master the intricacies of buoyancy; and similarly, the air would still exist if the principles of flight had not been discovered. Cyberspace would not exist were it not for the ability of human beings to innovate and manufacture technologies capable of exploiting the various properties of the EMS.

(c) Cyberspace can be constantly replicated. As an entity, there is only one air, one sea, one space, and one land (although divided by the boundaries created by us). In contrast, there can be as many cyberspaces as one can possibly generate. For warfare, there is only one portion of the air, sea, or land that is important: that portion that is being contested.[9] However the same is not the case with cyberspace. Vulnerability detected at one place becomes a global phenomenon in a matter of no time.

(d) The cost of entry into cyberspace is relatively cheap. The resources and expertise required to enter, exist in, and exploit cyberspace are modest compared to the resources and expertise required for exploiting the land, sea, air, and space. Generating strategic effect in

8 On Cyberwarfare by Fred Schreier

9 Deciphering Cyberpower: Strategic Purpose in Peace and War published in Strategic Studies Quarterly Summer 2011.

cyberspace does not require a budget of billions, manpower in the thousands, tracts of land, or divisions/fleets/wings/constellations of hardware that cost yet more billions of tax payers' money. Rather, modest financial outlays, a small group of motivated individuals, and access to networked computers that are accessible to a large portion of the world's population can provide entry to the cyber domain.[10]

(e) Cyberspace is qualitatively different from the sea, air, and space domains, yet it both overlaps and continuously operates within all of them.

Cyberspace as the newest and most important of the global commons has been widely available for less than thirty years, yet more than a quarter of the world's population now uses it in some form or the other every day, and that number continues to expand. Thus, cyberspace has become the center of gravity for the globalised world; and for nations, not only for military operations but for all aspects of national activity, to include economic, financial, diplomatic, and other transactions.

Cyberpower

It is a fact that cyberspace has changed the way we create and share information and how humans interact and communicate. Undeniably, information today is like raw material that fuels economies and societies. While power based on information resources in not new, the term cyberpower certainly is. According to one widely used definition, "*Cyberpower is the ability to use cyberspace to create advantages and influence events in other operational environments and across the instruments of power.*"[11] Thus cyberpower is not restricted to just the realms of warfighting but will encompass much more than that. Cyberpower is the capability to control information systems and networks in and through cyberspace.

Like cyberspace draws analogy to land, sea, air and space, in a similar manner we need to check out if the concept of cyberpower is analogous to sea power, airpower and space power.

---

10 See Col Stephen W. Korns, USAF, "Cyber Operations: The New Balance," Joint Force Quarterly 54 (3rd Qtr. 2009): 97–98.

11 Kuehl, in Kramer, op. cit., p. 38.

Cyberpower is shaped by multiple factors. While cyberspace just exists as an environment, cyberpower is a measure of the ability to use that environment. Technology is one important aspect, because the ability to 'enter' cyberspace is what makes its use possible. Technology is constantly changing, and some users – countries, societies, non-state actors, etc. may be able to leap over old technologies to deploy and use new ones to their dramatic advantage. Organisational factors also play a role, because organisations reflect human purposes and objectives, and their perspectives on the creation and use of cyberpower are shaped by their organisational mission, be it military, economic or political. But the element most closely tied to cyberpower is information. Cyberspace and cyberpower are dimensions of the informational instrument of power, and there are myriad ways that cyberpower links to, supports, and enables the exercise of the other instruments of power. Thus, information is the currency or DNA of cyberpower. [12]

The world today is a global village and cyberspace has created the new buzz word called *global economy* by linking nations together, offering supply chain models not heard of before, boosting productivity and opening new markets. The world today is much more flat than it was in 2005 when Thomas L Friedman published his bestseller "*The World Is Flat*". How information is created and transported across the globe is transforming economies and societies at a very rapid pace. The impact of cyberpower today has forced nations to adapt to new ways of the wired world in which traditional borders are being altered and new relationships among not only people but also governments are being forged, across national borders.

Cyberpower is capable of producing the desired outcomes not only within the cyberspace, but also in other domains outside the cyberspace. This is because the world today is much more dependent on technology of electronics than ever before. Every facet of life today has some hardware and software associated to it making it vulnerable to cyberattacks.

Cyberpower has three main characteristics:

(a) **It is Omnipresent**. Land, sea, air, and space power are able to generate strategic effect on each of the other domains. But

12 From Cyberspace to Cyberpower, Defining the Problem, Dr Dan Kuehl, available at http://www.carlisle.army.mil/DIME/documents/Cyber%20Chapter%20Kuehl%20Final.doc

nothing generates strategic effect in all domains so absolutely and simultaneously as cyberpower.

(b) **It is Complementary**. Like space power, cyberpower too is a complementary instrument because the coercive power of cyberpower is still limited.

(c) **It can be Stealthy**. This characteristic of cyberpower makes it attractive to a large number of users both state actors as well as others.

Threats in the Cyberspace

Having understood what cyberspace and cyberpower are, it is time to analyse the threats that one faces in the cyberspace. Cyberspace is a borderless domain available to anyone and everyone across the globe and as discussed earlier, it does not cost much to enter and exploit this domain. Due to large scale proliferation of ICT systems into all aspects of life, the importance of information for political matters has also increased manifold. Because of this reason, state and non-state actors can use this power to achieve objectives not only in cyberspace but also the physical world. Low cost, high potential impact and general lack of transparency makes cyberpower attractive to both powerful and less powerful actors. While a powerful state can combine cyberpower with existing military capabilities, economic assets, and soft-power means to their advantage; a not so powerful nation today has the tools available to gain asymmetrically in cyberspace by inflicting damage on vulnerable targets of powerful states. As our dependence on cyberspace goes on increasing, threats, vulnerabilities and risks that stem from this domain also increase exponentially. As a result, cyberspace has become a warfighting domain with the intrinsic potential to destroy or render useless physical, technical, and virtual infrastructure across the globe. Capabilities are being acquired to damage critical national infrastructure, such as economic, government, military, educational, health, social etc. of a nation state.

Therefore, threats that emanate from cyberspace need to be clearly understood. Threats within and from cyberspace are disparate, drawn-out, and some may also be disproportionate in the harm they could cause. Threats, dangers, and risks arising from action in cyberspace have three general characteristics as explained below :[13]

(a) The nature of the threat in cyberspace is as broad as cyberspace itself. Any aspect of the world that is dependent on the cyber domain is potentially at risk. Hence, of concern are adverse actions that threaten the integrity and security of critical national infrastructures; destabilise the financial system; enable access to nationally significant classified information or commercially exploitable trade secrets; or undermine in any other significant way the ability to rely upon ICT systems for relevant national security objectives.

(b) Threats to the integrity of information and security in cyberspace are deeply embedded in the cyber domain. They arise from vulnerabilities inherent, or from malware placed, in complex software operating systems, and from malicious hardware. They are embedded because the threat is an intrinsic feature of cyberspace, which may never be fully eradicated.

(c) The threat in cyberspace is as diverse as the plethora of potentially hostile actors who exploit these vulnerabilities, the actions they take, and the targets they attack. Among the great diversity of actors are nation state actors, ideological and political extremists, terrorist organisations, well-organised criminal gangs, and all sorts of state-sponsored, mercenary or individual hackers. Each poses a distinct threat, requiring a differentiated response.

Going by the above analysis, it seems that from a personal computer at your home to the National Information Infrastructure; from a mobile phone used to access mails to private networks owned by big business houses, anything and everything connected to the cyberspace is vulnerable to threats emanating from various sources. It also indicates that although a number of threats do exist outside the confines of cyberspace which can have an impact on our national security, yet the cyberspace too poses a number of challenges to national security today. Due to the widespread integration of the cyberspace into the economy, society, government and even the armed forces and the peculiar nature of architecture of the internet, the "virtual world" today poses serious challenges to the policy makers

13 National Security Threats in Cyberspace, Post-Workshop Report by Paul Rosenzweig– September 2009

and law enforcement agencies just as the "real world" does. Rosenberg, the rapporteur of a workshop on national security threats in cyberspace, further argues that the nature of cyberspace makes threats from that domain fundamentally different from those existing in the 'real world.'[14] Following nine factors contribute to this difference :-

(a) The span of cyberspace is global, creating conflicting and overlapping realms of control by nation-state actors with differing legal and cultural approaches and distinct strategic interests.

(b) The world has become so dependent upon the cyber domain that to disassociate from it is impossible. Cyber globalisation cannot be undone; neither can our reliance on cyberspace for national security functions.

(c) The now globalised production of both cyber hardware and software in many different countries makes it virtually impossible to provide reliable supply chain assurance or good product assurance.

(d) The scalability of the cyber domain makes it qualitatively different. We do not deal with kinetic force of physically limited range, but with mechanism by which operations on a global scale are controlled.

(e) Operations within the domain are controlled by a small number of people. Everyday users cannot modify or control software and hardware they use, thus only few have control of the cyber universe.

(f) Because of the interconnectedness and interoperability of cyberspace, no locus of positive control is feasible. Efforts to mitigate the threat, if possible at all, will require close international cooperation.

(g) Changes in the cyber domain occur ever more rapidly. The interconnectedness of cyberspace enhances this acceleration, but each change creates again a new cycle of vulnerabilities.

(h) The distribution of cyber assets spans all types of organisations, from private to government controlled systems to those operated

14 ibid

by the public, each with different resources, capabilities, and concerns.

(j) The nature of cyberspace is such that the technical capacity to attribute actions to the responsible actor with a sufficient degree of confidence is still lacking. Hence, anonymity is easily achievable.

Cyberattack

Having understood the vulnerabilities of the cyberspace and the threats, let us examine what is a cyberattack and how can cyberattacks be classified. Cyberattacks are socially or politically motivated attacks carried out primarily through the cyberspace. Attacks target the general public or national and corporate organisations and are carried out through the spread of malicious programs, unauthorised web access, fake websites, and other means of stealing personal or institutional information from targets of attacks, causing far-reaching damage. Unlike a physical attack, a cyberattack can be relatively innocuous and in most cases may not even cause any type of damage to any equipment or systems, though there have been cyberattacks in the past which have resulted in physical damage to systems also. Stuxnet, a cyber worm attack in 2009 from an unknown origin (probably collaboration of US and Israel) on a highly protected nuclear site at Natanz, in Iran is perhaps an example which clearly indicates the extent of damage that a cyberattack can cause. The details of such cyberattacks will be discussed later.

Taxonomy of a Cyberattack

Cyberattacks over the years have become both increasingly numerous and sophisticated. Many attacks are now relatively "user-friendly" and in-depth technical knowledge is no longer required to launch an attack. A Google search of "Tools to attack a website" produces 80,000,000 results and a search for "Learn to carry out a web attack" produces 3,200,000 results. Even if ten percent of these sites can actually teach you how to use the internet for a network attack, yet this number is alarmingly large. This has led to the rise of various groups of attackers, such as "*script-kiddies*", who while ignorant of how their attack works, can cause great damage. The exponential rise in the rate of cybercrime can also be attributed to this. Figure below further clarifies the aspect of nature of attack and why the quantum of attacks has increased over the last thirty years.

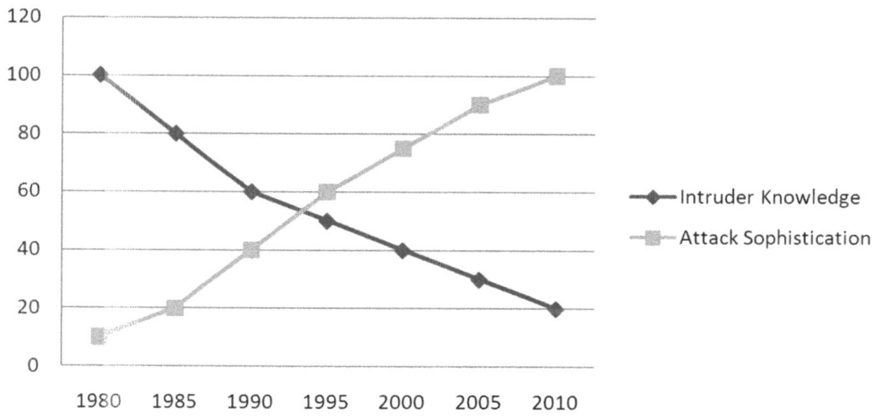

Figure 3: Attack Sophistication *versus* Intruder Knowledge Curve

(Note: The above data has been collated from a number of internet sources as well as from experience of various Information Security Officer working with some of the reputed private companies in India.)

What clearly emerges from the above is that while the sophistication and the nature of cyberattacks have constantly become better with time, the knowledge required to carry out such lethal attacks has become minimal. Today anyone who is connected to the internet can easily learn to carry out disruptive activities as compared to thirty years back. If that be so, it is difficult to even imagine what kind of damage can be caused by motivated and knowledgeable hackers not just to the individual networks but also to the nation as a whole. Before analysing this, it is essential to classify what are various types of computer and network attacks as well as establishing the people who can undertake such attacks. Taxonomy of both these aspects allows for previous knowledge to be applied to new attacks as well as providing a structured way to view such attacks. The purpose of a classification or taxonomy is also to provide a useful and consistent means of doing so for better understanding and response.

Hostile actions against an IT system or network can take two forms: cyberattack and cyber exploitation. Both these terms can be defined as under:

(a) A cyberattack is the use of deliberate actions to alter, disrupt, deceive, degrade, or destroy adversary IT systems and networks or the information and programs resident in or transiting these systems.

(b) Cyber exploitation is the use of operations to obtain information, usually clandestinely and conducted with the smallest possible intervention that still allows extraction of the information sought.

A number of taxonomies of cyberattacks have been promulgated by various experts. The two most important early taxonomies in the security field were the Protection Analysis (PA) (Bisbey and Hollingworth, 1978) taxonomy and the Research in Secured Operating Systems (RISOS) (Abbott et al., 1976). Since computer attacks were a highly skilled area, both these focussed on vulnerabilities rather than attacks and provided a good background to proposing new taxonomies. Both focused on categorising security flaws and both resulted in similar classification schemes. Some of the other important milestones in classifying computer and network attacks are:

(a) **Bishop's Vulnerability Taxonomy (1995).** As per Bishops Taxonomy, Six "axes" are used to classify the vulnerabilities. They are the nature of the flaw, Time of introduction, Exploitation domain, Effect domain, Minimum number of components necessary to exploit the vulnerability and the Source of identification of the vulnerability.

(b) **Howard's Taxonomy (1997).** It has five stages: attackers, tools, access, results and objectives. Howard attempts to focus attention on process driven taxonomy, rather than a classification scheme.

In 2001, Lough proposed another taxonomy called VERDICT[15] (Validation Exposure Randomness Deallocation Improper Conditions Taxonomy) which was based on the characteristics of attacks instead of a tree-like taxonomy. According to him majority of attacks on modern computers have been successful due to the exploitation of the same errors and weaknesses that have plagued computer systems. Lough proposed his taxonomy using four characteristics of attacks:

(a) **Improper validation**: insufficient or incorrect validation results in unauthorised access to information or a system.

(b) **Improper exposure**: a system or information is improperly exposed to attack.

15 A Taxonomy of Computer attacks with application to wireless networks by Daniel Lowry Lough.

(c) **Improper randomness**: insufficient randomness results in exposure to attack.

(d) **Improper deallocation**: information is not properly deleted after use and thus can be vulnerable to attack.

Most of these and many others had some common shortcomings. The first problem was: how to deal with blended attacks? The second was that attacks often do not have many common traits. This makes the creation of broad categories difficult. One of the most accepted taxonomies ever proposed is the one done by Simon Hansman and Ray Hunt in June 2004. It works by using the concept of dimensions. Dimensions are a way of allowing for a classification of an attack to take a more holistic view of such an attack. Hansman and Hunt taxonomy proposes four dimensions for attack classification.[16] These are as follows:

The First Dimension

The first, or base, dimension is used to categorise the attack based on the attack vector. Attack vector is the means by which an attack reaches its target, for example, the Melissa "Virus" uses email as its main form of propagation, and therefore is, in the first dimension, a mass-mailing worm. If an attack vector is not present or is too trivial then the attack can be categorised by finding the category closest to how the attack works. The following definitions assist in categorising attacks which lack obvious attack vectors. The category that best matches with the definitions below is chosen. Once the general class has been established, the attack may be further classified by using the sub-classes, if they exist. Some of the commonly well-known attack vectors are discussed as under :[17]

(a) **Virus:** A self-replicating program that propagates through some form of infected files. It replicates by inserting copies of itself into other computer programs, data files, or the boot sector of the hard drive. Viruses often perform some type of harmful activity on infected hosts, such as stealing hard disk space or CPU time, accessing private information, corrupting data, displaying political or humorous messages on the user's screen, spamming their contacts, or logging their keystrokes. Subtypes: file infectors,

16 A taxonomy of network and computer attacks, Simon Hansman, Ray Hunt

17 Definitions as available on Wikipedia

system/boot record infectors, macros.

(b) **Worms**: A self-replicating program that propagates without using infected files. Usually worms propagate through network services on computers or through email. Worms spread by exploiting vulnerabilities in operating systems. Worms almost always cause at least some harm to the network, even if only by consuming bandwidth, whereas viruses almost always corrupt or modify files on a targeted computer. Subtypes: mass mailing via botnets, network aware.

(c) **Trojans**: A program made to appear benign that serves some malicious purpose. A Trojan horse, or Trojan, in computing is a non-self-replicating type of malware program containing malicious code that, when executed, carries out actions determined by the nature of the Trojan, typically causing loss or theft of data, and possible system harm. A Trojan often acts as a back door, contacting a controller which can then have unauthorized access to the affected computer. Subtypes: remote access, data destruction.

(d) **Buffer Overflows**: In computer security and programming term, a buffer overflow, or buffer overrun, is an anomaly where a program, while writing data to a buffer, overruns the buffer's boundary and overwrites adjacent memory. This is a special case of violation of memory safety; a process that gains control or crashes another process by overflowing the other process's buffer. Buffer overflows can be triggered by inputs that are designed to execute code, or alter the way the program operates. This may result in erratic program behavior, including memory access errors, incorrect results, a crash, or a breach of system security. Subtypes: stack-based overflows, heap-based overflows.

(e) **Denial of Service Attacks**: In computing, a denial-of-service (DoS) or distributed denial-of-service (DDoS) attack is an attempt to make a machine or network resource unavailable to its intended users. Although the motives, means to carry out an attack and targets may vary, it generally consists of efforts to temporarily or indefinitely interrupt or suspend services of a host connected to the network. It is an attack, which prevents legitimate users from accessing or using the network. There are two general forms of

DoS attacks: those that crash services and those that flood services. In computing terms the Subtypes are referred to as : host (resource hogs, crashers), network (TCP, UDP, ICMP flooding), distributed.

(f) **Network Attacks**: Attacks focused on a network or the users on the network by manipulating network protocols, ranging from the data-link layer to the application layer. Subtypes of network attacks are:-

(i) **Spoofing**: In the context of network security, a spoofing attack is a situation in which one person or program successfully masquerades as another by falsifying data and thereby gaining an illegitimate advantage. A spoofing attack could be Caller ID spoofing, E-mail address spoofing or GPS spoofing attack.

(ii) **Web/email Phishing**: Phishing is the act of attempting to acquire information such as usernames, passwords, and credit card details (and sometimes, indirectly, money) by masquerading as a trustworthy entity in an electronic communication. Phishing emails may contain links to websites that are infected with malware and direct users to enter details at a fake website whose look and feel are almost identical to the legitimate one. Phishing is an example of social engineering techniques used to deceive users.

(iii) **Session Hijacking**: In computer terminology, session hijacking, sometimes also known as cookie hijacking is the exploitation of a valid computer session—sometimes also called a session key—to gain unauthorized access to information or services in a computer system. In particular, it is used to refer to the theft of a magic cookie used to authenticate a user to a remote server. It has particular relevance to web developers, as the HTTP cookies used to maintain a session on many web sites can be easily stolen by an attacker using an intermediary computer or with access to the saved cookies on the victim's computer.

(iv) **Wireless WEP Cracking**: Wired Equivalent Privacy (WEP) Wi-Fi Protected Access (WPA) and Wi-Fi Protected Access II (WPA2) are security protocols and security certification programs developed by the Wi-Fi Alliance to secure wireless computer networks. Hackers can crack weak Pre-Shared Keys by using brute-force cracking tools and/or Rainbow Tables to crack weak keys in a very short amount of time.

(v) **Web Application Attacks**: With the emergence of Web 2.0, websites are often attacked directly as information sharing through social networking has increased and the Web is increasingly being used as a means of doing business and delivering services. Hackers either seek to compromise the corporate network or the end-users accessing the website by subjecting them to drive.

(g) **Physical Attacks**: Attacks based on damaging physical components of a network or computer. Subtypes: basic, energy weapon (HERF gun, EMP/T bomb, LERF), Van Eck (Van Eck phreaking is the process of eavesdropping on the contents of a CRT or LCD display by detecting its electromagnetic emissions. It is named after Dutch computer researcher Wim van Eck.)

(h) **Password Attacks**: Attacks aimed at gaining a password. Subtypes: guessing (brute force, dictionary attacks), exploiting implementation.

(i) **Information Gathering Attacks**: Attacks in which no physical or digital damage is carried out and no subversion occurs, but in which important information is gained by the attacker, possibly to be used in a further attack. Subtypes: packet sniffing. A packet analyzer also known as a network analyzer, protocol analyzer or packet sniffer, is a computer program or a piece of computer hardware that can intercept and log traffic passing over a digital network or part of a network. As data streams flow across the network, the sniffer captures each packet and, if needed, decodes the packet's raw data, showing the values of various fields in the packet, and analyses its content according to the appropriate RFC or other specifications, host mapping, security scanning, port scanning, OS fingerprinting.

The first dimension is summarised in Table below:

Level 1	Level 2	Level 3
Viruses:	File infectors System/bootrecord infectors Macro	
Worms:	Mass mailing Network aware	
Buffer overflows	Stack Heap	
Denial of service attacks:	Host-based: Network-based:	Resource hogs Crashers TCP flooding UDP flooding
Network attacks:	Distributed Spoofing Session hijacking Wireless attacks: Web application attacks	 WEP cracking Cross site scripting Parameter tampering Cookie poisoning Database attacks Hidden field manipulation
Physical attacks:	Basic Energy weapon:	HERF LERF EMP
Password attacks:	Van Eck Guessing:	 Brute force Dictionary attack
Information gathering attacks:	Exploiting implementation Sniffing: Mapping Security scanning	Packet sniffing

Table 1: The 1st Dimension of Cyberattacks

The Second Dimension

The attack target is covered in the second dimension. It can be classified as Sendmail 8.12.10 or can cover a class of targets, such as Unix-based systems. As an attack may have multiple targets, there may be multiple entries in this dimension. For example, if worm Code Red attacked Server A, the target would not be Server A, but the Internet Information Server (IIS) service running on this server. There would be a wide range of potential targets and the list will only constantly increase. Instead of working out an exhaustive list, a generalised way of classifying the targets is shown in the table below, with a few specific examples.

Level 1	Level 2	Level 3	Level 4	Level 5	Level 6
Hardware	Computer:	Hard Disks	……		
		Network Equipment	Routers Switches Hubs Cabling …….		
		Peripheral devices:	Monitor Keyboard …….		
Software:	Operating system:	Windows family:	Windows XP Windows 2003 Server …….		
		Unix family	Linux:	RedHat Linux 6.0 RedHat Linux 6.5 ……	
		FreeBSD:		9.2 10.0 ……	
		MacOS family	MacOS X:	10.8 10.9 ……	

Level 1	Level 2	Level 3	Level 4	Level 5	Level 6
	Application:	Server: User:	Database Email Web: ..... Word processor	 IIS MS Word:	 8.0 8.5 ...... 2010 2013
	Network:	Protocols:	Transport-layer:	IP Network-layer:	..... TCP ....

Note: "......." indicates extra categories can be added to the classification.

Table 2: The 2nd Dimension of Cyberattacks

The Third Dimension

The third dimension covers the vulnerabilities and exploits, if they exist, that the attack uses. The vulnerabilities and exploits do not have a structured classification due to their infinite possibilities. Hence, a list defined by the Common Vulnerabilities Exposures (CVE) is used. CVE is a dictionary of standard terms related to security threats. These threats fall into two categories, known as vulnerabilities and exposures. Vulnerability is a fact about a computer, server or network that presents a definite, identifiable security risk in a certain context. An exposure is a security-related situation, event or fact that may be considered vulnerability by some people but not by others. CVE was developed and is maintained by the MITRE Corporation to facilitate the sharing of data among diverse security interests. The vulnerability could be of three types:

(a) **Vulnerability in Implementation**: Sometimes the design of the system is secure, but the implementation fails to meet the design and thus vulnerabilities are introduced. Buffer overflows often exploit such vulnerabilities. For example program may have been securely designed, but its implementation may contain bugs that could be exploited.

(b) **Vulnerability in Design**: The fundamental design of the system is flawed, so that even a perfect implementation will have vulnerabilities. For example, a system which allows users to choose weak passwords will have vulnerability in its design.

(c) **Vulnerability in Configuration**: The configuration of the system introduces vulnerabilities. The system itself may be secure but if configured incorrectly, renders itself vulnerable. An example would be, installing a secured operating system and then opening a number of vulnerable ports.

The Fourth Dimension

The fourth dimension takes into account the possibility of an attack to have a payload or effect beyond itself. For example, a virus that installs a Trojan is still clearly a virus, but has a Trojan as a payload. The payload may be another attack itself and so the first dimension can be used to classify the payload if this is the case. The ultimate aim of the payload could be corruption of information, disclosure of information, theft of service or subversion.

Let us now examine some of the known cases of cyberattacks and try and classify them as per the above taxonomy.

The Morris Worm: In 1988, the Morris worm was one of the first computer worms which spread through the Internet and gained significant media attention. It was written by Robert Tappan Morris, a student at Cornell, and launched on 02 Nov 1988 from MIT. The Morris worm worked by exploiting known vulnerabilities in Unix send mail, finger, and rsh/rexec, as well as weak passwords. The worm used each of these methods to spread, and thus it had three attack vectors. Using the above described taxonomy, the attack can be classified as under:

- **1st Dimension**: Network aware Worm. The attack propagated without using infected files and had multiple attack vectors.
- **2ndDimension**: BSD 4 Sun 3 & VAX variants.
- **3rd Dimension**: Vulnerability in Implementation & design.
- **4th Dimension**: Theft of service & subversion.

Some of the other attacks have been summarised in the table below:

Attack	Year	1st Dimension	2nd Dimension	3rd Dimension	4th Dimension
Blaster	August 2003	Network-aware worm	MS Windows NT 4.0, 2000, XP, Server 2003	CAN-2003-0352	TCP packet flooding DoS
Melissa	March 1999	Mass-mailing worm	MS Word 97 & 2000	Configuration	Macro virus & TCP packet flooding DoS
Michel angelo	February 1991	System boot	DOS family		Corruption of information
Rootkit Sirefef Gen	November 2012	Virus	Windows Operating system, Flash Player	Design	Subversion (Capable of downloading other malware, display fake information about threats)
Sobig.F	August 2003	Mass-mailing worm	Email client	Configuration	Trojan

Table 3: Classification of Some Known Cyberattacks

As can be seen from above, cyberattacks starting way back in 1999 till as recently as 2012 can easily be classified using the above four dimensions of the taxonomy. Hence the taxonomy is very useful in better understanding of an attack. As always, as the nature of attack continues to change, there is room for improvement. However, the above taxonomy does provide a basic framework which acts as a starting block for any future refinement.

Taxonomy of Cyber Adversaries

Having categorised the cyberattacks, it is also essential to understand who are these people or organisations who undertake these attacks. The study of cyber adversaries was initiated in the early 1980's, when personal computers began to come into the mainstream and the term "hacker" entered the lexicon as a person skilled at programming and manipulating operating systems. The issue of Attack Sophistication *versus* Intruder Knowledge over the years has already been analysed. The use of the word 'hacker' to describe an individual engaging in malicious activity emerged after the arrest of six teenagers known as the 414 gang, who broke into a number of computer systems, including those of the Los Alamos National Laboratory in the early eighties. Within the computer science community today, there are many who prefer the term "cracker" to describe individuals engaging in malicious behaviour and breaking into security systems. What then is the difference between hackers and crackers?

> *A hacker can be referred to as a 'white hat'. Someone who doesn't use a system illegally but exposes holes within systems. Their aim is to fix flaws within systems and to improve its security. 'White hats' may be security professionals, who are hired by companies to audit network security or test software.*
>
> *A cracker can be referred to as a 'black hat'. They break into systems illegally for personal gain, vandalism, or bragging rights.*

For any network to be secure against cyberattacks, it is essential to understand the motivation and the methodology used by an attacker for carrying out such cyberattacks. Today, cyber threat models are little more than a progression of semi-descriptive labels: hackers, hacktivists, scriptkiddies, nation states, cyber terrorists, organized crime, or malicious insiders. These labels reinforce preconceived notions regarding motivation and resources. Taxonomy of cyber adversaries has been suggested by C Meyers, S Powers, D Faissol in April 2009 which very clearly classifies cyber adversaries and is as under :[18]

18 Taxonomies of Cyber Adversaries and Attacks: A Survey of Incidents and Approaches, C. Meyers, S. Powers, D. Faissol, April 2009

Adversary Class	Skills	Malicious ness	Motivation	Method
Script kiddies, newbies, novices	very low	low	boredom, thrill seeking	Download and run already-written hacking scripts known as toolkits.
Hacktivists, Political activists	Low	Moderate	promotion of a political cause	engage in denial of service attacks or defacement of rival cause sites
Cyber punks, crashers, thugs	Low	Moderate	prestige, personal gain, thrill seeking	write own scripts, engage in malicious acts, brag about exploits
Insiders, user malcontents	Moderate	High	disgruntlement, personal gain, revenge	uses insider privileges to attack current or former employers
Coders, writers	High	Moderate	power, prestige, revenge, respect	write scripts and automated tools used by newbies, serve as mentor

Adversary Class	Skills	Malicious ness	Motivation	Method
White hat hackers, old guard, sneakers	High	Very low	intellectual gain, ethics, respect	non-malicious hacking to help others and test new programming
Black hat crackers, professionals, elite	Very high	Very high	personal gain, greed, revenge	sophisticated attacks by criminals/ thieves; may be "guns for hire" or involved in organized crime
Cyber terrorists	Very high	Very high	ideology, politics, espionage	well-funded cyber attacks against target nations
Non state actors	Very high	Very high	politics, espionage state policy	Covert state sponsored operations
Nation State	Extremely high	Extremely high	As part of national policy	Outright cyber war

Table 4: Classification of Cyber Adversaries

Script kiddies, Newbies, Novices: This is the least sophisticated category of adversaries, comprising of individuals with limited programming skills. They are new to hacking and rely on pre-written scripts known as "toolkits" in their exploits; examples of these include NeoSploit (2007), WebAttacker (Russian origin 2009), and IcePack (Chinese origin 2007). With the increasing sophistication of the available toolkits, their ability to pull off larger-scale attacks is on the rise, as in the case of the denial-of-service attacks perpetuated by "Mafia Boy" in Canada (2000)[19].

Hacktivists, Political Activists: These adversaries are different from the other classes in that they are motivated by a political cause rather than personal gains. Some examples of hacktivism include the "virtual sit-ins" perpetuated by Electronic Disturbance Theater against the Pentagon and other agencies, in protest against perceived civil rights violations from 2006 to 2010; email bombs used by the Internet Black Tigers (IBT) throughout Sri Lanka to gain publicity for the Tamil Tigers (most likely funded by the Liberation Tigers of Tamil Eelam). In 1997 IBT attacked the email systems of several Sri Lankan embassies throughout the world; and worm propagation by Worms Against Nuclear Killers (WANK) on computers in NASA's Goddard Space Flight center, protesting an upcoming launch (created by Melbourne-based hackers in 1989).

Cyber Punks, Crashers, and Thugs: They are capable of writing their own (limited) scripts and engaging in malicious acts such as spamming, defacing, and identity theft. These hackers seek attention and prestige such as media attention. For example Kevin David Mitnick who combined his hacking skills with social engineering to gain access to restricted systems. At the time of his arrest, he was the most-wanted computer criminal in the United States. Today he runs a security firm named Mitnick Security Consulting, that helps test a company's security strengths and weaknesses, and is the Chief Hacking Officer of security awareness training company KnowBe4.[20]

Insiders, User Malcontents: This group of adversaries represents arguably the greatest risk to companies, and yet is often the least publicised. Insiders are most frequently motivated by revenge; usually in response to a negative work-related event. This frustration leads them to deliberately attack their own company/ organisation networks. The most talked about insider sabotage is perhaps the case of Michael Lauffenberger who was working for General Dynamics Corporation and was arrested on charges that he planted a destructive program in a plot to wipe out vital data on a rocket project and then got hired back as a high-priced consultant to repair the damage.[21]

19 As available on http://en.wikipedia.org/wiki/MafiaBoy

20 Kevin Mitnick as available at http://en.wikipedia.org/wiki/Kevin_Mitnick

21 Computer Programmer Charged in Sabotage Plot, Newyork Times, June 27, 1991

Black Hat Crackers, Professionals, Elite: The adversaries in this category are professional criminals, who use their technical skills in pursuance of their criminal activities. Similar to criminals outside the cyber domain, they are motivated by money and greed. These hackers are both rare and very dangerous, as they have strong technical skills and are often able to support themselves through their criminal exploits. Some of the well known crackers in the recent history have been:-[22]

(a) Cyber criminal Albert Gonzalez accused of masterminding the biggest ATM and credit card theft in US history. From 2005 to 2007, he and his cyber group had allegedly sold more than 170 million card and ATM numbers.

(b) Jonathan James, a 16-year-old black hat hacker, who became the first juvenile imprisoned for cybercrime in the United States, gained notoriety by implementing a series of successful intrusions into various systems. At a young age of 15, James specialized in hacking high-profile government systems such as NASA and the Department of Defense. He was reported to have stolen software worth over $1.7 million. He also hacked into the Defence Threat Reduction Agency (DTRA) and intercepted over 3,000 highly secretive messages passing to and from the DTRA employees, while collecting many usernames and passwords.

Cyber Terrorists: The most dangerous and skilled of all cyber adversaries are the cyber terrorists. Cyber terrorists engage in state-sponsored cyber warfare. Their job is to conduct attacks that destabilise, disrupt, and destroy the cyber assets and data of an enemy nation or government organisations. Attacks by cyber terrorists are typically well-funded and highly secretive; individuals engaging in such activities have extremely high skills and are motivated by ideology.

Cyberwarfare

Every era brings with it new techniques and methods of warfare. The Romans perfected the art of infantry field combat. The staffing norms developed during the Napoleonic era and the concept of use of artillery in conjunction with tactical deployment of infantry and cavalry are still

22 Top 10 Notorious Black Hat Hackers, as available at http://listverse.com/2012/05/08/top-10-notorious-black-hat-hackers/

relevant. World War I saw the introduction of poisoned gas attacks and use of tanks for the first time. Employment of air power, missiles and rockets in the battle field took the centre stage during World War II. The world was suspended in an uneasy equilibrium when the threat of nuclear weapons was introduced at the beginning of the cold war. Sri Lanka and Vietnam are examples of the use of the guerrilla warfare to subdue a superior force and technology. The terror wars in Jammu and Kashmir and the North Eastern parts of India and also many other parts of the world have seen use of suicide bombers and IED's as effective weapons. Mumbai attacks gave the meaning of low intensity conflicts another dimension. While defacing websites and disabling government's official channels may not be recognised as warfare, it is apparent that networks, which have an immense bearing on the communication, commerce and social interaction, are also vulnerable to attacks. Attack on and across the networks are poised to become the defining innovations of twenty first century.

So far we have learnt the meaning of terms cyberspace and cyberpower and how cyberattacks are carried out by various groups of people. Let us now establish what constitutes cyber warfare. Does the concept of cyberwar exist or is it only a myth, a term created by the western powers in their own interest?

The world is increasingly becoming more and more digital. Large amount information today is stored in the form of digital data either on computers or in some other electronic form. Transactions of this information take place on networks across the globe, usually unencrypted. When such a massive vulnerable reservoir of information is available to be tapped and misused, why would the nation states not be willing to join the race to dominate and exploit it? Perhaps this is the single most important reason why nation states have recognised the cyber space as an important domain which could be militarily exploited for furtherance of national interest both during peace and war.

There are not many definition of cyber war and cyber warfare that are available. While most scholars agree that a cyber war is a reality, Thomas Rid, a famous British scholar, on the contrary has written a book "Cyber War will not Take Place". Rid, in his book has compared the term "war" in cyber war to war against obesity. Hence, there is a need to delve deeper into this aspect of cyber warfare. What makes the cyberspace a domain where militaries need to fight? While information warfare and information operation have been spoken of for a long time, what is the difference between information warfare and cyber warfare? What acts of a nation will constitute cyber war so that the affected party can retaliate militarily against them? Chapter 5 will cover these aspects in detail.

Like any other form of warfare, can cyber warfare too be defined at both strategic as well at operational levels? Perhaps yes. At strategic level, it is that form of asymmetric warfare where a campaign of cyberattacks is launched by a nation against another state and its society, primarily but not exclusively for the purpose of affecting the target state's behaviour. Operational cyber warfare will consist of wartime cyberattacks against military targets and military related civilian targets. Impact of these forms of cyber warfare on national security and organisation of the armed forces will be dealt with in detail in Chapter 5.

The United Nations Integrated Crime and Justice Research Institute (UNICRI), a premier UN entity established in 1967 to support nations worldwide in preventing crime and facilitating criminal justice, has been running structured programmes on cybercrime and has acknowledged that cyber warfare is a reality. The organisation defines Cyber Warfare as any action by a nation-state to penetrate another nation's computer networks for the purpose of causing damage and the phenomenon also includes 'cyber hooliganism', cyber vandalism and cyber terrorism undertaken by a nation state. As per UNICRI Cyberwarfare can consist of many threats, namely :[23]

(a) **Online acts of espionage and security breaches** – These are done to obtain national material and information of a sensitive or classified nature through the exploitation of the internet (e.g. exploitation of network flaws through malicious software).

(b) **Sabotage** – The use of the internet by one nation state to disrupt online communications systems of another nation state (e.g. military communication networks) with the intent to cause damage and disadvantage.

(c) Attacks on SCADA networks and National Critical Infrastructures.

23 Cyberwarfare as available on http://www.unicri.it/special_topics/cyber_threats/ cyber_crime/ explanations/ cyberwarfare/

The above definitions clearly indicate that cyber warfare refers to conducting military operations in the cyber domain. Hence, like any other form of warfare, the intent of undertaking such operation in this virtual domain is aimed at influencing the will and decision making capabilities of the enemy's political leadership, economic might, armed forces and the nation's war waging capabilities. Cyberwar is a warlike conflict in virtual space with means of information and communication technology and networks. These operations in the virtual world are often referred to as "Computer Network Operations".

A century ago, when one nation's army mobilised and massed at another's border, war was imminent. Outbreak of hostilities was a matter of time in such a situation. Most acknowledged that the threatened nation had a right to defend itself. But today, technology has confused the application of old rules. In cyberspace, where attacks can be launched in milliseconds, a nation might not have enough time to detect an attack and mount a defence. So let us understand what constitutes computer network operations? Three distinct forms of operations in the cyber domain are :-

(a) **Computer Network Attack**: Operations designed to disrupt, deny, degrade, or destroy information resident in computers and computer networks, or the computers or networks themselves.

(b) **Computer Network Exploitation**: Operations designed towards retrieving intelligence-grade data and information from enemy computers using the networks.

(c) **Computer Network Defense**: This consists of all measures necessary to protect own ICT and infrastructures against hostile Computer Network Attack and Computer Network Exploitation.

The law of conflict management, *Jus ad Bellum*, is a set of rules that have for centuries governed the right to resort to armed conflict and determining whether the conflict is lawful or unlawful in its conception. Article 2(4) of the charter of United Nations was the *coup de grace* for this theory that recognised the right of a state to go to war as just. The article overrules *Jus ad Bellum* and requires all member states of the UN to refrain from use of force against the territorial integrity and political independence of any other state. Article 2(4) is so important to the maintenance of international peace and security that it has often been described as "critical legal obligation" outlawing war. The only exception where force can be used and is not unlawful as per the UN charter is an exercise of that state's inherent right of self defence or unless the use of force is authorised by the Security Council under the Chapter VII. Can the UN charter be applied to cyber warfare also? We shall examine this aspect in Chapter 5.

Conclusion

The dependence of mankind on cyberspace is increasing with each passing day. The kind of impact it has had on our lives is unprecedented. It is, therefore, but natural that nations will try and exploit this domain to their advantage not only for economic aspects but also for political and military advantage. It is for this reason that cyberspace is being termed as the fifth domain of warfare, though this domain was never created with the intentions of only waging a war.

Cyber warfare is all about disrupting, if not destroying, the critical infrastructure which is dependent on information and communications systems. It means trying to know all about an adversary while denying it the same advantage. It means turning the "balance of information and knowledge" in one's favour, especially if the balance of forces is not. It means using knowledge so that less capital and labour may have to be expended. Cyberwar also refers to preparing and conducting military operations according to information-related principles. This implies that cyber warfare is a subset of information warfare. We shall examine all these aspects in succeeding chapters.

2 Global Cyber Hotspots

The world has awakened to a new threat. China, Russia and North Korea's test of a cyber weapon, Iran's cyber weapon ambitions, the renewed defense industry's emphasis on the use of computers as a weapon have all combined to accelerate the rate of development of what we can call "the most destructive weapon on the planet."

– Kevin G Coleman

Cyberspace, the global communications and information ecosystem is deeply embedded in all aspects of our society, economics and politics. As individuals, we virtually live online. Our economies have started to depend more and more on virtual online businesses. Governments are trying to implement e-governance models across the globe for effective governance. 'Digital India' is one such initiative of Government of India to integrate the government departments and the people by 2019. It aims at ensuring the government services are made available to citizens electronically by reducing paperwork. Many more such initiatives are on, around the world.

As more systems get automated and networked, more challenges are being thrown up like cybercrime, cyber espionage and threats to confidentiality and integrity of personal data. Who are these people exploiting the cyberspace to their advantage? Are these nations which can use the cyber domain to wage a war through it? While in the previous chapter, we dwelt on what exactly is cyberspace and the actors operating in it, in this Chapter we will try to determine what are the indicators of the cyber power of a nation, where are the cyber power hotspots on the globe and analyse some of the recent cyber conflicts.

Indicators of Cyber Warfare Capabilities

When nuclear technologies came into being, the capabilities to develop and use nuclear power, whether for peaceful use or destruction, was limited to a few developed nations because of the very nature of the technology. If a nation wanted to go nuclear, not only was the technology not easily available but also the chosen few powers ensured that enough impediments were put in their path. Then there was the threat of nuclear deterrence which prevented nations from using nuclear technologies for warfare. Thus, the number of countries which possessed a nuclear weapon system remained few. Some nations like North Korea and Iran which covertly tried to develop a nuclear weapon could be easily identified as there were very few counties capable of developing the technology for weapon system and also there was an embargo on transfer of such technologies. All these factors put together ensured that any nuclear power remained bastion of a chosen few.

However, this is not the case with cyber technologies. Unlike any other weapon system technology, the very nature of information technology and ease of its availability makes it unique. It is perhaps the first commercial technology which can be put to military use too. It is for this reason that the factors which spell out the might of a nation to wage a cyberwar will be different from the factors contributing towards conventional or nuclear power. While it is easy to determine the nuclear and conventional war waging capabilities of a nation, it's difficult to determine the cyber might of a nation. Therefore it is essential to establish what all factors contribute towards cyberwar waging capabilities. Is it just the peaceful use of this technology or are there more factors that determine the power of a nation to wage a cyberwar? Let us determine some common denominators which could indicate how strong would the cyber warfare capabilities of the nation be.

The factors which are indicators of the cyber warfare capabilities of a nation can be divided into two broad categories: The Government Sector and the Private Sector. Let us examine each one of them in more detail.

The Government Sector

Available Cyber Warfare Doctrine. If a nation has declared cyber warfare doctrine, it is evident that the nation possesses a formidable cyber might.

During cyberattacks, there is no time to deliberate on a comprehensive response. A Cyber Warfare Doctrine spells out the role of all stakeholders in the event of a cyberattack; brings about a decisive conclusion about the national response when such attacks occur, and serves to deter future conflicts through a unified national security policy. As on date, not many countries have come out with a cyber warfare doctrine.

Active Cyber Warfare Units. If a nation wants to undertake offensive cyber operations and also protect its own infrastructure, specially military infrastructure, it needs to be well organised for it. The armed forces of such nations will therefore have organisations capable of undertaking cyber warfare. An active cyber warfare organisation could be anything from a national cyber command to a discrete unit capable of undertaking cyberattacks. A number of nations have already raised or are in the process of creating such units. Some nations on the other hand have covert units capable of undertaking cyber operations. The former Defence Minister of India, Shri AK Antony, in May 2013 announced that India too will soon form a cyber command to handle the online threats being faced by the country[1]. Though the cyber command has still not seen the light of the day, the armed forces remain hopeful that the present government will soon allocate the necessary budget for raising this strategic asset in India.

Computer Emergency Response Teams (CERT). CERT is a government-mandated information technology security organisation. The purpose of CERT is to respond to computer security incidents, report on vulnerabilities and promote effective IT security practices throughout the country. CERT could be at various levels, starting from national level to individual organisation level. A number of armed forces across the globe alos have their own CERT.

Cyber Crime Prevention / Investigation Teams. While the task of such teams may be to prevent and investigate cybercrimes, yet due to the very nature of their task, they can be an effective tool for undertaking defensive cyber operations.

Government-run Academic Institutions with Cyber Programs. Such institutions clearly indicate that the government has intentions of creating a trained pool of manpower which can be employed for undertaking cyber operations, both defensive as well as offensive. A large number of countries

1 Cyber Command for Country Soon: Antony TNN May 26, 2013, 03.09AM IST.

including India for example run programs on Ethical Hacking to train white hat professionals.

Government Sponsored Cyber Projects. A large number of countries sponsor defence related information technology projects akin to conducting cyber training programs. The aim of such projects could be to carry out R&D in the field of cyber technologies which can then be successfully employed in strategic and operational cyber warfare activities. Some countries mandate such projects to undertake cyber espionage and surveillance in the garb of R&D.

Intelligence Service Capabilities. Intelligence, as we shall see in subsequent chapters, is a very important part of cyber operations. The moment a nation state or its armed forces start investing in cyber intelligence gathering, it can be assumed that the country is investing into cyber warfare capabilities.

Military Command and Control, Communications, Computers and Intelligence (C^4I) and Information Warfare Capability. To be a force multiplier, cyber warfare needs to form part of the overall war waging strategy of a country. Cyber operations therefore need to be integrated with overall information warfare and C4ISR strategy of the armed forces. If the armed forces of a country, for example USA have well developed C4ISR capabilities, they will be able to undertake cyber operations with much more ease, than a nation with no or little C4ISR assets.

Military Intelligence Units. When a nation is trying to develop offensive cyber warfare capabilities, its military intelligence units would certainly be tasked to gather information about enemy's operational networks and IT systems. Without this piece of critical information, it would be impossible to carry out any wartime cyberattacks.

Military Units Capabilities. Military capabilities around the globe are being upgraded to monitor the constantly changing cyber domain, to launch and to defend against cyberattacks. Armed forces are being trained and equipped to defend against enemy's cyber warfare capabilities. Development of such capabilities is the biggest indicator that a nation is trying to develop offensive cyber warfare assets.

Overall Use of IT. The mere fact, that the armed forces of a nation have a predominance of networks and rely on information technology for its day to day functions, is itself an indicator that the nation is equipped for cyber warfare. A well networked army/ navy or air force is bound to invest in cyber defence. If defensive cyber warfare capabilities exist, it is but certain that some outfit for offensive cyber operations too would be available with such a force.

The Private Sector

While potent armed forces are a pre-requisite for war fighting for a nation, so is not the case with cyberwar. Unlike other forms of warfare, an offensive cyber war/ cyber operations can be undertaken by non-state actors, cyber terrorists or even state sponsored hackers. Such elements, which shall be discussed in detail in Chapter 5, may or may not be trained and sponsored by the state. Private IT infrastructure of a country is adequate to ensure that the nation is equipped for cyberwar. The state of development of the private sector is therefore, equally important as an indicator of cyber warfare potential of a nation. Some of the aspects are as under:

(a) Academia - Developed educational system for computer science/ engineering helps the youth of the country to be available for various IT related tasks. The same youth can be employed for building a sound cyber warfare base.

(b) Accessibility of network to general public – The more the penetration of facilities like internet, the more are the chances that the nation would have cyber warfare capabilities.

(c) Computer security programs – If the nation is capable of developing or even implementing sound computer security programs, its cyber defence will be better than others.

(d) Expatriate students studying in technologically advanced countries – China is a classic example of this. According to the Minnesota Daily, the US universities enrolled nearly 100,000 Chinese students between 2009 and 2012, and Chinese students now comprise about a quarter of all foreign students in the United States.[2] China, as we shall see a little later, today has one of the most potent offensive cyber capabilities.

2 Department of Homeland Security, Study in the States as available at http://studyinthestates.dhs.gov/2014/01/number-of-chinese-students-studying-in-the-united-states-increases

(e) Fiber optic cable/copper wiring – The extent of physical network ensures reach of voice and data networks to the remotest corners of the country. The greater the reach, more will be the number of people who have access to cyberspace.

(f) Hackers – hackers could be state-sponsored, condoned black hats and cyber criminals who are enrolled with specific political aims. Many nations are running ethical hacking schools to train security personnel. The larger the number of schools, the bigger will be pool of hackers available to the nation.

(g) Hardware production capabilities – The hardware production capabilities reflect on the overall growth of the country in the field of IT.

(h) Some of the other factors could include:

  (i) High speed internet availability to the public

  (ii) IT cooperation of the private sector with other countries

  (iii) IT infrastructure in the country

  (iv) Presence of IT security firms in the country

  (v) Number of ISPs and main nodes

  (vi) Number of satellite links providing network connectivity across the nation

  (vii) Density of telephone lines

  (viii) Overall state and integration of IT

  (ix) Process control systems including SCADA systems

  (x) Software development capabilities

  (xi) Transnational corporations active in the IT sector / using IT

What the above indicators signify is that, the more developed the private IT and telecom sectors are in a nation, the more are the chances that the nation will be capable of undertaking cyber warfare. In any case, if a nation has well developed telecom and IT sectors, for example Japan,

Taiwan and India, they will have to prepare themselves against cyberattack from rogue nations and rogue elements. What this means is that defensive cyber capability becomes an inherent part of well-developed IT and telecom sectors of a country.

The geopolitical reality of the cyberspace today is that while great powers are actively engaged in developing their armies to undertake cyber operations in a new battleground, the real innovation in orchestrating cyberattacks is occurring in regional conflicts like Russia-Ukraine, Israel-Iran, Japan-China, India-Pakistan et al. This is primarily because cyberattacks are easy, effective and can be carried out even when the two states are not at war. Based on some of the above discussed factors, McAfee Labs in October 2013 released a report on Cyber Warfare capabilities of nations across the globe. The details are summarised in the table below :-[3]

	Cyber Warfare Doctrine	Cyber Warfare Strategy	Cyber Warfare Training	Cyber Warfare Exercises / Simulation	Collaboration with IT industry/ Technical Universities
Albania		X	X	X	
Argentina	X		X		
Australia		X	X		
Austria	X		X	X	
Belarus	X		X		
Brazil		X	X	X	
Bulgaria		X		X	
Canada				X	
China	X		X	X	X
Cyprus		X	X	X	X
Czech Republic		X	X	X	
Denmark		X		X	

3 Hacking Summit Names Nations With Cyberwarfare Capabilities by Francois Paget as available at https://blogs.mcafee.com/mcafee-labs/hacking-summit-names-nations-with-cyberwarfare-capabilities

	Cyber Warfare Doctrine	Cyber Warfare Strategy	Cyber Warfare Training	Cyber Warfare Exercises / Simulation	Collaboration with IT industry/ Technical Universities
Estonia		X	X	X	
Finland	X			X	
France	X		X	X	X
Germany	X		X	X	
Ghana		X			
Hungary		X	X	X	X
India	X		X	X	X
Iran			X		X
Israel	X		X	X	X
Italy			X	X	X
Japan			X		
Jordan		X	X		
Kenya			X		
Latvia		X	X	X	
Lithuania		X		X	
Malaysia		X	X		
Netherland		X	X	X	
New Zealand		X	X		
North Korea			X		X
Norway		X		X	
Pakistan			X		
Philippines		X	X		X
Poland		X		X	
Russia	X		X		X

	Cyber Warfare Doctrine	Cyber Warfare Strategy	Cyber Warfare Training	Cyber Warfare Exercises / Simulation	Collaboration with IT industry/ Technical Universities
Slovak Republic		X		X	
South Korea		X			
Spain				X	
Sweden				X	
Switzerland		X		X	
Turkey		X	X	X	
United Kingdom		X	X	X	
USA	X	X	X	X	X

('X' indicates presence of the capability)

Table 5: Cyber Warfare Capabilities of Nations

If the McAfee report is to be believed, then Australia, Belarus, China, France, India, Iran, Israel, North Korea, Pakistan, Russia and USA are nations with complete gamut of offensive cyber warfare tools, while the other nations mentioned in the table have defensive cyber warfare capabilities. Let us therefore examine how well prepared are some of these nations in waging a cyber war.

United States of America

The US reserves the right... to respond to serious cyberattacks with an appropriate proportional, a justified military response."

– Inside Cyber Warfare by Jeffrey Carr P.273

The United States of America is truly the world leader in the field of cyber security as well as cyber warfare. Some of the factors which contribute towards this are:

- The US has the most advanced software and IT services industry in the world.
- The industry has increased its revenue by an average of six per cent between 2012 and 2014. The details are as under :[4]

Sub Industry	1997	2000	2005	2010	2012
Computer Science Design and related industry	\$75,259	\$113,596	\$134,964	\$189,882	\$229,792
Software Publishers	\$43,831	\$66,171	\$78,482	\$103,958	\$115,435
Data Processing, Hosting, & info. Services	\$30,314	\$23,970	\$71,822	\$69,224	\$80,186
Total	\$149,404	\$203,737	\$285,268	\$363,064	\$425,413

Table 6: Value-Added Produced by the Software Industry, 1997-2012 (\$ millions)

- The US accounts for more than 55 per cent of global ICT research and development.
- There are more than 100,000 software and IT companies in the US.
- Over 80 per cent of the US is connected to the internet. It is amongst the best networked nations in the world.
- From 2007 to 2014, as overall private-sector employment has declined at an average annual rate of 0.1 per cent, software industry employment grew on an average by 3.1 per cent per year.

Owing to the vast proliferation of the public and private networks, the US is amongst the most attacked nations in the cyber space. Some of

4 The U.S. Software Industry As an Engine for Economic Growth and Employment by Robert J. Shapiro published in September 2014 as available at http://www.sonecon.com/docs/studies/Report_for_SIIA-Impact_of_Software_on_the_Economy-Robert_Shapiro-Sept2014-Final.pdf

the recent attacks on the US will be analysed later. The Office of **Cyber Security and Communications** (CS&C), within the National Protection and Programs Directorate, Department of Homeland Security, is responsible for enhancing the security, resilience, and reliability of the Nation's cyber and communications infrastructure.[5] CS&C leads efforts to protect the federal ".gov" domain of civilian government networks and to collaborate with the private sector—the ".com" domain—to increase the security of critical networks. In addition, the National Cybersecurity and Communications Integration Center (NCCIC) serves as a 24/7 cyber monitoring, incident response, and management center and as a national point of cyber and communications incident integration. To protect the cyber infrastructure, it has identified two overarching objectives:

- To build and maintain an effective national cyberspace response system;
- To implement a cyber-risk management program for protection of critical infrastructure.

To check the cyber defence preparedness especially of the critical info-infrastructure of the country, The Department of Homeland Security runs biennial exercise series called 'Cyber Storm', which provides the framework for the most extensive government-sponsored cyber security exercise of its kind anywhere in the world. Cyber Storm participants perform the following activities :-[6]

- Examine organisations' capability to prepare for, protect from, and respond to cyber attacks' potential effects;
- Exercise strategic decision making and inter-agency coordination of incident response in accordance with national level policy and procedures;
- Validate information sharing relationships and communications paths for collecting and disseminating cyber incident situational awareness, response and recovery information, and;

5 Office of Cybersecurity and Communications as available at http://www.dhs.gov/office-cybersecurity-and-communications

6 Cyber Storm: Securing Cyber Space as available at http://www.dhs.gov/cyber-storm-securing-cyber-space

- Examine means and processes through which to share sensitive information across boundaries and sectors without compromising proprietary or national security interests.

The US armed forces too are well organised for undertaking cyber operations. United States Cyber Command (USCYBERCOM) is an armed forces sub-unified command subordinate to United States Strategic Command. The command is located in Fort Meade, Maryland. USCYBERCOM plans, coordinates, integrates, synchronises and conducts activities to – direct the operations and defence of specified Department of Defence information networks and; prepare to, and when directed, conduct full spectrum military cyberspace operations in order to enable actions in all domains, ensure US/Allied freedom of action in cyberspace and deny the same to our adversaries.[7] The organisation and tasking of the USCYBERCOM will be discussed later in Chapter 6. It is said to be manned by approximately over 6000 personnels, both in uniform and from the civil street. The task of USCYBERCOM is to:-

- Fuse the full spectrum of cyberspace operations;
- Plan, coordinate, integrate, synchronise, and conduct activities to lead day-to-day defence and protection of Department of Defence (DoD) information networks;
- Coordinate DoD operations providing support to military missions;
- Direct the operations and defence of specified DoD information networks;
- Prepare and when directed, conduct full spectrum military cyberspace operations.

On 01 Oct 2010, the US Army re-designated the inactive Headquarters of the Second US Army, as US Army Cyber Command, with its headquarters at Fort Belvoir, Virginia. Army cyber mission is to:

- Plan, coordinate, integrate, synchronise, direct, and conduct network operations and defence of all Army networks.

7 United States Cyber Command as available at http://en.wikipedia.org/wiki/United_States_Cyber_Command

- When directed, to conduct cyberspace operations in support of full spectrum operations to ensure US and allied freedom of action in cyberspace, and to deny the same to adversaries.

US Department of Defense (DoD) released a new strategy on 23 April 2015, to rewire the Pentagon for cyber operations. It is a more comprehensive and detailed articulation of the 2011 strategy. As per the document, US DoD has sets five strategic goals for its cyberspace missions:[8]

1. Build and maintain ready forces and capabilities to conduct cyberspace operations;

2. Defend the DoD information network, secure DoD data, and mitigate risks to DoD missions;

3. Be prepared to defend the US homeland and US vital interests from disruptive or destructive cyberattacks of significant consequence;

4. Build and maintain viable cyber options and plan to use those options to control conflict escalation and to shape the conflict environment at all stages;

5. Build and maintain robust international alliances and partnerships to deter shared threats and increase international security and stability.

The seriousness of the efforts of the USA on cyber security issues can be also be judged from the fact that amongst the first few things which Mr Barak Obama did after winning his second term as President of the USA, was to take out executive order No 13636 on 12 Feb 2013. The order deals with the aspect of Improving Critical Infrastructure Cyber Security. In March 2013, Director of National Intelligence, James Clapper identified cyberattacks as the greatest threat to the US national security. Great amount of work is being done on protecting the critical infrastructure of the country. Adequate budget is also allocated for such tasks. In the President's budget request 2016, overall IT spending is tabbed at US $86.4 billion (US $37.3 billion for defense IT and US $49 billion for non-defense).[9]

8 The DoD Cyber Strategy April 2015 http://www.defense.gov/home/features/2015/0415_cyber-strategy/Final_2015_DoD_CYBER_STRATEGY_for_web.pdf

9 Cybersecurity gets big boost in 2016 budget, Feb 03, 2015 as available at http://gcn.com/articles/2015/02/03/budget-cybersecurity.aspx

Russia

"US officials do not rate China as the biggest threat to the US in cyberspace. The Russians are definitely better, almost as good as we are"

– Richard Clark in his book Cyber War

To obtain reliable information on the IT and software industry of Russia, the quality of its leading participants, its capacity, growth and prospects for sustainability poses more of a challenge. The Russian Ministry of Economic Development reports that the Russian IT market grew by 6.7 per cent in 2012 as compared to 2011, to reach 732 billion Roubles (USD 22.46 billion).[10] As per some estimates, the Russian IT companies control one per cent of the global market, worth roughly USD 16 to 20 billion. IT export services industry is made up of three distinct sectors in Russia: Outsourcing Services, Independent Software Vendors and Captives.

It is expected that by 2015, the Russian internet economy will be approximately 3.7 per cent of its GDP (India would be USD 10.8 trillion by then at 3.4 per cent). In 2013 there were only 90 million internet users (India had 165 million internet users in the same period).

Russia's first real exposure to information and cyber domain was during the Chechen war in 1999. It was during this war that Russia felt left out of a major facet of information propagation. However, Russian cyberattacks on Estonia in 2007 and Georgia in 2008 clearly indicated how effective and visible cyber warfare capability Russia was capable of developing in a matter of few years. Both the incidences would be dealt with in detail subsequently. Today, cyber warfare in Russia includes allegations of denial of service attacks, hacker attacks, dissemination of disinformation over the internet, participation of state-sponsored teams in political blogs, internet surveillance using SORM technology (System for Operative Investigative Activities, is a technical system for search and surveillance in the internet in Russia. SORM-1 system was established in 1996 to monitor telephone communications. In July 1998 the system was replaced by SORM-2 to allow monitoring of the internet, in addition to telephone communications) and persecution of cyber-dissidents.

10 Software Industry Overview as available at http://www.software-russia.com/why_russia/industry_overview

According to some unconfirmed reports, Russia has integrated cyber operations into its military doctrine; though not fully successful. Putin's Information Security Doctrine 2010 empowers the state to control information. The objectives of this directive are:

- Protect strategically important information
- Protect against deleterious foreign information
- Inculcate patriotism and values

A 2012 analysis by an Israeli defense analyst highlighted that Russia supports cyber warfare capabilities, especially providing such capabilities in the Russian Army.[11] The nature of cyber warfare and information warfare requires that the development of a response to these challenges must be organised on an interdisciplinary basis and include researchers from different branches – political analysts, sociologists, psychologists, military specialists, and media representatives. Russia feels that the ability to achieve cyber superiority is essential to victory in cyberspace.

In Aug 2013, the head of the Foundation of Advanced Military Research announced that Russia will create a cyber security command in the near future.[12] The present status of the cyber command is not known, though a large number of unconfirmed reports indicate that Russian armed forces are capable of undertaking cross domain operations with cyber being one of the domains.

Russia is not keen to introduce an international treaty on cyber governance and prevention of cyberwar. Russia and the US fundamentally disagree on the nature of treaties to prevent cyber warfare. Russia is in favour of total cyber weapon disarmament; something similar on the lines of nuclear disarmament. Also, Russia is not willing to sign the European Convention on Cybercrime primarily because it does not agree upon appropriate terms for cross-border access to data-processing networks.[13]

---

11 A Brief Analysis of Russian Cyberwarfare Capabilities – Past, Present, and Future by Matthew Crosston as available at http://www.billslater.com/writing/DET_630_Week_08_Writing_Assignment_from_W_F_Slater_v1.pdf

12 Russia Setting up Cyber Warfare Unit Under Military, International Business Times, 20 August 2013 as available at http://www.ibtimes.co.uk/russia-cyber-war-hack-moscow-military-snowden-500220

13 Putin defies Convention on Cybercrime, 27 March 2008 as available at http://eng.

On the other hand, Russia had joined China and a few others in plying proposals aimed at enhancing information security across the globe.

Russians have progressively demonstrated that they have the will, the vision, the doctrines, the tools, the knowledge, and experience with which to successfully wage serious cyber warfare. Latest in the list of countries who have blamed Russia for undertaking cyberattacks is Ukraine. Mobile phone networks and internet connections in Ukraine were severely hampered; government websites were overwhelmed with denial of service attacks; social networks were corrupted, and some of Ukraine's phone and internet cables were cut by pro-Russian forces during the annexation of Crimea in March 2014.[14] Over all, Russians are considered to be a potent threat in the cyberspace.

People's Republic of China

China should become a Cyber Power

– Xi Jinping

People's Republic of China has the most extensive and practiced cyber-warfare capabilities in the world. It began to implement an Information Warfare plan in 1995, and since 1997 has conducted numerous exercises in which computer viruses have been used to interrupt military communications and public broadcasting systems. The present government in China feels that internet security and informatisation is a major strategic issue concerning a country's security and development as well as people's life and work.[15]

China has emerged as a global power in information and communications technology guided by a 15-year (2006-2020) development strategy. In China, the telecom industry is dominated by three state-run businesses – China Telecom, China Unicom and China Mobile while the manufacturing industry is led by the private players like Huawei Technologies and ZTE. Zhongguancun, located in Haidian District

---

cnews.ru/news/top/indexEn.shtml?2008/03/27/293913

14 Russian cyber attacks on Ukraine: the Georgia template, 4 News, 03 May 2014 as available at http://www.channel4.com/news/ukraine-cyber-warfare-russia-attacks-georgia

15 Xi Jinping: China Should Become a Cyber Power, The Diplomat, 04 March 2014

of Beijing and also known as the silicon valley of China and is a major technology hub in China.

According to a report, in March 2012, there were 284.3 million Chinese fixed-line and 1.01 billion mobile customers. The size of the software industry including software and information services in 2012 was worth 2502 billion RMB (about USD 416 billion). In December 2013, China had 618 million Internet users. The penetration rate of internet in 2014 was approx. 45.8 per cent. Unlike the rest of the world, Kylin, an operating system developed by National University of Technology, PRC is China's own operating system. In 2013, China announced release of yet another operating system with the same name using Ubuntu, a Linux based operating system. Most Chinese use Kylin operating system. Baidu is the leading search engine in China. Soso.com and Google China are also present in the Chinese market. A quick comparison of PRC and India as per data of 2013 – 14 is as under :

	China	**India**
Number of Internet users	600 million (43 per cent of population)	152 million (12.5 per cent of population)
Internet based IT business	10 per cent of the GDP	3.3 per cent of the GDP
Value of e-business	$ 1.4 trillion	$ 100 billion

Table 7: Internet growth Data: PRC *versus* India

The Chinese Government's programme of censorship of the Chinese people is unprecedented. The Chinese Government has a surveillance and content control system, which it launched in November 2000, and became known as the *Great Firewall of China.* All major western social media platforms are blocked in China. Twitter, Facebook, YouTube, Vimeo, Google Docs – most of them shut down in July 2009.

PLA and Cyber Warfare. China, at a very early stage of its development, realised that it cannot match the technological might of the USA. Out of this was born the strategy of 'Asymmetric Warfare'. Information dominance, a part of this strategy whether for political, economic, or military purposes, requires mastery of both the electromagnetic spectrum and the global cyber sphere. The PLA GSD Third Department (Signals Intelligence) and Fourth Department (Electronic Countermeasures) are considered to be the two largest players in China's burgeoning cyber-infrastructure.[16] In 2000, China established a strategic IW unit designed to "wage combat through computer networks to manipulate enemy information systems spanning spare parts deliveries to fire control and guidance systems". In July 2010, PLA announced that it had established an "Information Protection Base" under the General Staff Department. The Western powers confirm that the PLA has consolidated the computer and network attack missions together with Electronic Warfare into an Integrated Network Electronic Warfare activity under the General Staff Department's 4th Department.

The Third Department of the GSH is responsible for monitoring the telecommunications of foreign armies and producing finished intelligence based on the military information collected. The Third Department command authorities also manage a complex infrastructure that exploits vulnerable computer networks around the world. Third Department has assumed the responsibility for ensuring the security of PLA computer systems in order to prevent foreign adversaries from gaining access to sensitive national security information[17]. Computer network defence has apparently been included with cyber-espionage in the 3rd Department.

In addition to their own capabilities, it is said that the PLA and cyber intelligence agencies are able to readily utilise the corporate sector, including the state-owned telecommunications carriers such as China Telecom Corporation and also private companies which provide telecommunications and IT services. It is perhaps for this reason that Chinese telecom giants such as Huawei Technologies, one of the biggest suppliers of telecom equipment in the world, has been effectively blocked from business in the US and India. It was only in July 2015, that the Government of India, Ministry of Home Affairs cleared the project of Huawei Technologies to set up a unit in Tamil Nadu as part of : "Make in India" programme.[18]

---

16 The Chinese People's Liberation Army Signals Intelligence and Cyber Reconnaissance Infrastructure by Mark A. Stokes, Jenny Lin and L.C. Russell Hsiao, 11 November 2011 as available at http://project2049.net/documents/pla_third_department_sigint_cyber_stokes_lin_hsiao.pdf

17 Ibid

18 Make in India: Chinese telecom giant Huawei to set up a unit in Tamil Nadu, The Economic Times 14 July 2015.

PLA IW units have reportedly developed detailed procedures for Internet warfare, including software for network scanning, obtaining passwords and breaking codes, stealing data, information paralysing software, information-blocking software, information-deception software, and other malware; and software for effecting counter-measures. These procedures have been tested in field exercises of the armed forces since the year 2000.

China is reported to have conducted cyber-intelligence operations against numerous countries, like the USA, the UK, Australia, New Zealand, Canada, Germany, France, the Netherlands, Portugal, Japan, South Korea, Taiwan, India, Pakistan, Iran, Thailand, the Philippines and Indonesia. PLA Unit 61398, a Military Unit Cover Designator of the PLA has been alleged to be the source of Chinese cyberattacks and cyber intelligence operations. The unit is said to be staffed by thousands of people, trained in network security, digital signal processing, covert communications and English. However, Unit 61398, more formally known as General Staff Department, Third Department, Second Bureau is just one of the dozens of similar groups based in China.

China all along has denied that its armed forces are capable of undertaking cyber operations. In fact it was only in March 2015, that for the first time PLA acknowledged that it did possess cyber warfare capabilities. A high-level Chinese military organisation formally acknowledged that the country's military and its intelligence community have specialised units for waging war on computer networks.[19] China finally has dropped the charade.

While the whole world talks about China's capabilities of undertaking cyber operations, China on the other hand feels and often points out that it is the biggest victim of hacking. As per Mr Cai Mingzhao, Minister of the State Council Information Office of China, between January and August 2014, more than 20,000 websites based in China were modified by hackers and more than 8 million servers, 14 per cent more than 2012, were compromised and controlled by overseas computers via zombie and Trojan programs[20]. These activities caused severe damage to their economy

19 China Reveals Its Cyberwar Secrets as available at http://www.thedailybeast.com/articles/2015/03/18/china-reveals-its-cyber-war-secrets.html

20 Cai Mingzhao delivering the keynote speech at the opening session of the EastWest Institute's 4th Worldwide Cyberspace Cooperation Summit, on 05 November 2013. Text

and the everyday life of the people. More than 80 per cent of Chinese Internet users have fallen victim to cyberattacks at some time or the other. The annual economic losses run into tens of billions of US dollars a year.

Islamic Republic of Iran

Iran is fully prepared to confront any kind of cyberattacks

– General Mohammad Aqakishi, Commander of the information technology and communication department at the General Staff of the Iranian Armed Forces

Iran's domestic consumer electronics market, including computing devices, mobile handsets and video, audio and gaming products was estimated at US $8.2 billion in 2010. It has been steadily growing ever since. 26 per cent of population of Iran uses the internet though the telecomm industry is almost entirely state-owned. Since 2005, Iran has been developing a "national Internet" to improve control over its content as well as speed of the data that moves around on the net.

The software and IT industry in Iran is not very well developed. Only about 150,000 people are employed in the ICT sector, including around 20,000 in the software industry. Despite lack of IT industry base, Iran has boosted its cyber capabilities in a surprisingly short amount of time and possesses the ability to launch successful cyberattacks. The Iranian regime has emerged as a "world class" cyber threat.

Prior to 2009, much of Iran's cyber efforts were focused internally on countering government dissidence. The influential Iranian Revolutionary Guard Corps (IRGC) proposed the development of an Iranian Cyber Army in 2005 to combat internal threats.[21] The Stuxnet attack that targeted Iran's nuclear infrastructure was the catalyst that changed the entire dynamics of Iranian cyber development. In early March 2012, Supreme Leader of Iran, Ayatollah Ali Khameni announced the creation by decree of a new Supreme Council of Cyberspace, "to oversee the defense of the Islamic Republic's computer networks and develop new ways of infiltrating or

---

available at http://www.ewi.info/idea/kicking-ewiper centE2per cent80per cent99s-cybersecurity-summit

21 Iran's Emergence as a Cyber Power by LTC Eric K. Shafa 20 August 2014, as available at http://www.strategicstudiesinstitute.army.mil/index.cfm/articles/Irans-emergence-as-cyber-power/2014/08/20

attacking the computer networks of its enemies". The council included heads of intelligence, militia, security, media chiefs, and the IRGC and was allocated an independent budget.

Today, Iran is a cyber power to reckon with. In 2011, Iran invested at least US $ 1 billion in cyber technology, infrastructure, and expertise.[22] In March 2012, the IRGC claimed it had recruited around 120,000 personnel over 3 years to combat "a soft cyber war against Iran." In early-2013, an IRGC General publically claimed that Iran had the 'fourth biggest cyber power among the world's cyber armies'. In December 2013, Iran unveiled 12 cyber products that were indigenously developed. Cyber defence products included secure cell phones, operating system, navigation system, telecommunications optical transmission system, anti-malware, cyber threats recognition and identification system, security operations centre, a high-speed and high-capacity firewall and a software firewall which showcased the kind of capabilities Iran had acquired in a very short span of time.[23]

While Iran may not be world-class cyber power like the US, China, and Russia, however, it is the will demonstrated by Iran to freely use cyberspace for launching cyberattacks all around the world, that makes it a credible cyber threat. In 2012, Iran was suspected of launching malware that wreaked havoc on 30,000 computers at the Saudi oil company, Aramco. In late-2013, Iran's infiltration of the US Navy's internet network garnered much attention because it indicated that Iran's capability had advanced.[24] Iranian armed forces too are being equipped to defend against enemy's cyberattacks. As per some reports, Iran's secret cyber war-room is supposedly located at Hizballah's secret internal security apparatus headquarters in the Shiite Dahya district. The sudden rise of Iran as a global cyber power could not have been achieved on its own. Western countries often blame Russia for providing clandestine support and training to Iran in its cyber expansion programme.

---

22 Iranian Cyber Army, The Offensive Arm of Iran's Cyber Force by Ashley Wheeler, September 2013, available at www.phoenixts.com/blog/iranian-cyber-army.

23 Iran Unveils 12 Cyber Products, TMC News, 16 March 2014, as available at http://www.tmcnet.com/usubmit/2014/03/16/7727038.htm

24 U.S. Says Iran Hacked Navy Computers, The Wall Street Journal, 27 September 2013, as available at http://www.wsj.com/articles/SB1000142405270230452620457910160235675 1772

Israel

In recent months, we have identified a significant growth in the scope of cyberattacks by Iran against Israel

– Israeli Prime Minister Benjamin Netanyahu

"If Israel decides it doesn't like this deal and it wants to sabotage an Iranian nuke program or facility, it can easily do so through the cyberspace

– US Senator Marco Rubio on Iran Nuclear Deal

Israel's tradition of scientific research, a near-absence of natural resources and an entrepreneurial spirit led the country to pursue knowledge-based industry. In 2009, software industry was worth US $ 6.2 billion. Today Israel's Tech-Investment has edge over the Silicon Valley. 75 per cent of Israeli population uses internet.

Israel's telecom sector has emerged as a world leader in developing innovative technologies, system and solutions for telecom provider and integrators. (Indian armed forces import a large amount of telecom equipment from Israel). In the coming years, Israel's technological advancement will continue leveraging its competitive advantages in such areas as mobile and Internet applications, home networking, storage area networks, and wireless IP networking

High degree of penetration of internet, dependence on information technology and being in the midst of constant conflicts, Israel becomes a natural target of cyberattacks. Israel faces roughly 100,000 cyberattacks each day and is considered a global leader in its ability to handle cyberattacks. From Hamas, Iran or hackers from China, in the past one decade, Israel has faced them all. A number of attacks have even resulted in breakdown of public services and infrastructure. For example, in Sept 2013, a major artery in Israel's national road network in the northern city of Haifa suffered a cyberattack.[25] The Trojan attack targeted the security camera apparatus in the Carmel Tunnels toll road on 08 Sept 2013. As a result of the cyberattack, the security cameras blacked out shutting down

25 Israeli road system hit by cyber-attack, 27 October 2013 as available at http://elderofziyon.blogspot.in/2013/10/israeli-road-system-hit-by-cyber-attack.html#.VQ0dWY6UeSo

the road network for daily travellers for hours and causing chaotic traffic situation. To ensure a secure cyber ecosystem in the country, private companies in Israel have created 'Cyber Gyms' to train their employees to handle cyberattacks and situations that arise out of such attacks.

Israeli Defence Forces have defined cyber warfare as the fifth realm of warfare. They have established a command dedicated to cyber warfare that brings together personnel from the Intelligence Branch and the Teleprocessing Branch to ward off cyberattacks.[26] In June 2012, the Israel Defence Forces' official website announced use of cyberspace to gather intelligence, attack enemies and conduct various military operations. Defence sectors related to cyber warfare have received increased funding and priority in selecting highly qualified inductees.

Military Intelligence Unit 8200, the equivalent of the US National Security Agency is said to be responsible for the Israel Defence Forces offensive cyber capabilities. The Israelis consider it the best intelligence gathering organisation in the world. Though the primary task of the unit is intelligence gathering, sigint to be more specific, many media reports alleged that Unit 8200 was responsible for the creation of the Stuxnet computer worm. Defending military networks is under the supervision of the C4I Directorate which has established a cyber war room in the Kirya military headquarters of Israel Defence Forces. It is said that, Israel Defence Forces have integrated cyber preparedness into their routine training.

A major factor in Israel's cyber security prowess is generous government support for both private and public endeavors. Recently, Prime Minister Benjamin Netanyahu established a new national authority for Operative Cyber Defense, which he stated, has major significance to the defense of the State of Israel in the future. Today Israel is believed to have some of the most advanced cyberwarfare capabilities in the world, to the point where the National Security Agency USA reportedly considered Israel to be a potential electronic and cyber warfare proliferator.

---

26 IDF forms new force to combat cyber warfare, Haaretz, Saturday, March 21, 2015 as available at http://www.haaretz.com/news/diplomacy-defense/idf-forms-new-force-to-combat-cyber-warfare.premium-1.506979

Pakistan

Pakistan is not a new player in the arena of cyber warfare; it has been engaged in a cyber war with India since 1998

– Jeffrey Carr, Inside Cyberwarfare

To promote the growth of information technology industry, the Government of Pakistan founded Pakistan Software Export Board in 1995. Since then, the IT industry in Pakistan has grown at a good rate. Today, it is regarded as a successful sector economically. Even during the peak of financial crisis, IT industry in Pakistan continued to grow. In 2012-2013, the Government of Pakistan spent INR 4.6 billion on information technology projects.

Like India, the telecom boom caught on very well in Pakistan too. In 2008 Pakistan was the world's third fastest growing telecommunications market. Presence of a huge market and active participation of big international brand names has resulted in good infrastructure-optical network and satellite links across the country. However, despite the presence of big brands and rapid growth of IT and telecom industry, Pakistan still does not have much of R&D facility in the country in both the fields. Also, the successive military and democratic governments have not been able to lay down a clear strategic direction for both these industries.

In 2013, approximately 10 per cent of the population of Pakistan was connected to the internet which is roughly about 20 million users. Internet service is primarily provided by State-owned Pakistan Telecommunication Company Ltd. To ensure cyber security for its internet users, Pakistan Government has approved e-mail and internet security policy and security guidelines for the country. In March 2014, Pakistani senate was informed by the Nawaz Sharif government that a cyber security strategy is being devised to counter cyberattacks or infiltration from other countries. Pakistan Senate Defence Committee Chairman, Senator Mushahid Hussai, in Feb 2015, listed the need for legislation, establishing a CERT, a Joint Inter-Services Cyber Defence Command, and Cyber 'rules of the game' within SAARC framework between Pakistan and India to ensure that neither side engages in cyber warfare against the other or hacks other's websites.[27]

27 Mushahid underlines need for cyber security strategy for Pakistan, Daily Times, 19 February 201

Pakistani Armed Forces are in the process of understanding the nuances of cyber warfare. As a first step towards it, the Pakistan's Military College of Signals has started hosting an annual National Conference on Information Assurance. Professor Alya Alvi in an article published on 18 Jan 2014 has stated that Pakistan army seems to have not followed the course of the US and India of establishing a cyber warfare branch.[28] According to him, "*Our armed forces need to be upgraded, modernised, sophisticated and well equipped to cope with the emerging challenges*".

Hackers in India and Pakistan seem to be in a constant state of war. In view of the differing religious, political and national views held by both sides, it is not surprising that there is an almost constant barrage of Internet attacks against each other's websites and information. Those attacks are probably not state sponsored but are just hacktivists demonstrating national pride with the tools available to them.[29]

Security experts in Pakistan feel that their Government is not adequately prepared to handle cyber threats.[30] According to them, neither Pakistan's legal framework is in place nor is the trained human resource available in the country to defend it against serious cyber threats. Yet despite this, as far as India is considered, Pakistan will remain a credible threat in the cyberspace as she is capable of integrating cyber operations with state sponsored terror activities. If ISI decides to unleash a mix of cyberattack with jihad, Indian security forces may find it difficult to handle such a threat.

Democratic People's Republic of Korea

The development of telecom sector in the Democratic People's Republic of Korea is seriously impeded by the country's parlous economic state and the regime's general repression of communications. According to a report, each time the Country's 3G subscribers crosses 2.5 million mark, its internet crashes.[31] In North Korea, access to internet remains privilege

---

28 Pakistan Observer 18 January 2014 as available at http://issuu.com/abidoon/docs/e-paper_17-01-2014__lhr_

29 Surviving Cyber War, Richard Stiennon P 55

30 Govt not prepared to handle cyber threats, Dawn, 01 October 2014 as available at http://www.dawn.com/news/1135486

31 North Korea - Telecoms Market Overview and Statistics as available at http://www.budde.com.au/Research/North-Korea-Telecoms-Market-Overview-and-Statistics.html

of the elite. There are not many software industries in North Korea. Though in the recent past, the government has started investing in telecom infrastructure, yet ordinary citizens have restricted access to the internet and many still do not own a PC.

Despite the lack of infrastructure and absence of institutions to train its manpower, North Korea has indulged in cyberattacks very often. The most recent case has been that of Sony Hack. On 24 Nov 2014, personal information about employees of Sony Pictures Entertainment and their dependents, e-mails between employees, information about executive salaries at the company, copies of unreleased Sony films, and other information were obtained and released by a hacker group going under the nickname "Guardians of Peace" (GoP). United States intelligence officials believe the cyber-attack was sponsored by the North Korean Government.[32] Initially North Korea agreed to cooperate in investigations to determine if the cyberattack originated from its soil, but later, on 21 Dec 2014, it backtracked and warned of strikes against the White House. The entire incidence resulted in loss of millions of dollars to Sony Pictures Entertainment.

According to a report published in The Telegraph in Jan 2015, "*North Korea is currently running its 6,000-strong workforce for cyber warfare and performing cyberattacks [to achieve] physical and psychological paralysis in South Korea, such as causing problems for military operations and national infrastructure*".[33] Despite being one of the poorest countries in the world, North Korea's hacking capabilities have become a global talking point. While most of the attacks are targeted towards South Korea, the recent Sony Pictures hack has shown the world that North Korea is capable of taking on the might of any nation including the USA.

32 Sony Hack: A Wakeup Call for the Private Industry against Cyberattacks by Sanjeev Relia as available at http://usiblog.in/2014/12/sony-hack-a-wakeup-call-for-the-private-industry-against-cyberattacks/

33 North Korea doubles its cyber warfare team to 6,000 troops, The Telegraph, as available at http://www.telegraph.co.uk/news/worldnews/asia/northkorea/11329480/North-Korea-doubles-its-cyber-warfare-team-to-6000-troops.html

Analysis of Some Cyberattacks

Having defined cyberattacks, how they are classified and the taxonomy of cyber adversaries in Chapter One, and having seen some of the global cyber powers, it is time to analyse some of the well-known cyberattacks which have come to light in the recent past and draw lessons from them. Thousands of cyberattacks take place over the internet each day. Some attacks also take place without using internet as a medium. However, most attacks go unreported. Recent history of cyberspace is replete with hundreds of examples of attacks which have resulted in significant losses of financial resources, intellectual property, personal information, and vital intelligence to private sector and government organisations at all levels across the globe. With each attack, we learn more and more about ways to prevent them altogether, mitigate the damage, or shorten the recovery time when attacks succeed. Let us first analyse some of the well-known cyberattacks.

Estonian Cyberattacks – 2007

The most talked about and discussed cyberattacks in the history of cyber warfare and cyberspace are the cyberattacks on Estonia in 2007. Republic of Estonia, with a population of a little over 1.3 million, has become a role model for nations on how to use the cyber space for good governance. As one of the most electronically advanced countries, the Estonian government has shifted its operations to the virtual domain since November 2005. Cabinet-level meetings are conducted online and documents are signed with e-signatures by the government officials. In a rare display of how well the country is networked and how robust the networks are, Mr Jaak Aaviksoo, the Minister for Education and Research of the Republic of Estonia casted his ballot online from the Oberoi Hotel, New Delhi on 14 October 2013 while addressing a gathering of over 200 delegates during CyFy 2013. Of course to maintain the secrecy of his selection of the candidate, he requested the organisers to blackout the projection systems for just about 10 seconds. The Minister, who incidentally was the Minister of Defence of Republic of Estonia in 2007, said that the cyberattacks, supposedly backed by the Russian Government on Estonia in 2007, were a wakeup call to the world about the threats that nations can face from the cyber domain. Unless we sit up and take note of this threat, nations will not be able to effectively use this domain.

In 2007, Estonia was ranked 23rd in e-readiness ratings. 61 per cent of the population enjoyed online access to bank accounts, and 95 per cent of banking transactions were electronically controlled by two major banks of the Nation. In Apr 2007, the Estonian Government's decision to relocate the World War II monument (a bronze Russian soldier commemorating the sacrifice made by the Soviet Armed Forces in liberating Estonia from the Nazi forces) from the capital Tallinn to a military cemetery outside the city sparked protests and riots among Estonia's Russian minority. The protests started on 27 Apr 2007 and were followed by a barrage of DDoS attacks ranging from single individuals using various methods like ping floods to rentals of botnets from all around the world (botnet is a collection of compromised computers (bots) running malicious programs that allow them to be controlled remotely. Botnet is a portmanteau of robot and network). The Government network was designed to handle 2 million megabits per second; the servers were flooded with nearly 200 million megabits per second of traffic. The longest attack lasted over 10 hours and created over 90 million megabits per second of data on the targets. As a result, the websites of the Ministries of Foreign Affairs and Justice had to shut down. The second phase of attacks came on 3 May; the botnets began attacking private sites and servers. This included banking, telecom and government infrastructure. Banks in Estonia were shut down, save a few, but it came at great monetary costs and also affected international banking. The climax of the attacks happened on 9 May, the Russian anniversary of the end of WWII.

The head of the Security at Swedbank's Estonian subsidiary reported that over 80,000 unique IP addresses were identified as the source of the attacks which included "Get Floods" and "Ping Floods". President Ilves alludes to evidence that some of the cyberattacks originated from within the Kremlin although subsequent investigations have yet to yield conclusive attribution to the Russian Government for the attacks. The plausible deniability of a crowd sourced attack was clearly demonstrated in Estonia.

Estonia's response to the cyberattacks was in three phases: communication, network response and server infrastructure hardening. In April 2007, the technical community of Estonia became cyber warriors. Within an hour of the start of the DDoS attacks, the major telecom providers, the banks and the university located at Tartu were talking to each other to determine what had to be done. They decided to filter out all communication from outside Estonia and essentially cut Estonia off the internet. Obviously, the attacker in response recruited bots inside Estonia and continued the DDoS against critical servers. The next step was to address a fundamental problem of the way the government servers were configured. The websites in Estonia succumbed not because the web servers could not handle the number of requests, but because the backend database was not designed to respond to repeated floods of requests. To overcome this, the system administrators got together a large number of cache servers to store static copies of web pages built from the backend database. These SQUID farms put in place within 72 hours brought most of Estonia's beleaguered websites back online.

Both US and NATO sent teams of computer security experts to help the Estonian authorities cope with the massive wave of DDoS attacks that paralyzed the country. What struck many network security experts as unusual about the cyberattacks was that they lasted for weeks, and their intensity was extremely high. Some botnets employed in the DDoS attacks on Estonian websites included up to 100,000 'zombie' PCs. The concerted efforts by its allies eventually stabilised Estonia's situation, but intermittent cyberattacks on government websites, including the State Chancellery and Federal Electoral Committee, continued well into the middle of May 2007. Estonia till date blames Russia for the cyberattacks. Moscow has always denied any involvement in the attacks.

These cyberattacks were also a pivotal moment in the rising of cyber warfare. NATO was called upon to consider the question: "At what point does a cyberattack become an act of war thus invoking Article V of the NATO treaty that requires member nations to come to the aid of the party under attack?" And if an act of war has been committed then what is the appropriate response?

The cyberattack on Estonia led NATO to establish the Cooperative Cyber Defence Centre of Excellence (CCD COE) in Estonia in May 2008. The Centre, with a staff of 30 specialists, became operational in August of that year, and is part of a NATO network of 13 accredited Centres of Excellence dedicated to training representatives from alliance member countries "on technically sophisticated aspects of NATO operations." The CCD COE focus is on coordinating cyber defence and establishing policy for aiding allies during cross-jurisdictional attacks.[34] We will discuss the relevance of CCD COE in Chapter 6.

The Pentagon under Constant Attack

The Pentagon is one of the largest office complexes in the world housing 23,000 military and civilian personnel who are responsible for control and administration of 1.4 million strong US defence department. It was designed to be an intelligent building. Unfortunately, the 'intelligence' catered only to heating, ventilation and air-conditioning of the building and not the networks housed in the building. The Pentagon had adopted an IP network in 1995. By 2003, there were thousands of network devices, desktop computers and servers including email servers as part of the computing infrastructure. The growth of the networks over a period could be at best described as 'helter-skelter'. The primary line of defence was a firewall backed by Intrusion Detection System (IDS). The IDS is a passive method used to alert the users. It does nothing to stop an attack. The IDS generates thousands, sometime million alerts each day based on suspicious events, sorting of which is a difficult task.

Because the pentagon represents the core of military operations in the US, it has many disparate networks, conflicting management hierarchies and houses hundreds of servers for command, control and administrative functions. It also perhaps has been one of the most desirable targets for cyber intelligence gathering and cyberattacks. The US officials over the past twelve years have agreed to a very large number of cyberattacks taking place on the Pentagon.

In June 2007, US Defence Secretary, Robert Gates admitted that email servers in the Pentagon had been compromised leading to those systems being taken off line. He downplayed the seriousness of the attacks, claiming that only low level personnel were affected. Yet, 1500 computers were taken off line to address the issue. To this date the length of time that the email servers were compromised has not been revealed. The content of the information that has been lost also has never been made public.

Again in July 2007, General Wesley Clark reported to a congressional committee investigating the dangers of Peer to Peer network, that data from Pentagon had made its way onto LimeWire, a file sharing service. His

34 On Cyberwarfare by Fred Schreier

testimony included that an investigator had found "the entire Pentagon's secret backbone network infrastructure diagram, including the server and IP addresses, with password transcripts for Pentagon's secret network servers, the DoD employees' contact information, secure socket layer instructions and certificates allowing access to the disclosing contractors' IT systems and ironically a letter from OMB which explicitly talks about the risks associated with P2P file sharing network".[35] This had happened due to malware which had been introduced into a network in the Pentagon.

In 2010 the Pentagon again reported that over 24,000 files from a defence contractor had been stolen. As usual no details were given of how these files were stolen and what was contained in them. But what can be assumed is that at least some of the files had secret content. Secret enough that Deputy Defense Secretary William J Lynn III felt compelled to admit it during a speech about the future of cyber policy. Once again cyberattacks were cited as the reason. Lynn said intrusions in the last few years had compromised some of the Pentagon's most sensitive systems, including surveillance technologies and satellite communications systems. According to him, penetrations of defense industry networks had targeted a wide swath of military hardware, including missile tracking systems and drone aircraft.

As late as May 2013, in a departure from the usually veiled suggestions of Chinese involvement in cyberattacks, the 92-page Department of Defense report released by the Pentagon, openly accused Peoples Republic of China of launching cyberattacks aimed at exfiltrating information from the US Government and military as well as from corporate entities. As per the report, the stolen information is supporting China's defence industrial base, helping Chinese policymakers and military planners build "a picture of US defence networks, logistics and related military capabilities that could be exploited during a crisis". Importantly, the report cautioned, the espionage activities are helping the country build out a sophisticated electronic warfare capability aimed at neutralising American technological superiority in traditional kinetic warfare and other areas.[36] US lawmakers too have, on numerous occasions voiced concerns about cyberattacks originating from China.

---

35 Surviving Cyberwar by Richard Stienno P 48

36 Pentagon accuses China of cyber attacks on U.S military, business targets, by JaikumarVijayan, available at http://www.computerworld.com/s/article/9238976/Pentagon_accuses_China_of_cyberattacks_on_U.S_military_business_targets

GhostNet: Dalai Lama under Cyberattack

Between June 2008 and Mar 2009 the Information Warfare Monitor (IWM) conducted an extensive and exhaustive two-phase investigation focused on allegations of Chinese cyber espionage against the Tibetan community. The IWM was an advanced research activity tracking the emergence of cyberspace as a strategic domain. The company closed down in Jan 2012. The Chinese suppression of Tibet is well known. The greatest threat to the Chinese hegemony in their vast territories is His Holiness the Dalai Lama, living in Dharamsala in exile since 1959. The Chinese believe that his teachings and activities of a worldwide Tibetan liberation movement could have cascading consequences that eventually could topple Communist rule in Tibet. In late 2008, the people in the monastery at Dharamsala, based on two incidents and the Chinese response to these incidents, suspected that their critical emails were not safe. The monastery contacted Information Warfare Monitor through University of Cambridge, to carry out discreet investigations of their IT infrastructure.

IWM conducted field-based investigations in India, Europe and North America. In India they worked directly with affected Tibetan organisations, including the Private Office of the Dalai Lama, and several Tibetan NGOs. In Europe and North America they worked with Tibetan missions in London, Brussels, and New York. Based on the analysis of the data, discovery of insecure, web-based interfaces in four control servers came to light. These interfaces were allowing attackers to send instructions to, and receive data from compromised computers. The research team successfully scouted these servers, revealing a wide ranging network of compromised computers. This extensive network consisted of at least 1,295 infected computers in 103 countries. The GhostNet, as it was called, was directing infected computers to download a Trojan known as ghost RAT through emails. The Trojan allowed attackers to gain complete, real-time control of the infected machines. These instances of ghost RAT are consistently controlled from commercial Internet access accounts located on the island of Hainan, People's Republic of China.

Thirty per cent of the infected computers were classified as high value targets by IWM. These included machines from the ministries of foreign affairs of Iran, Bangladesh, Latvia, Indonesia, Philippines, Brunei, Barbados and Bhutan. Computers from embassies of India, South Korea, Indonesia, Romania, Cyprus, Malta, Thailand, Taiwan, Portugal, Germany and Pakistan; the ASEAN Secretariat, SAARC, and the Asian Development Bank, also formed part of the list. Here is an example of the Chinese Internet SIGINT in practice which was reveled in the IWM detailed report:-[37]

> During the course of our research, we were informed of the following incident. A member of Drewla, a young woman, decided to return to her family village in Tibet after working for two years for Drewla. She was arrested at the Nepalese-Tibetan border and taken to a detention facility, where she was held incommunicado for two months. She was interrogated by Chinese intelligence personnel about her employment in Dharamsala. She denied having been politically active and insisted that she had gone to Dharamsala for studies. In response to this, the intelligence officers pulled out a dossier on her activities and presented her with full transcripts of her Internet chats over the years. They indicated that they were fully aware of, and were monitoring, the Drewla outreach initiative and that her colleagues were not welcome to return to Tibet. They then released her and she returned to her village.

The final investigation report stated that GhostNet not only took full control of infected computers but also searched and downloaded specific files, and covertly operated attached devices, including microphones and web cameras. How long had the Trojan been working for and the extent of loss of data can never be specified. After the IWM report was published, several of the command and control servers listed in the report and part of the network blamed for the attacks went offline.

The First Cyberwar: Georgia 2008

The extent to which cyberattacks can be optimally exploited, in conjunction with conventional operations on land, sea and air, was demonstrated for the first time during the campaign against Georgia in Aug 2008. It was perhaps the first occurrence of cyberwar with the outbreak of simultaneous military and cyber hostilities against Georgia on 07 Aug 2008. Russia invaded Georgia, a small mountainous country in the region that separates Europe

37 Tracking GhostNet: Investigating a Cyber Espionage Network, Information Warfare Monitor, 29 March 2009, available at http://www.nartv.org/mirror/ghostnet.pdf

and Asia, in response to Georgia's attack against the separatists in South Ossetia. The first cyberattack began in July 2008, when a botnet called Machbot was found communicating with servers for taking instructions of DDoS attacks against presidential websites. Massive scale cyberattacks though were launched only on the evening of 07 Aug 2008 just before Russia invaded. Regardless of who launched these attacks, the aim of these attacks was very clear, to prevent Georgia from using the cyberspace for communicating with its populace and the outside world.

The speed of action and the multidirectional nature of these cyber strikes adhered to a classical military swarming technique, overwhelming the cyber defences of the Georgian targets. The attacking forces were highly decentralised, but were able to synchronise and concentrate their operations in a way that made any Georgian defence response nearly impossible. The speed with which these cyberattacks were launched made it difficult for the Georgian cyber experts to even gauge what was happening. The attacks continued as the Russian tanks and troops were crossing the border and bombers were flying sorties. The attacks peaked at approximately 0.5 million network packets per second, and upto 200 to 250 Mbits per second in bandwidth. They consisted mainly of HTTP queries to the http://mfa.gov.ge website. These requests were generated to overload the web server in a way where every single request would need significant CPU time. The inability of the Georgians to keep their websites up and running was instantly damaging to the national morale. These attacks also served to delay any international response to the kinetic conflict unfolding in the South Ossetia region.

The attacks did not end in 2008. On the first anniversary of the Georgian War, another attack occurred. This time it was on Georgian bloggers. Massive DDoS attacks were launched by a name Cyxymu and targeted social networking sites like Facebook, Google Blogger, Live Journal and Twitter, taking them offline for two to three hours. Four of the biggest online social networking communities, despite huge spending on infrastructure and cyber security, could not withstand a DDoS attack.

The 2008 cyberattacks on Georgia demonstrated that conventional operation and cyber operations can happen concurrently. Though the cyber attack did not cause any physical damage, yet they kept the decision makers occupied taking their attention off from the kinetic war that was taking place simultaneously.

Strike of the Stuxnet

Perhaps the most successful and widely quoted cyberattack in the recent times is "Stuxnet", a nickname coined by Microsoft security experts, an amalgam of two files found in the worm's code (".stub" and "mrxnet.sys"). The attack was against highly protected Iranian nuclear facilities and was launched in 2009 – 2010. Unlike most malware, Stuxnet did not use internet for propagation and also inflicted little harm to computers and networks that did not meet the configuration requirements of the worm. The attackers took great care to make sure that only their designated targets were hit. In other words "It was a marksman's job". While the worm was promiscuous, it made itself inert if Siemens software was not found on infected computers, and contained safeguards to prevent each infected computer from spreading the worm to more than three others, and to erase itself on 24 Jun 2012

Stuxnet contained a code for a man in the middle of the attack that faked industrial process control sensor signals on the target. It ensured that once infected, the system did not shut down due to detection of abnormal behaviour. Such complexity is very unusual for malware. The worm consisted of a layered attack against three different systems:

- Windows operating system: Stuxnet attacked Windows systems using an unprecedented four, zero day attacks. The number of zero-day exploits used was unusual, as they are highly valued and malware creators do not normally waste the use of four different ones in the same worm. Stuxnet was unusually large at half a megabyte in size and written in several different programming languages (including C and C++) which is also not a routine for malware.

- Siemens PCS 7, WinCC and STEP7 industrial software applications that run on Windows. Once installed, Stuxnet infected project files belonging to Siemens 'WinCC/PCS 7 SCADA control software and subverted a key communication library of WinCC called s7otbxdx.dll.

- One or more Siemens S7 PLCs: The entirety of the Stuxnet code has not yet been disclosed, but its payload targeted only those SCADA configurations that met criteria that it was programmed to identify. It monitored the frequency of the attached motors, and only attacked systems that spun between 807 Hz and 1210 Hz.

Three variants of Stuxnet are believed to have hit various targets between 2005 and 2010. Based on a study of the spread of Stuxnet by Symantec (an American computer security, backup and availability solutions software corporation) the main affected countries in the early days of the infection were Iran, Indonesia and India. Details as per Symantec are as under:[38]

Country	Infected computers
Iran	58.85 per cent
Indonesia	18.22 per cent
India	8.31 per cent
Azerbaijan	2.57 per cent
United States	1.56 per cent
Pakistan	1.28 per cent

Table 8: Countries Affected by Stuxnet

Experts on Iran and computer security specialists were convinced that Stuxnet was meant "to sabotage the uranium enrichment facility at Natanz – where the centrifuge operational capacity has dropped over the past year by 30 per cent." On 23 Nov 2010 it was announced that uranium enrichment at Natanz had ceased several times because of a series of major technical problems. A "serious nuclear accident" (supposedly the shutdown of some of its centrifuges) occurred at the site in the first half of 2009, which is speculated to have forced the head of Iran's Atomic Energy Organisation, Gholan Reza Aghazadeh, to resign. Statistics published by the Federation of American Scientists (FAS) show that the number of enrichment centrifuges operational in Iran mysteriously declined from about 4,700 to about 3,900 beginning around the time of the nuclear incident as mentioned by WikiLeaks. Another report published in December 2010 suggests that Stuxnet may have destroyed up to 1000 centrifuges (10 per cent) sometime between November 2009 and late January 2010.[39] The report says:

38 "W32.Stuxnet". Symantec. 17 September 2010.

39 "Did Stuxnet Take Out 1,000 Centrifuges at the Natanz Enrichment Plant?"Institute for Science and International Security. 22 December 2010.

> *The attacks seem designed to force a change in the centrifuge's rotor speed, first raising the speed and then lowering it, likely with the intention of inducing excessive vibrations or distortions that would destroy the centrifuge. If its goal was to quickly destroy all the centrifuges in the FEP [Fuel Enrichment Plant], Stuxnet failed. But if the goal was to destroy a more limited number of centrifuges and set back Iran's progress in operating the FEP, while making detection difficult, it may have succeeded, at least temporarily.*

On 29 Nov 2010, Iranian President Mahmoud Admandinejad stated for the first time that a computer virus had caused problems with the controller handling the centrifuges at its Natanz facilities. At a news conference in Tehran he said, "They succeeded in creating problems for a limited number of our centrifuges with the software they had installed in electronic parts."

The number of successful cyberattacks happening on a daily basis is very large. One thing that clearly emerges from the examples discussed above is that cyberattack can support covert action designed to influence governments, events, organisations, or personnel supporting foreign strategy and policy in a manner that is unlikely to be attributable to the own government. The range of possible cyberattack options is very large. We have reached an era where cyberattack can support military operations too. This aspect will be dealt with at length in Chapter 5.

What has the World Learnt from these Cyberattacks?

Millions of cyberattacks have been carried out and millions are yet to follow. Most cyberattacks whether intended to steal money, information or threaten the critical infrastructure, have some things in common. Based on the lessons learned from analysis of various cyberattacks, let us analyse what these common factors are.

- **People are the Weakest Links.** Even with all its technical sophistication, Stuxnet could not have succeeded without some sort of human failure. The insider threat, resulting from either complacency or a lack of understanding of the possible ramifications, is frequently cited in most after-action reporting of cyberattacks. Even the most advanced technologies can be rendered useless without well-informed, attentive people serving as the first line of defence.

- **Policy and Process**. Most attacks are able to succeed because the policy and processes which are meant to protect the networks are not properly put in place. This is applicable both for public sector networks as well as the private sector networks. In most cases, the basic cyber security policies and strategy itself are missing. In a number of cases, if the policy has been framed, it is not implemented thus bringing the entire effort to a null.
- **Technology**. While it's critical to exert strong leadership, train and educate employees, and implement sound cyber security policy, it's equally important to smartly employ technical solutions in securing your networks. After all cyberspace is derived out of technology. Hence it is technology which will play a very important part in ensuring its safety.

Conclusion

Every cyberattack has new elements and different motivations. While all big nations have acquired cyber weapon capabilities, it is the small scale attacks by smaller states or non-state actors, which are of concern. What could be the impact of these attacks on strategic and military targets? Can cyberattacks really have tangible effects? Can they cause destruction? In the next chapters we will examine the types of attacks that can threaten our critical infrastructure and defence networks.

3 National Critical Information Infrastructure and its Relevance to National Security

Critical infrastructure protection is an essential element of a resilient and secure nation.

- Barak Obama

President of the United States of America

Studies of recent military history campaigns reveal that non-military infrastructure of nations played an important role in contributing towards their war waging potential. Hence, during war such infrastructures are always an obvious target for the adversary. No matter at what depth such targets are located, extensive air campaigns and special operations have been undertaken to downgrade the war waging capability by destroying such critical infrastructures. The two gulf wars are replete with examples of this. In the first Gulf war, the coalition air forces flew over 100,000 sorties, dropping 88,500 tons of bombs with the aim of destroying variety of Iraqi military and non-military critical infrastructure. These bombing raids destroyed variety of Iraqi civilian infrastructure. 11 of Iraq's 20 major power stations and 119 substations were totally destroyed; while six major power stations were damaged. At the end of the war, electricity production was at four percent of its pre-war levels. All major dams, most major pumping stations, many sewage treatment plants, telecommunications equipment, port facilities, oil refineries and distribution, railroads and bridges were also destroyed.

What was the aim of undertaking such massive air campaigns against targets which had little military significance? It was a part of the overall military strategy to defeat the enemy by destroying his morale and his economic ability to produce and transport material to the theatres of military operations, or both. Use of such awe-inspiring airpower was aimed to change the adversary's behaviour — in line with Clausewitz's dictum that war is fundamentally "an act of force to compel our enemy to do our will." Attacking the enemy's armed forces is necessary but not always sufficient. Attacking economic targets in large numbers will have added effects, the results of which are exponential. In other words, the complete might of a nation needs to be targeted in all future wars.

What Makes a Nation a Great Power?

A great power is presumed to enjoy certain advantages that most other states are denied. States are placed in the top rank because they excel in one way or another. The power is composed of many elements which include both tangible and intangible components. There are a number of ways in which the national power can be determined. The Chinese concept of Comprehensive National Power (CNP) is amongst the most preferred model for determining the national power of a state.

CNP is a concept which refers to the overall power of a nation state and is an accumulation of a wide range of national assets, capabilities and potential. As per the Chinese Academy of Social Sciences indexing system, the following eight factors contribute towards CNP index framework :-[1]

(a) Natural resources.

(b) Economic activities capability.

(c) Foreign economic activities capability.

(d) Scientific and technological capability.

(e) Social development level.

(f) Military Capability.

(g) Government regulation and control capability.

(h) Foreign affairs capability.

Similarly as per the "Ray Cline Model", the Perceived Power of a nation is calculated using five factors, namely; Critical Mass (population and territory), Economic Capability, Military Capability, Quality of Strategy

1 Comprehensive National Power A Model For India, P K Singh, Y K Gera and Sandeep Dewan, p 32

and Will to Pursue Strategy.[2] In both the above models and many other such models available for calculating the CNP of a nation state, besides the military capability, economic might and technological capabilities are also contributing factors. Infrastructural development and ICT base of the nation are deciding factors for economic and technological growth and hence assume pronounced importance.

The two Gulf Wars clearly demonstrated the significance of targeting enemy's CNP. While during both these wars, extensive air campaigns were undertaken to target such infrastructures, the question arises, can this be achieved in today's times using the cyber domain? If yes, then cyberattacks will play a pivotal role in the future wars. Hence, there is a need to analyse what constitutes critical infrastructure and what are the threats to such infrastructure from cyberattacks.

What is Critical Infrastructure?

Infrastructure is the prerequisite for the development of any economy. The fabric of modern life at individual, national and international levels is getting increasingly dependent on a number of interrelated and interdependent infrastructures. Transport, telecommunications, energy, water, health, housing, and educational facilities have become an integral part of human existence. It is difficult to imagine a modern world without these facilities. Provision and maintenance of adequate infrastructure facilities are absolutely necessary if rapid economic growth is to be achieved and sustained. The development of a country's infrastructure is vital to the growth of its sectors and the overall economy. Table below shows the planned and actual investments made by the Government of India in infrastructure development in the country during the 10th and the 11th Five Year Plans.

2 Ibid, p 49

	10th Plan		11th Plan	
	Original Projections Rs 8,71,445 Crore	Actual Investments Rs 9,19,225 Crore	Original Projections Rs 20,56,150 Crore	Revised Projections Rs 20,54,205 Crore
Oil & Gas	1.1%	3.5%	0.8%	6.2%
Storage	0.6%	0.6%	1%	0.4%
Airports	0.8%	0.8%	1.5%	1.8%
Ports	1.6%	2.5%	4.3%	2%
Water Supply	7.4%	6.5%	7%	5.4%
Irrigation	12.8%	13%	12.3%	12%
Railways	13.7%	11.1%	12.7%	9.8%
Telecom	11.9%	11%	12.6%	16.8%
Roadways	16.6%	13.8%	15.3%	13.6%
Electricity	35.5%	37%	30.4%	32%

Source: Planning Commission

Table 9: Sector vise Investment figures 10th and 11th Five Year Plans

According to experts, spending on the critical infrastructure sectors such as Railways, Roadways, Electricity, Telecom and Irrigation & Water Supply needs to remain over 10 per cent of GDP by 2017 to achieve and sustain 8 to 9 per cent economic growth. In fact Finance Minister Mr. Arun Jaitley, while presenting the national budget for financial year 2015 – 16, said that the country would spend an additional 700 billion rupees, or US $11 billion, on roads, railways, ports and other projects in 2016.[3] This has been aimed at bringing the growth figure to double digits.

Figure below represents projections data for the 12th Five Year Plan as released during the midterm appraisal of the 11th Five Year Plan.

3 India's Budget Focuses on Infrastructure as available at http://www.wsj.com/articles/india-budget-focuses-on-infrastructure-1425111915

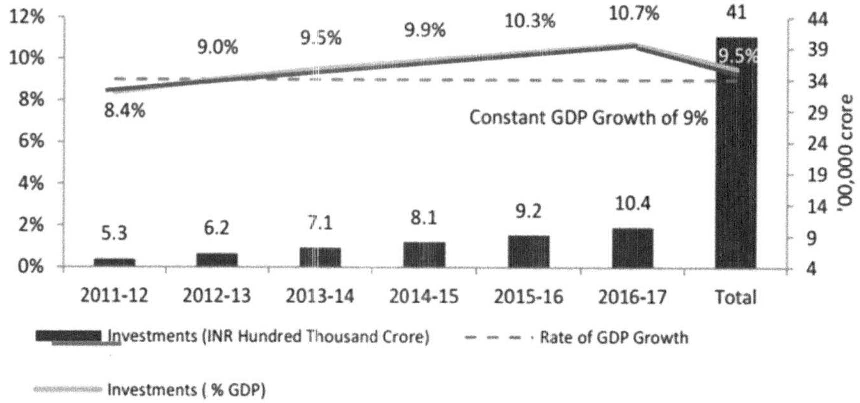

Source : Planning Commission

Figure 4: Projected Investment in Infrastructure in 12th Five Year Plan

The above table and statistical figure clearly display the importance that a country like India gives to development of infrastructure. What out of this is critical infrastructure, needs to be seen.

While, there is no universal definition of Critical Infrastructure, all the above sectors which contribute towards the growth of the nation can be termed as critical. It includes a range of engineered systems, assets and facilities which are essential for day-to-day societal functions, as well as continued economic and societal functioning in the aftermath of a disaster event including war. Some nations have defined critical infrastructure as under:-

Australia	"Critical Infrastructure is defined as those physical facilities, supply chains, information technologies and communication networks which, if destroyed, degraded or rendered unavailable for an extended period, would significantly impact on the social or economic well-being of the nation, or affect Australia's ability to conduct national defence and ensure national security." (Australian Government 2010)

Germany	"Critical Infrastructures are organisations and facilities of major importance to the community whose failure or impairment would cause a sustained shortage of supplies, significant disruptions to public order or other dramatic consequences."(German FMI 2009)
European Union	"Critical Infrastructure means an asset, system or part thereof located in Member States which is essential for the maintenance of vital societal functions, health, safety, security, economic or social well-being of people, and the disruption or destruction of which would have a significant impact in a Member State as a result of the failure to maintain those functions" (Art. II a, 2008/ 114/ EC)
United States	"Critical" Infrastructure is defined as systems and assets, whether physical or virtual, so vital to the United States that the incapacity or destruction of such systems and assets would have a debilitating impact on security, national economic security, national public health or safety, or any combination of those matters (Sec. 1016(e) of The USA PATRIOT and Homeland Security Acts, 2001)" (United States: Department of Homeland Security 2009)
United Nations International Strategy for Disaster Reduction (UN/ISDR),	The primary physical structures, technical facilities and systems which are socially, economically or operationally essential to the functioning of a society or community, both in routine circumstances and in the extreme circumstances of an emergency. Critical facilities are elements of the infrastructure that support essential services in a society. (UN/ISDR 2009, p.8)

Table 10: Definitions of Critical Infrastructure

The way critical infrastructure is defined differs from one nation to the other. However, major consistencies and key similarities can be found in all the above definitions.

What constitutes a critical infrastructure also varies according to organisational or national perspective. In the United States, the President's Commission for Critical Infrastructure Protection (PCCIP) identifies five main critical infrastructure sectors, namely Information and Communications; Banking and Finance; Energy (electrical power, oil and gas); Physical Distribution; and Vital Human Services.[4] This definition was coined in 1997. What was considered to be "critical" has changed over the past decade. Today critical infrastructure will also include things as transport systems, air and sea ports, water, hospitals and health clinics, and centres for fire, police and public administration services. Critical infrastructure therefore includes all sensitive elements of a larger ecosystem, encompassing the public and private sectors and society at large.

An important feature of critical infrastructure, is its interdependence, direct or indirect on other infrastructures. Figure below shows interdependence of some of the critical infrastructures. What clearly emerges from the diagram below is that all sectors today are dependent directly on information which itself has emerged as a critical infrastructure.

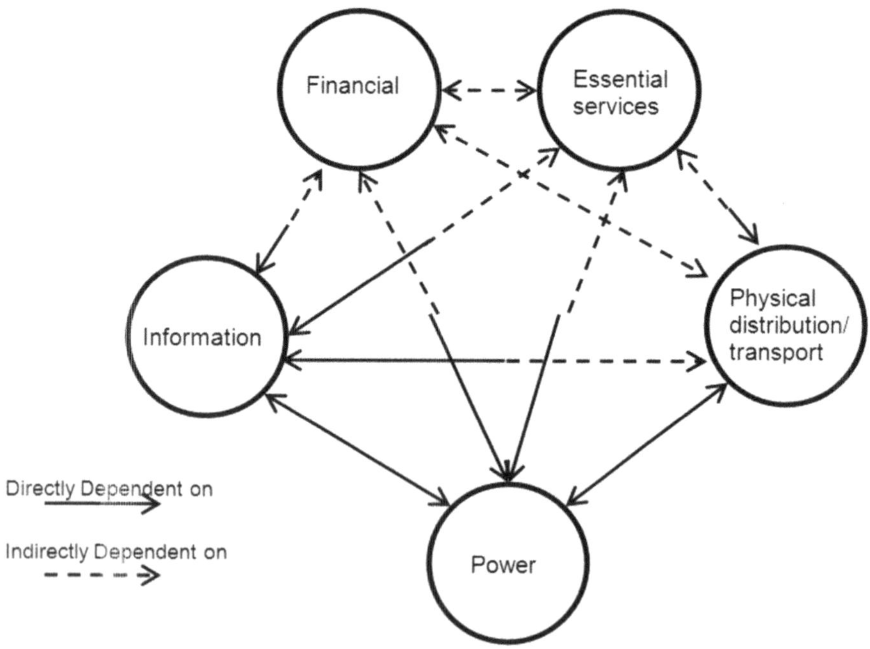

Figure 5: Interdependence of Critical Infrastructure

4 Ware, WH. The cyber posture of the national information infrastructure. Santa Monica, CA: RAND Institute, 1998.

The critical infrastructures and their interdependence form a network of nodes and links as shown above. A node or a link is critical if:-

(a) It alone can exert such influence on other nodes so as to cause serious disruption of governmental or societal infrastructure.

(b) It forms an integral part of an ensemble of nodes, which can be attacked or otherwise influence in a similar manner, such that aggregate malfunction can lead to serious disruption.

What is Information Infrastructure?

The idea of information as an infrastructure came about in the 1990s. The term infrastructure goes beyond physical infrastructure to include data – which can be considered a form of logical infrastructure or 'information infrastructure'. Thus an infrastructure came into being which is purely information-based. This includes the networks and computer databases that house volumes of critical data such as records of capital in banking system, scientific and technical intellectual property and so on. Today, Internet is the default global information infrastructure. Cyberspace, various aspects and properties of which have been discussed at length in Chapter 1, now has truly become the global information infrastructure.

Critical Information Infrastructure

As discussed earlier, one of the properties of an infrastructure is the dependence of various spheres of activity on it. In the past, the dependence stemmed from physical or geographical relationships only. With the advent of cyberspace there are additional relationships that have been created. These are dependent on computers for command and control of the infrastructure by remote electronic means and logical relationships such as the international financial market as a factor influencing inputs and outputs of critical infrastructures. Such dependence would not exist without technology. In the information age therefore, there is a difference between infrastructure in the traditional sense and the modern use of this concept which includes a cyber dimension.

This critical infrastructure that reinforces our daily lives, increasingly depends on networked online systems. Although cyberspace itself is categorised as a discrete sector, in practice it is so deeply embedded into other sectors that the two become difficult to distinguish. It can be visualised as a nervous system running through all other sectors, enabling them to function and interconnect. Such infrastructure in the information age can be categorised as Critical Information Infrastructure.

> *Critical Information Infrastructure (CII) therefore can be defined as those interconnected critical infrastructures (CI) and information infrastructures (II), the disruption or destruction of either of which would have a serious impact on the health, safety, security, or economic well-being of citizens, or on the effective functioning of government or the economy.*[5]

In other words damage or disruption of CII will have overwhelming impact on National Security.

The above three terms i.e. Critical Infrastructure, Information Infrastructure and Critical Information Infrastructure and their interdependence can be represented as under:-

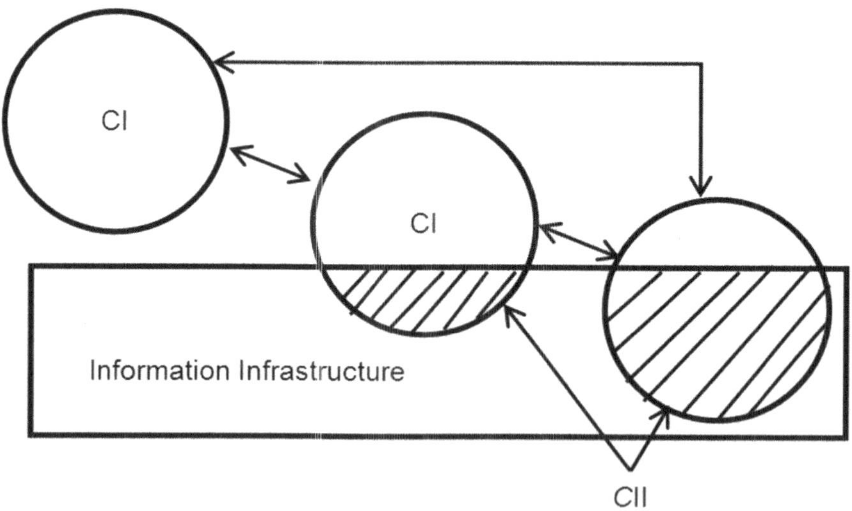

Figure 6: Critical Info-Infrastructure

5 www.enisa.europa.eu/act/res/files/glossary

A look at the figure clearly brings out the following:-

(a) Despite the information revolution, there may still be CI of a nation which may not be dependent on the cyber space for effective functioning. This is especially applicable for nations where the growth and penetration of information technologies has been slow. However, with the accelerated pace of development of the IT sector, it will be difficult for these critical systems to isolate themselves from the outside world, and eventually they too will get networked in the times to come.

(b) CIs are interdependent, directly or indirectly. Hence disruption of one CI may have cascading effect on the performance of others CIs. Power and Information are two such infrastructures, the disruption of which today can result in major breakdown of other infrastructures.

(c) Most infrastructures are dependent on II or the cyber space for Industrial Control System (ICS) using computers for effective functioning though with varying degrees of dependence. For example, large technical systems such as railways or electricity supply system today depend greatly on information technologies for smooth day to day functioning. As the load varies, electricity supply to a city can be remotely controlled through a networked system. Similarly the opening and closing of sluice gates of a dam can be controlled through remotely located computes. However the transportation sector such as road infrastructure in India is not as dependent on networks yet as it is perhaps in the developed nations.

The reliance on technology, communication and the interconnectivity of IT and ICS has changed and expanded the potential vulnerabilities and has increased potential risks to operations. Experts today are of the opinion that any sector or infrastructure which relies on networking and IT and is critical to the nation can be attacked and degraded through the cyberspace. We shall delve into this aspect in greater detail subsequently. But if the claim of researchers is true, then there is a need to protect such infrastructure against threats emanating from the cyber domain.

The World Economic Forum (a Swiss nonprofit foundation committed to improving the state of the world by engaging business, political, academic, and other leaders of society to shape global, regional, and industry agendas), in its report "Global Risks 2013" has listed out the top five risks that the world has faced in the last seven years. The tabulated representation shows how the global risks in terms of likelihood have changed in the last seven years.[6]

	2007	2008	2009	2010	2011	2012	2013
1st	Break down of CII	Asset price collapse	Asset price collapse	Asset price collapse	Metrological catastrophes	Severe income disparity	Severe income disparity
2nd	Chronic diseases in developed countries	Middle east instability	Slowing Chinese economy	Slowing Chinese economy	Hydrological catastrophes	Chronic fiscal imbalances	Chronic fiscal imbalances
3rd	Oil price shock	Failed and falling states	Chronic diseases	Chronic diseases	Corruption	Rising greenhouse gas emission	Rising greenhouse gas emission
4th	China economic hard landing	Oil and gas price spike	Global governance gaps	Fiscal crisis	Biodiversity loss	Cyber attacks	Water supply crisis
5th	Asset price collapse	Chronic diseases in developed countries	Retrenchment from globalization	Global governance gaps	Climatological catastrophes	Water supply crisis	Mismanagement of population ageing

Table 11: Top Global Risks 2007 – 2013

In the year 2007, breakdown of critical information infrastructure was the top most crises that the world faced. In 2012, cyber-attacks formed part of the top five. The report states that cyber-attacks, a massive incident of data fraud or theft, or an incident of massive digital misinformation could all lead to critical systems failure and eventual global governance failure.

While significant resources have historically been needed to cause

6 World Economic Forum, Global Risks 2013 Eighth Edition available at www.weforum.org/docs/WEF_GlobalRisks_Report_2013.pdf

devastating consequences for geopolitical powers, it is increasingly possible for skilled individuals to do so remotely and anonymously through networked computer systems. Cyberspace therefore poses challenges to our National Security today. Therefore, it is increasingly becoming essential to identify India's critical information infrastructure and ensure its protection from threats emanating from the cyberspace.

National Critical Information Infrastructure Protection Centre (NCIIPC), an organisation created under the National Technical Research Organisation (NTRO) issued "Guidelines for Protection of National Critical Information Infrastructure" in June 2013. As per the document, NCIIPC has laid down factors which help in identifying the criticality of an information infrastructure in India.[7] These factors are:-

(a) **Functionality**: It is a dynamic concept which comprises a set of functions, procedure and or capabilities associated with a system or with its constituent parts. It may be viewed at two levels- Functional Uniqueness and Functional Dependency.

(b) **Criticality Scale**: It is a heuristic rule for impact assessment based on multidimensional approach that includes availability, access, delivery and consummation of essential services.

(c) **Degree of Complementarities**: The distinguishing characteristic of the Information Infrastructure is that it is all-embracing - it links other Information Infrastructure Systems together. Failure of one system has potential to shut down other Critical Information Infrastructure relatively quickly in a cascading manner.

(d) **Political, Economic, Social and Strategic Values**: It includes what is held important for political stability, economic prosperity, fraternity, unity and integrity of a Nation.

(e) **Time Duration**: Time duration has an important significance in the identification and categorisation of CII. A system may or may not be critical at all the times. Systems or their constituents need to be identified in their alignment with period.

---

7 Guidelines for Protection of National Critical Information Infrastructure, VERSION 1.0 (JUNE 2013), issued by National Critical Information Infrastructure Protection Centre

NCIIPC has identified seventeen subsectors which it classifies as CII. Details of these will be discussed subsequently. Having identified what CII is, let us now analyse how a cyberattack can impact some of the CII's, thereby, resulting in a catastrophic failure which ultimately may impact the national security; both during peace as well as war.

Where is the Threat From?

In Chapter 1 we have discussed in detail who are the cyber adversaries. All these cyber actors do not pose a threat to a nation's CII. While the black hats and hacktivists are cyber criminals whose motive behind cyberattack is money, it is the cyber terrorists, non-state actors and nation states who pose the real threat to CII. Cyber terrorists use cyberspace and network technologies to spread terror among public. CII would be an obvious target for such players. On the other hand, non-state actors are group of volunteers sponsored by the state, who on behalf of the state are willing and able to use cyberattacks to achieve political goals of the state.

By and large a nation state would target another nation state's CII in the event of a conflict between the two; something that would be a part of strategic offensive cyber warfare policy of the state. Cyber terrorists and non-state actors on the other hand would pose a constant threat both during peace and war to the CII. Employment of non-state actors in cyberspace operations is a very attractive option for nation-states, especially when pursuing limited strategic goals. Also, recruiting non-state actors as a technically competent force on behalf of a nation can be achieved at little or no cost. The additional advantage of employing a non-state actor is that even if attribution is successful, i.e. the attacker is identified by the nation under attack, the nation undertaking such attacks can always deny it. Lack of applicable international laws covering cyber warfare creates a further useful shield of legal ambiguity in case of such attacks being accurately identified. Both the examples of Estonia and Georgia clearly indicate how non-state actors successfully carried out effective cyber attack while the Russians denied any connection with these attacks.

Nation-states have little incentive to openly take credit for cyberattacks. Doing so could lead to political or military recrimination, and might expose individuals to criminal prosecution if their illicit actions were deemed to be against the laws and customs of war. On the other hand cyber terrorists and non state actors face no such threat. Even if the international community was successful in codifying cyber warfare into alignment with international law, and thereby implement limitations of its use, it would probably still not be very effective as the employment of non-state actors in cyberspace operations is still in effect a gray area.

Hence, both during peace time as well as in the scenario of an impending full-fledged war between two states, employment of cyber terrorists and non state actors for targeting CII as part of overall sabotage strategy poses the most serious threat. There is enough evidence that is sited at various forums about China, Russia and Iraq having trained an army of such non-state actors in waging a successful cyber war by targeting CII of another nation.

Let us now examine what are the kinds of threats that various CII face from all such cyber terrorists, non state actors and nation states. While NCIIPC has identified seventeen sectors, only few of these are being discussed; although other sectors too face comparable threats.

Cyberattack on a Smart Grid

Let us first analyse the impact of a cyberattack on one of the most important critical infrastructure – the power sector. Power or electricity is a resource importance of which is felt much more when there is a breakdown. Power has come to be known as a `strategic commodity' and any uncertainty about its supply can threaten the functioning of the economy, particularly in a developing economy like India. The electricity sector in India had an installed capacity of 245.394 Giga Watts (GW) as of Apr 2014, the world's fourth largest. Captive power plants generate an additional 39.375 GW. The per capita average annual domestic electricity consumption in India in 2012 was 96 kWh in rural areas and 288 kWh in urban areas for those with access to electricity, in contrast to the worldwide per capita annual average of 2600 kWh and 6200 kWh in the European Union respectively. The demand for power is constantly increasing and is being met with newer, conventional and nonconventional methods of producing power including nuclear power.

To reduce transmission losses and supply power more efficiently as per varying requirement of the consumers at different times of the day, smart grids are increasingly being used all across the world. Even in India 14 smart grid pilots were approved for immediate execution in 2013 and are at various stages of completion. Interestingly all these projects are being implemented in smaller cities like Panipat and Mysore and not in the four metros. Though now under the smart city project, 100 cities are being targeted including the four metros. Smart grids will form part of the smart city project.

So what is a smart grid? A smart grid is an electrical grid that uses digital information and ICT to gather and act on information, such as information about the behaviour of suppliers and consumers in an automated fashion to improve the efficiency, reliability, economics, and sustainability of the production and distribution of electricity. Using communication, control and computation technologies a smart grid can enhance the reliability of the power grid, reduce electricity costs and provide new real-time customer services. The diagram below explains various components of a smart grid:

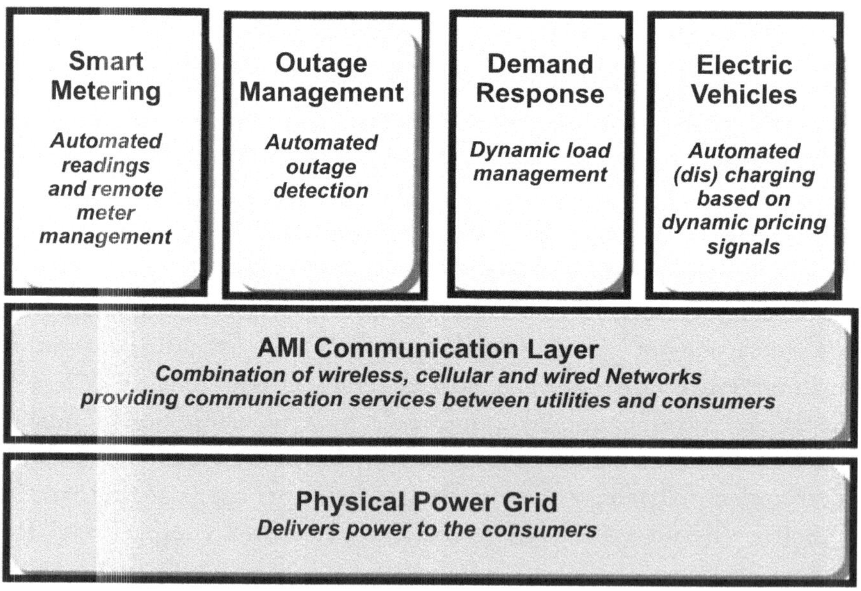

AMI : Advanced Metering
Infrastructure

Figure 7: Components of a Smart Grid

How deep is ICT embedded in each of the above smart grid sub systems needs to be seen.

Smart Metering. Automated remote metering requires meters to send readings to a central utility at a fixed frequency. This function depends on reliable and timely delivery of meter data to the utility by the underlying Advance Metering Infrastructure (AMI) communication layer. Long term disruption of the functioning of the meter impacts the operational resilience of the smart grid. Remote metering is resilient if data from some percentage of the meters is always delivered to the utility and within a specified time.

Outage Management. Automated outage management requires smart meters to send outage information in a "last gasp" message on detection of an outage by the meter. The utility uses the information such as time and location of the outage from the message to restore power in a timely manner. A disruption of this function directly affects the operational resilience of the grid by delaying the recovery and restoration of power to end users. Outage management is resilient if the utility can always identify and recover from outages within a specified time.

Demand Response (DR). DR is a critical component of automated load management and relies on the ability of the Advanced Metering Infrastructure (AMI) communication layer to reliably send load curtailment requests to smart meters and other end devices for dynamically managing the overall system load. DR signals to the Home Area Network (HAN) could travel through the Internet or the AMI system. Unlike metering, disruption of DR operations can have near-term effects on operational resilience of the smart grid by destabilising the power grid. DR is resilient; if required kWh of load is always curtailed within short span of time, where the required load and time are dependent on utility-specific requirements.

As is evident from above, the dependence of a smart grid on ICT and networks is considerable. Hence it is essential to protect smart grids against cyberattacks. For this, another module for the protection of such grids needs to be added. The final configuration of a smart grid would look like this:

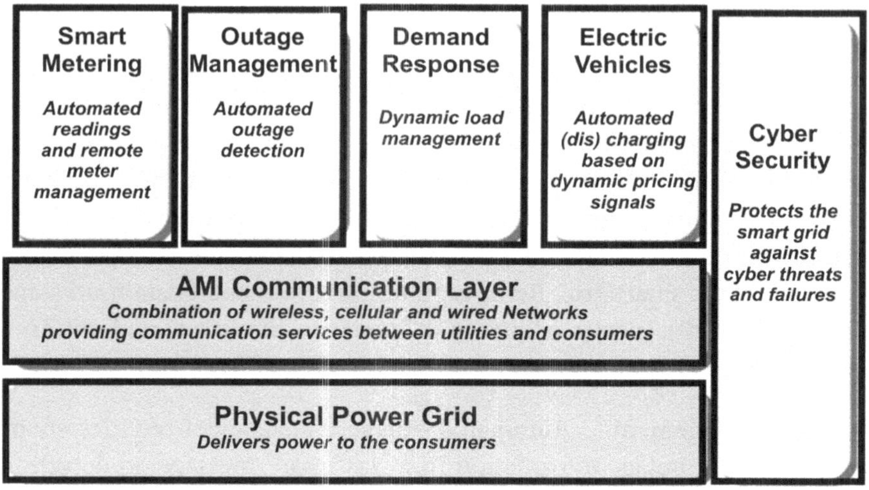

Figure 8: Smart Grid with Cyber Security Module

The Cyber Security (CS) component protects the smart grid system against attacks and failures and provides integrity, availability and confidentiality services for the smart grid. CS functions like detection, diagnosis and response depend on the underlying communication layer for tasks such as transporting monitored data from different critical points in the system, exchanging detection and diagnosis messages across its components and communicating response actions for responding promptly to adverse situations. Disruption of these functions has direct consequences to the security of the smart grid and impacts its overall resiliency. Cyber security component is resilient if it always detects and responds to security threats before performance and security requirements of other functions are violated.

Let us now analyse how a simple DoS attack can impact a smart grid. As discussed in Chapter 1, DoS or DDoS attack is an attempt to make a machine or network resource unavailable to its intended user; in this case the smart meters and the dynamic load management system. On a smart grid, following data would constantly be flowing on the AMI communication layer:-

- All meters send their readings to the central collector, where each meter read is approx. 1000 bytes, according to a preconfigured sending interval set by the utility.

- Dispatch of a DR load curtailment signal from the collector to a group of enrolled homes requesting that they curtail certain amount of load. Upon receipt of a DR request, the smart meter immediately responds by sending a DR reply to the collector.

An attacker can generate a DoS attack targeting the collector in a certain RF mesh. The attacker can take advantage of the large number of meters within the geographical region to generate a DoS attack on the collector node by simultaneously generating low bit-rate traffic (hundreds of Kbits/s) from individual meters. Realistically, an attacker can accomplish this attack by using different means; for example, an attacker could compromise smart meters in a certain RF mesh and reprogram them to increase the frequency at which they send meter reads. Or, an attacker could take control of other customer devices such as the service gateway within an area to send spurious traffic creating a DoS attack.

An experiment was carried out by the USC Information Sciences Institute in the US to simulate a DoS attack and check its impact on a smart grid and the following were its findings :-[8]

(a) It requires an attacker to compromise only a small fraction of the meters in a typical RF mesh region to disrupt the communication resilience within the region.

(b) A compromise of about 5% of the meters was sufficient to reduce the Packet Delivery Ratio (PDR) to 10% and the successful DR request ratio to zero. Although these figures apply to a single RF mesh region on which the attacks were simulated, in reality, an attacker can easily scale-up this attack by replicating it over multiple RF mesh regions.

(c) Remote Metering Utilities expect to receive a certain percentage of meter reads per reading cycle and within a specified time. Missing readings from meters may not be severe as far as billing operations are concerned but the periodic meter reads are also used in a continuous manner as an input to important demand response functions such as load monitoring and forecasting. Disruption of

8 Analyzing Resiliency of the Smart Grid Communication Architectures under Cyber Attack, Anas AlMajali, Arun Viswanathan and Clifford Neuman as available at https://www.usenix.org/system/files/conference/cset12/cset12-final13.pdf

these continuous inputs has consequences for the stability of the overall power grid thereby impacting its resilience.

(d) DR functionality depends on the ability to successfully curtail load within a given time period. This requires DR requests to be successfully communicated and acknowledged within a specified time. A DoS attack can cause successful DR transactions (request-response pairs) to reduce to zero. Thus an attacker can easily disrupt the automated load management functions in the smart grid which can eventually lead to consequences such as large-scale blackouts.

An attacker needs to compromise only a small fraction of meters to launch a DoS attack. Cyber security functions at the utility may not be able to detect and brand the impact of the attack immediately and thus result in a delayed response. In addition, the DoS attack could disrupt critical meter events from reaching the utility which could cause additional delays in detection and response.

A number of simulations carried out all over the world where smart grids are installed show that a simple DoS attack in a smart grid can result in large scale blackouts. The blackouts continued to persist till corrective measures were initiated against the DoS attack.

On 30 Jul 2012, parts of North India came to a standstill, crippled with power failure that affected the states of Delhi, Punjab, Haryana, Himachal Pradesh, Uttar Pradesh, Rajasthan and Jammu and Kashmir. This power failure was attributed to overdrawing of power by some states and took 15 hours to restore. On 31 Jul 2012, the northern grid collapsed again. This time, a cascading effect saw the collapse of the Eastern and North Eastern power grids as well. While the power was being overdrawn as a routine, could this failure have been triggered by a cyberattack?

Cyber Attacks on Nuclear Power Plants

The Stuxnet attack, the most lethal and most quoted cyberattack in the recent times on Iran's nuclear facility at Natanz, demonstrated to the world that a well-protected and guarded installation like a nuclear fuel enrichment facility too is not secure from cyberattacks. The details of the attack have already been discussed in Chapter 2. India too has 20 operational nuclear power plants having an installed capacity of 4780 MW and seven more are under construction. Once functional they will generate over 10,000 MW of electricity.

Consequences of a cyberattack on a nuclear power plant attack can be catastrophic as it may result in nuclear fallout. Ensuring cyber security of a nuclear power plant or a nuclear reactor is therefore one of the most precarious tasks. Let us examine in greater detail, what are the vulnerabilities and challenges of this task.

The spread of ICT in the new generation of nuclear reactors has brought forth many advantages as well as risks. While Generation II reactors are still based on analog control rooms, increasingly powerful computers are becoming prevalent, not just in the control rooms, but also in the field in the form of Intelligent Electronic Devices in the next generation of Nuclear Power Plants. They allow for efficient network based communications, the use of Supervisory Control and Data Acquisition (SCADA) systems, and more efficient operation of the plants.

Supervisory Control and Data Acquisition, or SCADA systems are specialised computer networks and devices that work in concert to monitor and control key processes involved in the management of machinery, equipment and facilities. Measurements taken from a variety of sensors (temperature, pressure, flow etc.) are used to make decisions, for example; to open a valve and release water from a tank when it fills up, or to initiate an emergency shutdown of a nuclear power plant. SCADA systems are therefore considered to be the nervous system of this most critical infrastructure. In a nuclear power plant they are usually composed of a set of network agents, consisting of sensors, actuators, control processing units such as Programmable Logic Controllers (PLCs), and communication devices. A typical SCADA system architecture of a nuclear power plant is depicted below:-

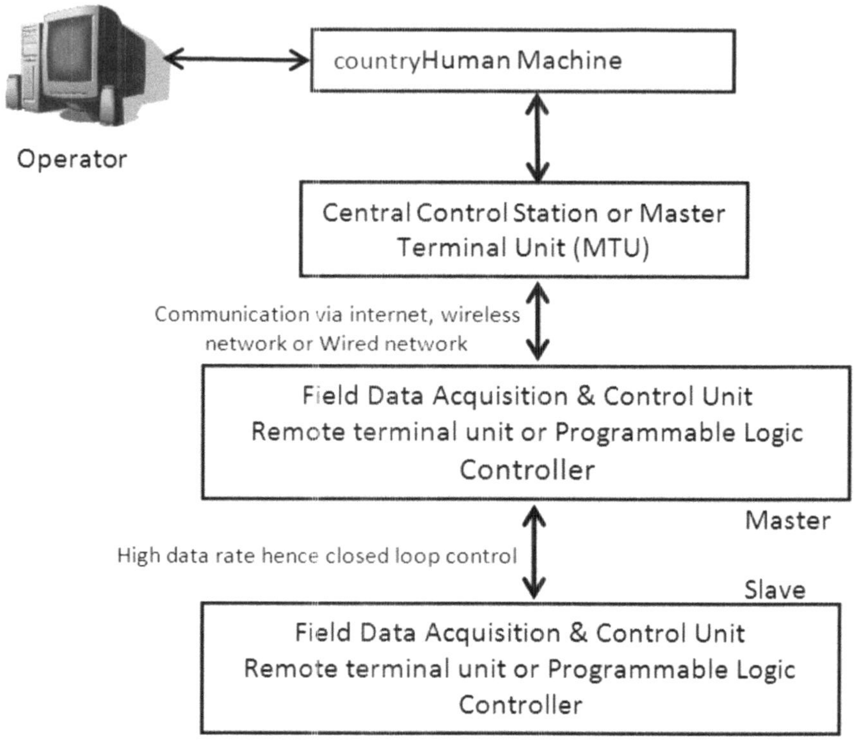

Figure 9: SCADA Architecture

Traditionally, SCADA networks have been segregated from other corporate networks to minimise exposure to unsecure areas, such as the Internet. Recently however, more organisations are connecting SCADA networks with other potentially unsecure networks in order to cut costs, share operational information, or distribute ordering/billing data. This makes SCADA even more vulnerable to cyberattacks.

Modern SCADA architectures rely heavily on standard protocols and digital data transmission. For example, a communications protocol such as the Foundation Fieldbus is applied in conjunction with industrial Ethernet radios. These Ethernet radios provide data rates of 512 kbps, a large increase over those provided by EIA-232 serial links. For security, industrial Ethernet access points use spread-spectrum frequency hopping technology with encryption. Most SCADA protocols were never intended for use on publically accessible networks, and in some cases, not even on IP networks. MODBUS, a common SCADA protocol, was originally designed for use only within simple process control networks to enable low speed serial communications between clients and servers.[9] In order to communicate on an IP network, MODBUS TCP merely encapsulates serial data within a TCP packet before sending it across the network. No additional protection has been added to secure communications sent using the protocol.

A nuclear power plant uses a number of SCADA systems. The diagram below shows various SCADA systems that would be functional in a nuclear reactor along with their network elements :-[10]

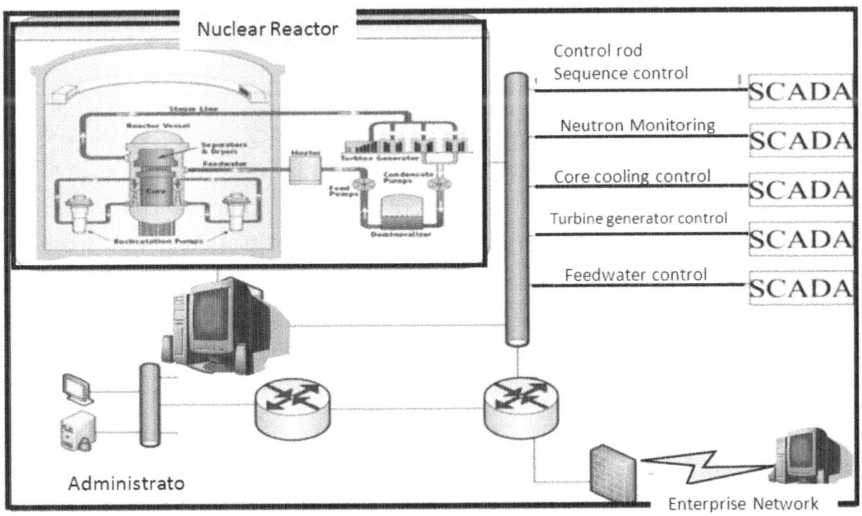

Figure 10: SCADA Systems in a Nuclear Power Plant

9 MODBUS as available at http://www.digitalbond.com/scadapedia/protocols/modbus-2/

10 A Testbed to Simulate Cyber Attacks on Nuclear Power Plants by Laith Mohammad Al-Barakat as available at https://ideals.illinois.edu/handle/2142/29718?show=full

Threats to SCADA Systems. For reasons of efficiency, maintenance, and economics, data acquisition and control platforms have migrated from isolated in-plant networks, using proprietary hardware and software, to PC-based systems using standard software, network protocols, and the Internet. The downside of this transition has been the exposure of SCADA systems to the same vulnerabilities and threats that plague Windows-based PCs and their associated networks. Some typical attacks that might be mounted against SCADA systems that employ standard hardware and software are:-

- Malicious code such as viruses, Trojan horses, and worms.
- Unauthorised disclosure of critical data.
- Unauthorised modification and manipulation of critical data.
- Denial of service attacks.
- Unauthorised access to audit logs and modification of audit logs.

Threat to Process Control System. There are several cyber threats that use low-level coding vulnerabilities to attack a large number of process control systems in production. Low-level coding vulnerabilities are defined as a programming error that corrupts the memory of a program. The exploitation of such vulnerabilities generally takes the form of control-data or Non-control attacks. Control data attacks are considered the most critical security threats. They alter the target program's control data (data that are loaded to processor program counter at some point in the program execution, e.g., return addresses and function pointers) in order to execute injected malicious code or out of context library code (in particular, return-to library attacks). The attacks usually make system calls (e.g., starting a shell) with the privilege of the victim process. Non-control data attacks corrupt a variety of application data including user identity data, configuration data, user input data, and decision-making data, i.e., computational data usually held by global or local variables in a computer program. Some examples of low-level coding vulnerabilities in process control systems include:-

- Buffer overflow.
- Format string vulnerability.

- Integer overflow.
- Double free attack.

Possible Consequences of a Cyberattack

Civil nuclear assets represent a special case of critical infrastructure given the grave consequences of possible radiation release in certain circumstances of attack. As opposed to conventional fossil fuel, which can be completely shut off by simply turning off the fuel supply, the fuel for a nuclear power plant is "kept" in the core before it needs refueling. The reaction rate in a nuclear power plant is controlled to maintain criticality (sustained chain reaction) as the fuel burns. Furthermore, even when a nuclear plant is shut down, radioactive decay still occurs and some amount of heat continues to be generated. This decay heat must be removed or the reactor core will melt, causing a situation similar to the accident at the Three Mile Island Unit 2 nuclear power plant, Pennsylvania, on 28 Mar 1979, or more recently at some of the plants at Fukushima, Japan. The fear is that a cyber attacker can recreate the situation by taking advantage of vulnerabilities in SCADA system of digitally controlled Nuclear Power Plants.

SCADA systems are responsible for controlling heat removal and handling other normal and emergency situations in the nuclear power plant. Therefore, any interference with the operation of the SCADA system can have dramatic and dangerous consequences. Another challenging situation is spent nuclear fuel, which also contains the radioactive products of the fission process. This spent fuel can be reprocessed to produce new fuel rods or it can be stored in pools in nuclear power plants. When stored in a pool on site, it must be cooled for nearly five years before it can be moved to dry storage on site, or to off-site locations. Vulnerabilities in the cooling system of the spent fuel pool may also become target of cyberattacks.

The Stuxnet attack showed that a cyberattack could yet be carried out on a nuclear site which was completely isolated from the internet. Tremendous amount of planning and resources would have gone into carrying out this attack. Finally it was just a tiny disk which was able to sabotage the uranium enrichment facility at Natanz where the centrifuge operational capacity dropped over thirty percent in one year by simply changing the centrifuge's rotor speed thereby inducing excessive vibrations or distortions.

On 05 Jun 2008, a news item in the US reported that a nuclear power plant in Georgia was forced into emergency shutdown for 48 hours after a software update was installed on a computer which reset the data of the control system.[11] This resulted in drop in the level of water reservoir that cools the radioactive nuclear fuel rods activating the automated safety system. It has still not been made public whether the software updates malfunctioned or if it was a case of malware installed with the update causing this problem.

South Korea in Mar 2015, blamed North Korea for a Dec 2014 cyberattack on nuclear power-plant operator Korea Hydro & Nuclear Power Co.[12] As per media reports, the cyberattacks aimed at stealing internal data that included plant blueprints and employees' personal information. So far, there are no known incidents of reactor meltdown and release of radiation owing to cyberattacks on nuclear power plants. Yet incorporating cyber security as a fundamental part of the overall security plan for nuclear facilities across the globe cannot be ignored anymore. This is more relevant as both cyberattacks and nuclear disasters do not recognise any national boundaries.

Cyber Threats to Telecom Sector

On 30 Dec 2013, *The Hindu* reported alleged role of Chinese telecom equipment giant Huawei in hacking into Bharat Sanchar Nigam Limited (BSNL) network and sabotaging its expansion plans in Rajahmundry in coastal Andhra Pradesh.[13] Investigations revealed that it was an intercompany rivalry between ZTE and Huawei about supply of equipment to BSNL which prompted the alleged hacking; nonetheless, it showed how vulnerable the government owned telecom giant is to cyberattacks.

In the information age, telecommunication is one of the most essential industries. It is considered as the backbone of industrial and economic development of a nation. Telecom sector has been aiding delivery of

11 The Washington Post, June 5, 2008

12 North Korea Blamed for Nuclear-Power Plant Hack as available at http://www.wsj.com/articles/north-korea-blamed-for-nuclear-power-plant-hack-1426589324

13 Centre to probe alleged hacking of BSNL network by Huawei by Sandeep Joshi, The Hindu, 30 December 2013

voice and data services at rapidly increasing speeds. In Chapter 2, while determining the cyber warfare capabilities of a nation, the reach and strength of telecom sector was weighed as an essential factor. Some of the direct and indirect benefits of the telecom industry in a growing economy of India are summerised in the diagram below:-

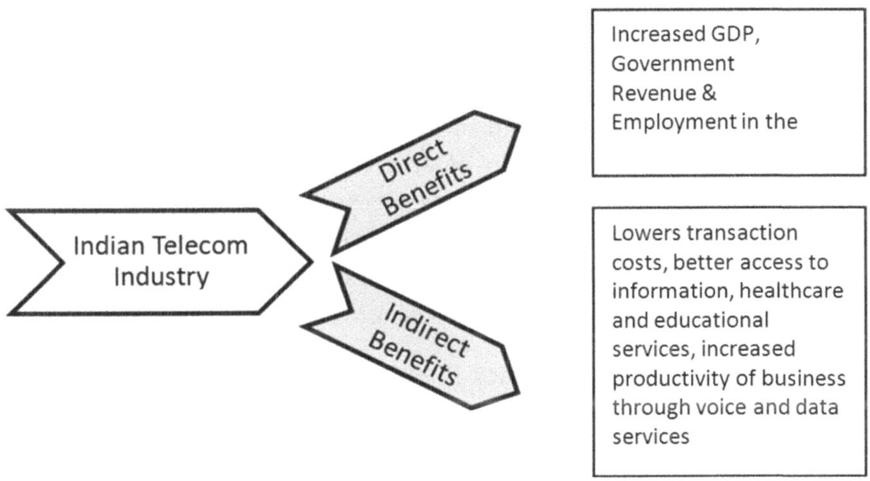

Figure 11: Benefits of Growth of Telecom Industry

The backbone or the core of the telecom network in India (and the rest of the world) today is based on Optical Fiber Cable (OFC) with radiating media as an overlay/ last mile connectivity. The radiating media could be point to point or point to multi point microwave radio or satellite overlay network. Hundreds of thousands of kilometres of OFC is laid in the Country not only by the public sector organisations but also private industry. Just for the Armed Forces, as part of the Network for Spectrum project, 60,000 km of OFC is being laid to provide connectivity for 219 Army, 162 Air Force and 33 Navy stations at a cost of approximately US $1.3 billion.[14] The coverage of the telecom networks in India is rather large with both public as well as private industry competing against each other.

14 PAN-India Optical Fibre Cable Network for Defence Forces at an Additional cost of $1.3 Billion, as available at http://www.defencenow.com/news/675/pan-india-optical-fibre-cable-network-for-defence-forces-at-an-additional-cost-of-$13-billion.html

A number of foreign companies have invested into the growth of this network. Diverse technologies are being used as various components of the network. Hence, the vulnerabilities are also bound to be numerous. It is therefore essential to determine the kinds of cyber threats this key industry faces.

Cyber Threats to Satellite Network

At any given time, there are over 3000 satellites orbiting the earth. The largest of them in orbit around the Earth is the International Space Station. Some satellites, called microsats, nanosats, or picosats, can be as small as 10 cm in diametre and 0.1 kg in mass. Military, civilian and commercial satellites deliver a broad range of services including voice, data and internet communications, broadcast services, mapping, space exploration, global positioning, meteorology, surveillance, navigation and emergency services. In some cases, the satellite produced or stored information can be highly sensitive, even putting national security at risk.

Till a few years back, legacy satellite systems were hardware based with dedicated hardware circuits and protocols. For a cyberattack on such a system, an attacker needed detailed knowledge of the proprietary system as well as physical access to them. Systems were often not connected to each other and seldom to the internet. Such systems were naturally shielded from cyberattacks. Modern satellites, as well as other communication systems today, are much more vulnerable to cyberattacks because:

(a) Most networks use open networking standards/ protocols such as TCP/IP. This not only cuts down the time required to carry out R&D but also makes implementation of networks more economical.

(b) Networks use less secure operating systems such as Windows instead of proprietary operating systems.

(c) Convergence of networks into one network including the internet brings in additional vulnerabilities.

A complex satellite communication network is based completely on ICT equipment. The two most critical elements in the satellite network, performance of which if degraded can adversely impact the entire network are, the satellite itself and the base station or the gateway. Configuration of a typical communication satellite network is as under:

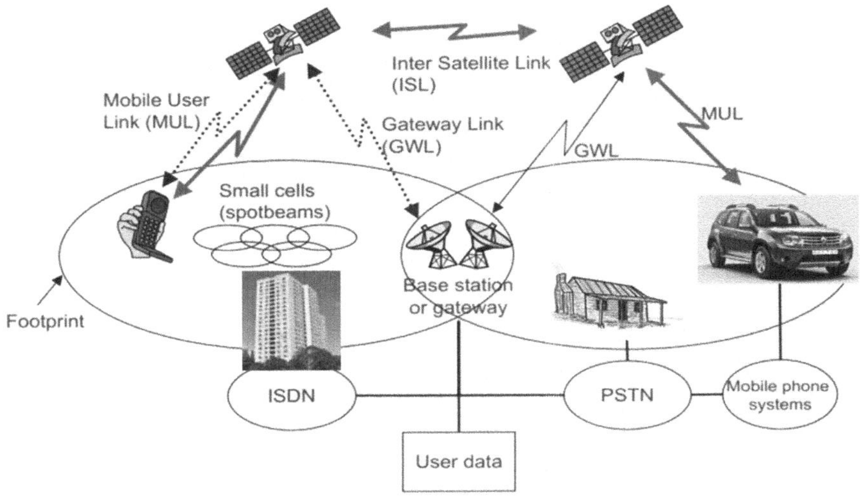

Figure 12: Configuration of Satellite Based Communication Network

A cyberattack on a satellite network will be with the aim of "soft" kill to the satellite. Though a cyberattack can also take the form of "hard" kill where the satellite system is permanently disabled or destroyed. The nature of kill would depend on the technical proficiency and the intention of the attacker. A satellite and the base station of any satellite network face the following types of cyber threats :-[15]

(a) Taking control of (or nullifying the ability to control) a satellite.

(b) Deliberately interfering with satellite transmissions, by jamming, denying, degrading, or forging (counterfeiting) signals, either from the ground or from other satellites.

(c) Key targets of communications link attacks are satellite uplink

15 global: satellites, security and the social graph by Randy S Segal and Steven M Kaufman as available at http://www.hoganlovells.com/files/Publication/186d7935-e551-43df-97fe-58f9250d7ebe/Presentation/PublicationAttachment/b2c7e23a-ad97-4911-bd1c-6bf5bcc8f8d4/Global%20Satellites%20security%20and%20the%20social%20graph.pdf

(transmitting information from ground station to satellite) and downlink (transmitting information from satellite to ground systems) facilities.

(d) Accessing (and potentially leaking) satellite-produced or stored information by implanting computer virus and logic bombs into satellite information systems.

(e) Compromised chipsets, ground systems, internet links and other system components or interfaces can be the vehicles for satellite cyberattack.

(f) Compromising other satellite or terrestrial based networks used by the satellite, or with which the satellite can in turn interfere.

Satellite communication has traditionally been used in the defence sector. For this reason, several anti-jamming technologies have been employed on military satellites. These may include Spread Spectrum, EHF frequencies, directional antenna beams and signal processing techniques for jamming mitigation, which are typically not used by commercial satellites. As the technologies exist though, this is related to commercial decisions rather than a technical research issue. Hence, satellite communication availability can easily be disrupted via cyber means, such as a network denial of service attack or malicious software. In 2010, cyber security investigative researcher Jeffrey Karr had shocked ISRO when he proved that India's INSAT 4B satellite which was put into orbit in 2007 was taken down by Stuxnet to serve Chinese business interests.[16] On 7 July 2010, INSAT 4B's power glitch forced India's leading DTH providers such as Sun Direct, Doordarshan and Tata Teleservices to shift to ASIASAT-5, a satellite owned by the Chinese government. ISRO is a Siemens customer. According to two former engineers who worked at the ISRO's Liquid Propulsion Systems Centre, the Siemens software in use to control the satellite was Siemens S7-400 PLC and SIMATIC WinCC, both of which will activate the Stuxnet worm. Some of the cyber threats which various satellite systems face are as follows:

16 India is a Sitting Duck in the Cyber Battlefield by Sai Manish as available at http://archive.tehelka.com/story_main51.asp?filename=Ne261111India.asp

Type of facility	Security Threat	Impact
Communication Satellite system	DoS attack	Loss of availability of the satellite
Satellite-based Sensing	GPS Spoofing	Misleading GPS coordinates used for positioning calculations
Communication Satellite and Satellite-based Sensing	On-board computer reconfiguration using malicious software	Cyber surveillance and loss of critical data
Communication Satellite and Satellite-based Sensing	SQL injection and other database attacks	Inaccurate database information, breach of data confidentiality
All types of satellite systems	Malicious software/ code	Take over control of satellite or even destroy the satellite

Table 12: Cyber Threats to Satellite Systems

Tabulated above are some of the threats that a commercial satellite network faces from a cyberattack. A simulation of cyberattacks against Harris BGAN satellite terminals being used by the NATO forces showed that an attacker could achieve the following on Falcon III RF-7800B :-[17]

(a) By exploiting the insecure protocols, an attacker injects malicious code into the terminal.

(b) The malicious code uses the built-in GPS to obtain the coordinates where the system is located. This would allow the attacker to compare the system's position with a fixed area (target zone) where an attack from enemy forces is planned.

(c) If a Packet Data Protocol (PDP) context is detected or the system enters the target zone, the malicious code disables communications or even damages the terminal

If such a system was deployed in the battle zone and an attacker was able to make a number of such satellite terminals nonfunctional for a long period of time, not only would it lead to breakdown of critical communication but also loss of life.

17 A Wake-up Call for SATCOM Security by Ruben Santamarta as available at http://www.ioactive.com/pdfs/IOActive_SATCOM_Security_WhitePaper.pdf

Cyber Threats to 3G and 4G Networks.

First and second generation wireless telecommunication networks were controlled by exchanging signaling messages on closed SS7 based networks. These networks were isolated because they did not provide connectivity to any public networks to which end subscribers had direct access. The vulnerabilities of these networks therefore were few and well assessed.

Today is the era of third generation (3G) networks while 4G rollout is also simultaneously taking place. At the heart of 3G networks lay IP technologies for session control and mobility management. 3G has opened up a new generation of IP-based services called Cross Network Services that must interwork with the 3G wireless telecommunication networks. This enables the mobile network operators to offer their subscriber's a host of multimedia services based on and built upon Internet applications, services and protocols. A 3G network actually allows for more data transmission and therefore the network enables voice and video calling, file transmission, internet surfing, online TV, view high definition videos, play games and much more. A typical configuration of a 3G network can be represented as under:

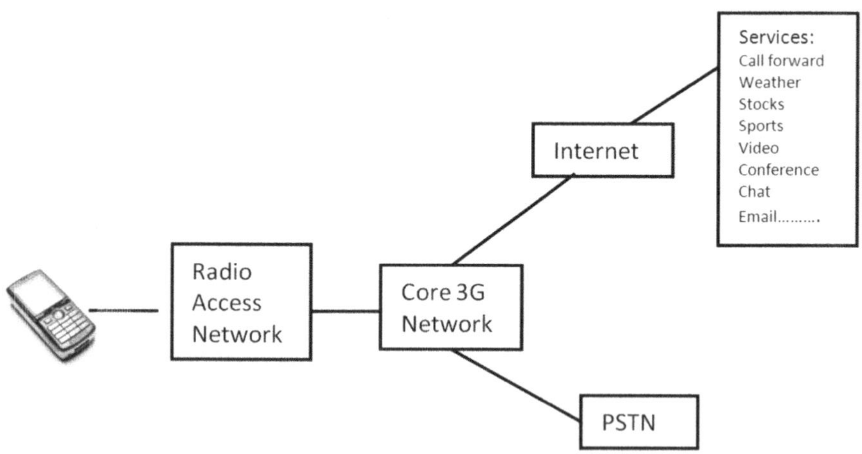

Figure 13: Architecture of 3G Network

The Core 3G network is connected to the Internet and the PSTN (Public Switched Telephone Network). Internet connectivity enables 3G users to receive the following services:

(a) Data services, such as weather reports, stock reports, sports information, chat, electronic mail;

(b) Cross Network Services such as Call Forwarding Services, Client Billing service and Location Based Instant Messaging;

(c) Location Based Services such as navigation, restaurant information, etc.

In 2G systems, network access is provided either to the PSTN or the Internet, so Cross Network Services are unavailable. With the integration of the core 3G networks, the PSTN and the Internet, the networks have opened up additional vulnerabilities and provided malicious attackers easy access through the Cross Network Servers. While 1G and 2G networks were vulnerable to Single Infrastructure cyberattacks, 3G networks are vulnerable to Cross Infrastructure cyberattacks also. Breaking into an Internet server providing Cross Network Service opens up possibilities for the attacker to invade the 3G core and PSTN networks. The Cross Infrastructure Cyber Attack is easy to execute by exploiting the vulnerabilities and sometimes serious enough to cause the breakdown of the telecommunication network services. If an attacker breaks into a 3G core network entity itself, the attacker can insert, modify and destroy data sources so that malicious subscribers may commit subscription fraud, collect confidential information from other entities and modify service logic to disrupt the network operation, thereby denying service.

Cyberattack on a 3G network could either be on the data stored in the system, on the signaling messages which are essential for running the network or service logic running in the various 3G core network entities. Let us now examine the extent of damage that can be caused by various types of cyberattacks on a 3G network :[18]

Interception. The attacker intercepts information for e.g., reads signaling messages on a cable, but does not modify or delete them.

18 A Taxonomy of Cyber Attacks on 3G Networks by Kameswari Kotapati, Peng Liu, Yan Sun, Thomas F. LaPorta as available at http://insr.cse.psu.edu/tech_report/NAS-TR-0021-2005.pdf

This is a passive attack. This affects the privacy of the subscriber and the network operator. The attacker may use the data obtained from interception to analyse traffic and eliminate the competition provided by the network operator.

Fabrication/Replay. In this case the attacker may insert spurious objects into the system. These objects depend on the level of the attacker's physical access to the system. For example, the attacker may insert fake signaling messages, fake service logic or fake subscriber data into this system. The effects could result in the attacker masquerading as a figure of authority.

Modification of Resources. The attacker causes damage by modifying system resources. For example, the attacker may modify signaling messages in and out of the cable. The attacker may also modify service logic or modify subscriber data in the entity.

Denial of Service. The attacker causes an overload or a disruption in the system such that network functions in an abnormal manner. The abnormal behaviour could be, legitimate subscribers not receiving service, illegitimate subscribers receiving service or the entire network may be disabled as a result of the attack.

Interruption. The attacker causes an interruption by destroying resources. For example, the attacker may delete signaling messages in and out of the cable or the attacker may delete a subscriber data in the entity such as an HLR thereby interrupting services of the users of the network.

According to a report, in 2014, the telecommunication companies in Europe registered close to one million hacker attacks daily on its grids alone. Two years ago this number was only 300,000.[19] Though no data is available about the number of such attacks against the telecom networks in India, in all probability, the data could be something similar. In the years to come, the number of attacks will only increase. The threat to the telecom infrastructure is therefore serious.

19 One million cyber attacks a day on Deutsche Telekom network as available at http://www.euractiv.com/sections/infosociety/one-million-cyberattacks-day-deutsche-telekom- network-309758

4G or Long Term Evolution (LTE) faces even more cyber threats than 3G. Still in the process of being rolled out in big cities, all assets on the 4G network will be running on top of Internet Protocol. Some of the cyber threats which a typical 4G network would face are:

Wireless APN Flooding: An attacker can enslave a number of devices that can quickly monopolise core bandwidth. This can flood the wireless Architecturally Private Network (APN) that connects the mobile devices of the 4G network to the Internet. The attacks can consume the "last mile" of scarce, wireless capacity and degrade service levels.

Mobile to Mobile Attacks: 4G traffic is all IP-based and can travel directly from mobile device to mobile device inside the wireless APN. This "peer to peer" (P2P) communication reduces backhaul traffic. However, it also permits mobile-to-mobile (Mob2Mob) attacks. The attack can also cause a DoS situation due to signaling congestion.

Voice over LTE (VOLTE) Service Assurance: Voice over IP (VoIP) attack tactics that have evolved on the Internet can be used just as effectively against VOLTE, even if the VOLTE infrastructure is not accessible from the Internet. Because VOLTE traffic remains largely within the wireless APN, carriers need different monitoring equipment to detect attacks as they move through the 4G infrastructure to the VOLTE service infrastructure.

As the 4G services are still not completely operational, the industry must build the security necessary to counter the 4G threats into the IP core and wireless networks. Unless this is done, the number of cases of cyberattacks taking placing from mobile devices will go up manifold.

Voice over IP

VoIP is a methodology and group of technologies for the delivery of voice communications and multimedia sessions over IP networks, such as the Internet. Other terms commonly associated with VoIP are IP telephony, Internet telephony, broadband telephony, and broadband phone service. VoIP has become very popular in the last few years as the cost of calls offered by VoIP service providers are much lower than those provided by regular telecom service providers. Now that VoIP is gaining wide acceptance and becoming one of the mainstream communication technologies, security has become a major issue. Let us have a look at the threats VoIP users face.[20]

Identity and Service Theft. Service theft can be exemplified by phreaking, which is a type of hacking that either steals service from a service provider, or uses service while passing the cost to another person. Encryption is not very common in SIP, which controls authentication over VoIP calls, so user credentials are vulnerable to theft.

Eavesdropping. This is how most hackers steal credentials and other information. Through eavesdropping, a third party can obtain names, password and phone numbers, allowing them to gain control over voicemail, calling plan, call forwarding and billing information.

Vishing. This is another word for VoIP Phishing, which involves fake calls requesting confidential and often critical information.

Viruses and Malware. VoIP utilisation involving soft-phones and software are vulnerable to worms, viruses and malware, just like any Internet application. Since these soft-phone applications run on user systems like PCs and PDAs, they are exposed and vulnerable to malicious code attacks in voice applications.

DoS. In VoIP, DoS attacks can be carried out by flooding a target with unnecessary SIP call-signaling messages, thereby degrading the service. This causes calls to drop prematurely and halts call processing.

Man-in-the-middle Attacks. VoIP is particularly vulnerable to man-in-the-middle attacks, in which the attacker intercepts call-signaling SIP message traffic and masquerades as the calling party to the called party, or vice versa. Once the attacker has gained this position, he can hijack calls via a redirection server.

Internet of Things and Smart Cities

The cases discussed above were cyberattacks on discreet systems and their impact on such systems. But what happens when many such smart digital

20 Security Threats In VoIP by Nadeem Unuth as available at http://voip.about.com/od/security/a/SecuThreats.htm

networked systems work together in a smart city? A large number of cities in the world can be classified as smart cities where a number of aspects such as traffic management, power supply, water management and many others have been automated. India under the present Government too has announced development of smart cities in the country. According to the Government of India, the aim is to develop 100 smart cities, for which INR 7,060 crores have been allocated in the budget for the financial year 2014 -15. Some of the key aspects of the smart cities being planned are.[21]

- Smart parking.
- Intelligent transport system.
- Tele care.
- Smart grids.
- Smart urban lighting.
- Smart waste management.
- Smart city maintenance.
- Digital signage.
- Smart water management.
- Women safety based on smart surveillance and smart policing

Besides the smart cities project, the Government also plans to roll out Internet of Things (IoT) program. The IoT has been defined as a seamlessly connected network of embedded objects/devices, with identifiers, in which M2M communication without any human intervention is possible using standard and interoperable communication protocols. Phones, Tablets and PCs are not included as part of IoT.[22] The vision of the Government is to develop connected and smart IoT based system for our Country's economy, society, environment and global needs. The IoT policy document lays down the details of how this ambitious project is to be implemented and steered.

---

21 IoT Policy Document Page 2 as available at http://deity.gov.in/sites/upload_files/dit/files/Draft-IoT-Policy%20(1).pdf

22 Ibid Page 4

At the heart of smart cities and IoT are self-aware and self-organising networks, storage and power networks, hybrid networking technologies, Data and Signal processing technology, platform interoperability besides next generation IoT based social software and enterprise applications. Statistics from the smart cities in the western world shows that the amount of data generated by various systems in a smart city can reach a considerable size. Big Data will need to be appropriately and centrally stored, managed, analysed, and protected. The city's operation centre will supervise the interaction between systems and will have to ensure continuity, integrity and resilience.

Like any other ICT system, the smart city's technological and communication environment, the network infrastructure and the IoT will present vulnerability to cyberattacks. The higher complexity and heterogeneity of these environments could in fact determine an even higher exposure, and need for more sophisticated protection strategies. As systems grow more complex, interconnected and handle more information, their exposure to vulnerabilities increases; whether due to malicious intent or human error.

When conceiving and building services, architectures and applications that leverage smart city information platforms, this should be done with high level security against cyber-attacks in mind, in order to guarantee service availability and continuity, data management and protection, as well as network resilience in case of severe incidents. When the reliance on networking and IoT would increase to a level that routine day to day activities will become impossible in the absence of these services, imagine the threat such technologies will face from cyber-attacks. Hence it is essential that while the core technologies for implementing these ambitious projects are being developed, cyber security forms part of the overall project and not an overlay implemented as an afterthought. Unless adequate number of layers of cyber security is put into place, one should not be surprised if in the future the news headlines read, "cyber terrorists hack into the electricity grid of Delhi causing a blackout". To prove the point, a researcher from security consultancy IOActive recently showed that vulnerabilities in road sensors relaying information to traffic lights could be exploited to turn them from red to green, or keep them on a certain colour.[23] The potential impact is all too obvious: traffic carnage and deadly accidents.

---

23 Smart or stupid: will our cities of the future be easier to hack? As available at http://www.theguardian.com/cities/2014/may/21/smart-cities-future-stupid-hack-terrorism-watchdogs

Another vulnerability which may be inherent to any smart city is availability of free wireless hotspots all over the city in addition to those provided by airports, hotels, and malls. With availability of the internet all the time and every place, more and more citizens will be exposed to vulnerabilities, especially the younger population who are at risk of being lured onto unsafe websites and chat rooms. Under such circumstances, it is but obvious that the rate of cyber crime will go up. Hence, smart cities will need smart policing to ensure that cyber crime is kept under check.

The world is full of people who are willing to use the cyberspace to wage terror and war by attacking the critical infrastructure. It is a place where individual actors backed by national will, with little technology and money can produce disproportionate results against other nation states by striking at their critical infrastructure thereby threatening public safety and security. Although the imminent threat of an all-out cyber war is not very likely, the prospect of bringing warfare to the cyber arena nevertheless promises significant asymmetric advantages to a nation-state with limited resources especially to those states that propagate terror as their agenda for achieving national objectives. This is even more significant if the attacker can remain anonymous. CII would therefore be an obvious target in such a scenario as the results of such attacks would not only impact the morale of the public but will also have political ramifications. Also, with a high degree of uncertainty about the origin of the attacks, it allows strategic political objectives of such nations to be achieved with ease. This is the reason that developed nations whose infrastructure relies heavily on networking and ICT are today finding newer methods of protecting critical infrastructure. New organisations are being raised to ensure the safety of such industry so that public safety and national security is not threatened from the cyber space.

Conclusion

Discussed above were some of the CII and how a cyber-attack can degrade their performance or even render them useless for a critical period of time. Cyber-attacks are ideal instruments of sabotage. The sabotage could be an attempt to deliberately weaken or disable an economic or military system. One of the recent examples of such an attack is when in Sept 2013, Israel's national road network located in the northern city of Haifa suffered a cyber-attack that caused massive traffic congestion in the city for hours.[24] As brought out in the previous chapter, the attackers used a malware to hit the security camera apparatus in the Carmel Tunnel toll road on 08 Sept 2013 to gain control over it. The tunnel is a strategic thoroughfare in the third largest city of the country. The attack caused an immediate 20-minute lockdown of the roadway. The next day, it again shut down the roadway during morning rush hour. The highway remained shut for eight hours, causing massive congestions.

An analysis of the attack revealed that most of the control systems on the highway are automated, especially as far as security is concerned. Also, they are remotely controlled, either over the Internet or otherwise, so they were vulnerable to cyberattacks. Imagine if such an attack was carried out against road networks in India in the Northern and the Western sectors while the Indian Armed Forces were mobilising. It could result in delay not only in occupation of critical defences but also may impact the offensive plans.

As more and more industrial control systems get automated and networked, protection of CII assumes a new dimension. The national and economic security of India today depends on the reliable functioning of critical info-infrastructure. The United States issued an Executive Order 13636, "Improving Critical Infrastructure Cyber Security," on 12 Feb 2013. The order establishes the Policy of the United States to enhance the security and resilience of the Nation's critical infrastructure and to maintain a cyber environment that encourages efficiency, innovation, and economic prosperity while promoting safety, security, business confidentiality, privacy, and civil liberties. It is time we, in India also awakened to the challenges that our infrastructure faces from the cyber domain and took measures to protect it. Unless we analyse this new threat to our national security on priority and institute measure to counter the threat, we may inadvertently be exposing our national assets to an enemy constantly lurking in the cyber domain, waiting to strike. Hence, there is a need to create a framework in the country to address and manage cybersecurity risks in particular and improve the cybersecurity posture of the Nation's critical info-infrastructure as a whole.

---

24 Israeli Road Control System hacked, caused Traffic jam on Haifa Highway as available at http://thehackernews.com/2013/10/israeli-road-control-system-hacked.html

Covert or overt employment of non-state actors in cyberspace operations, such as volunteers in state-to-state conflicts, cyber-militia, cyber-mercenaries or organised cyber-criminals raise many new questions to which the world is yet to find answers. Although there have not yet been any concrete instances where cyber actions, or cyberattacks, have resulted in physical injury or extended destruction of property of another nation, the heavy cyber-dependency of modern day infrastructure makes more damaging cyberattacks plausible or even probable in future scenarios. Finding ways to mitigate these types of hazardous events, before they evolve into real threats to national security, is thus an increasingly pressing issue for any government as well as the private infrastructure sector. A lot of work needs to be done, especially in India before we can confidently claim that our critical infrastructure is relatively secure from cyberattacks.

4 CII Protection in India

"Cyber security should be an integral part of National Security"

- Shri Narendra Modi, Prime Minister of India

India's security environment is determined by its geopolitical attributes, historical legacy, socio-economic circumstances as well as regional and global development. While national security is the requirement to maintain the survival of the nation state through the use of economic, military and political power, new factors seem to have added lately to this list which too impact national security. To be secure, a nation today needs to ensure economic security, energy security, environmental security, cyber security and so on. Shri P Chidambaram, Finance and Home Minister in the UPA Government while talking about India's National Security - Challenges and Priorities had this to say: "*National security is, caught in a complex spider's web and unless we recognise that each strand of this web is connected to other strands, we would not be able to do justice to our fundamental obligation to protect and defend the security of the nation*"[1]. The ex-minister clearly indicated that the concept of national security has been enlarged to encompass not just military but also non-military, conventional as well as non-conventional threats and challenges to the state and society.

With the growing economic uncertainty and complexities plaguing the country, it has never been more challenging for India from an internal security perspective. As per a report "Emerging Dynamics and Challenges of Internal Security in India" published jointly by PHD Chamber of Commerce and Industry and KPMG India in Jun 2013, the internal security

1 India's National Security - Challenges and Priorities, February 6, 2013 by Shri P Chidambaram, available at http://www.idsa.in/keyspeeches/IndiasNationalSecurity ChallengesandPriorities

ecosystem in India is impacted by following seven factors[2]:

(a) Terrorism and naxal management;

(b) Critical infrastructure protection;

(c) Border security;

(d) Maritime security;

(e) Police modernisation;

(f) City Surveillance;

(g) Intelligence and cyber security.

Though in the above report, critical infrastructure protection is primarily from physical threats, as has emerged in the previous chapters; our CII can be threatened from cyberspace as well. What is significant about the report is that both protection of critical infrastructure and cyber security are today considered as challenges to our internal security and stability as well as national security and therefore need to be given due importance. Hence, while formulating our National Security Policy, both these aspects will have to be given a due consideration. Shri Shyam Saran, former Foreign Secretary of India and currently Chairman of the National Security Advisory Board during his talk on "Revamping India's National Security Architecture for Optimum Synergy in the Use of its Instruments of National Power" held at USI on 22 Sep 2014, brought out the aspect of cyber security and the threat it poses to the nation. He indicated that the Government of India is aware of the threat to the National Security from the cyberspace and is trying to ensure that the people of India are able to use the cyberspace without facing any intimidation whatsoever. He further went on to say that "*Cyberattacks on critical civilian infrastructure may have consequences far more significant than damage to military installations. In any case military activities are heavily reliant on civilian infrastructure such as the transport network*[3]." What clearly emerges from the talk of Chairman of the National Security Advisory Board is that cyber security today is an

2 Emerging dynamics and challenges of internal security in India, June 2013, p4

3 Revamping India's National Security Architecture for Optimum Synergy in the Use of its Instruments of National Power, The 18th Pyara Lal Memorial Lecture, 2014 by Shri Shyam Saran, IFS (Retd)

important ingredient of our national security framework.

The PHD Chamber of Commerce and Industry and KPMG report "Emerging Dynamics and Challenges of Internal Security in India" summarises the focus areas and the agencies responsible to deal with each of the above seven factors as under:

	Terrorism and Naxal Management	Critical Infrastructure protection	Border Security	Maritime Security	Police Modernisation	City Surveillance	Intelligence and cyber security
Focus Areas	Integrated action plan LWE district development SRE Special infrastructure scheme Anti terrorism	Airports Surface transportation Power plants Govt. buildings	Border surveillance Border fencing, roads and flood lighting BOPs Integrated check posts BADP	Coastal Security vessels traffic management Coastal Police Stations	State police modernisation National police mission IV fort CCTNS	Safe city projects	Cyber security Intelligence collection Terrorism financing investigations
Agency Responsible	CRPF IRB NSG RR	CISF DSC Private organisations	BSF ITBP SSB Assam Rifles	Indian Navy Coast Guard Coastal police CISF	State police departments Coastal police	PM division of MHA State police departments	NATGRIG NIA IB Multi agency centers

Table 13: Agencies Responsible for Focus Areas of Internal Security

An analysis of the above factors clearly indicates that the country's internal security ecosystem is multilayered and complex system with a number of stakeholders contributing towards our national security. These stakeholders not only fall in the category of government organisations, but also semi government organisations and corporate houses. This is because a large number of critical infrastructures today are privately owned. Therefore the responsibility of ensuring security of such CII also lies with these companies. The term security here does not just refer to physical security but cyber security as well. For example under the head Critical Infrastructure protection, both government and private organisations have been listed. This brings in the factor of multi-stakeholder approach for protection of critical infrastructure and cyber security, a concept that needs to be deliberated upon in detail.

Till a decade ago, the responsibility of ensuring security of the nation was that of the democratically elected Government of India. Not that the Government is not responsible for it anymore. But with the inclusion of CIIs as a factor which impacts our national security and the threat that it faces from the cyber domain, private industry too now needs to be a partner in overall security environment. An analysis of the CII reveals the following:-

- Private sector has made inroads to most of the CIIs in the country. A few years back, the public sector undertakings had a monopoly over all critical infrastructure sectors, but that is not the case anymore. With the globalisation of the economy, today private industry plays an equally important role in creation and operation of such critical sectors. It is a matter of time when more efficient and better organised private sector overtakes the public sector in all critical areas of infrastructure.

- In certain sectors such as aviation, mobile telecommunication and banking, the dominance of private sector is much more than the public sector undertakings.

- More and more areas are being opened to investment by the private sector including foreign investors. Even a sector like defence has been opened to private sector. In August 2014, the NDA Government raised the FDI to 49 per cent from the earlier 26 per cent, subject to the Indian owners exercising management control. A large number of foreign private players would now be manufacturing critical defence equipment and supplying it for the three services.

- Nuclear energy is perhaps the only sector where the Government has maintained 100 per cent control. All other energy sectors today have private players, both for production of the energy as well as its distribution.

- The role of private sector in the overall growth of the country's economy is significant. Any threat or attack on the private sector will therefore have an impact on the safety and security of the general public.

If that be so, the impact of a cyberattack through or on the cyber space will affect all spheres of the society. In fact the consequences of such attacks on private sector may be much more noticeable than governmental sector. Hence there is a need to protect the private sector infrastructure in the country as much as the public sector infrastructure. The security of Nation's CII therefore requires the interaction of multiple governmental departments and agencies, as well as operational collaboration across national, state, local, nongovernmental organisations, and the private sector. Before going into the details of how this can be achieved, let us examine what could be the tangible and intangible impacts or impacts in the cognitive domain of cyber attacks on both government as well as private sector.

Impact on Government. A large number of Indian public sector undertakings have suffered cyberattacks. The attacks have varied from defacing of government websites to trying to disrupt the smooth conduct of Common Wealth Games in 2010 to stealing of sensitive information. Any Cyberattack on government owned infrastructure can not only result in breakdown of public services, but have the following impact too :-

(a) Direct attacks on national security seek to undermine government by degrading its ability to ensure the safety and security of its constituents. Typically, adversaries seek to attack critical systems and government functions to destroy society directly. The Russian cyberattacks on Georgia in 2008 are an example of such direct attacks where the Russians in conjunction with their ground offensive launched cyberattacks to undermine Georgia's Government.

(b) The reactions of national leadership to attacks on CII targets in their homeland could be pronounced. Unexpected collateral damage caused by an attack on CII may weaken international support, produce a negative domestic reaction, and stiffen resistance in target country. As James A. Lewis in his article "Thresholds for Cyberwar" sums it up, "A cyberattack is a tactical weapon with strategic consequences[4]". This statement will be analysed in Chapter 5.

(c) Indirect attacks on government manipulate messages or

4 Thresholds for Cyberwar by James A. Lewis, p3

information to undermine trust held by citizens, other governments, and non-governmental organisations. These types of attacks seek to affect the morale of the society. Once again the Russian cyberattacks on Estonia can be classified under this category where the cyberattacks were aimed to bring down the banking system thereby impacting the trust of the Estonian public in the democratically elected government.

Impact on Private Sector. On 15 Aug 2012, Saudi Aramco, the national oil company of Saudi Arabia came under cyber-attack which knocked out 30,000 of its workstations.[5] The malware deleted data base and made infected computers unbootable. Many of its websites remained down and emails bounced back. It took ten days to restore normal operations. Although the virus attack did not impact field operations, nor were there any explosions on the oil fields, yet Saudi Aramco's reputation as one of the biggest oil exploring and refining companies in the world took a hit and its image in the eyes of the customers took a blow. The biggest impact on the private sector is to its credibility and trustworthiness in providing essential public services.

The private sector as discussed above is a key player in CII. Cyberattacks on the private sector owned CII could impact society very broadly. This could include loss of credibility as well as impact on business. There have been a few cases where the business had to be shut down temporarily because of loss of faith of the customers. While in the government sector, basic security parameters can be controlled, however, the same parameters may be difficult to implement in the private sector. As the private sector is driven by profits, protecting commercial cyberspace may require greater controls, as well as incentives, than are currently in place in India.

Building a Secure Cyber Ecosystem

In the previous chapter we analysed what is CII and also established the need to protect it. But how does a nation protect its CII from cyberattacks? The best method would be perhaps to create an environment where cyberattacks cannot take place on national assets. In other words create a cyber ecosystem in the country where each device can work with immunity while the environment takes care of all the security needs. Given

5 Cyber war will not take place by Thomas Rid, p55

the potentially catastrophic consequences that cyberattacks can cause, it is imperative for us to build such an environment where critical infrastructure is automatically safeguarded from coming under attack.

As we have seen above, cyber ecosystem of India will comprise of a number of diverse participants such as private firms, government and nongovernment organisations and even individuals. The idea of a healthy, resilient and secure cyber ecosystem is one in which all above participants are able to work in near real time to anticipate and prevent cyberattacks, limit the spread of attacks and recover to a trusted state. It is essential to jointly build a secure cyber ecosystem for the country. A ecosystem which will bring in higher degree of cyber security thereby ensuring not only protection of the CIIs but also other cyber assets. The strategic concept of secure cyber ecosystem in the US is of two complementary focus areas as under:[6]

- The 1st focus area, "*Protecting Critical Information Infrastructure*," concentrates attention on systems and assets within the cyber ecosystem that are vital to the US. This information infrastructure can best be protected by reducing exposure to risk, ensuring priority response and recovery, maintaining shared cyber situational awareness, and increasing resilience.
- The 2nd focus area, "*Strengthening the Cyber Ecosystem*," is designed to drive fundamental change in the way people and devices work together to secure cyberspace. This evolutionary change in the computing environment will be achieved by empowering individuals and organisations to operate securely, making and using more trustworthy cyber protocols, products, services, configurations, and architectures, building collaborative communities, and establishing transparent processes.

In India, NCSP 2013 too talks of creating a secure cyber ecosystem in the country. The vision of the NCSP 2013 is to build a secure and resilient cyberspace for citizens, business and government. Its overall action plan looks as under:

6 Blueprint for Secure Cyber Future, November 2011 as available at https://msisac.cisecurity.org/resources/reports/documents/blueprint-for-a-secure-cyber-future.pdf

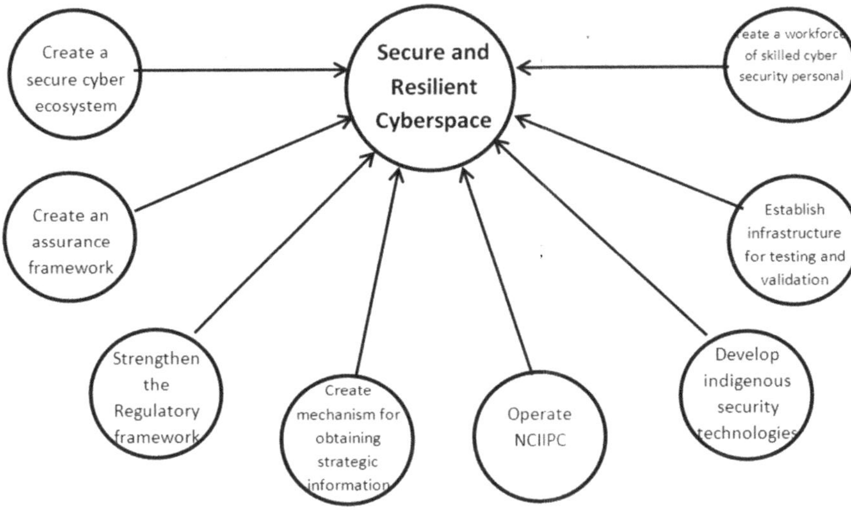

Figure 14: Building Secure and Resilient Cyberspace

The first objective drafted by the Government of India in the policy is "**To create a secure cyber ecosystem in the country**, generate adequate trust and confidence in IT system and transactions in cyberspace and thereby enhance adoption of IT in all sectors of the economy".[7] Being the objective Number One, creation of a secure cyber ecosystem in the country is the key focus area of NCSP 2013. For creation of secure cyber ecosystem, NCSP 2013 recommends eight aspects as under:

1. *To designate a National nodal agency to coordinate all matters related to cyber security in the country, with clearly defined roles and responsibilities.* Presently NTRO has been entrusted with this job and has been made responsible for coordination of all cyber security related matters. How far has NTRO succeeded in this task yet remains to be seen. Eventually this job will be taken over by the National Cyber Coordination Centre, which is likely to be raised and made operational by end of 2015/ mid 2016.

7 National Cyber Security Policy 2013 P3, Para III : Objectives

2. *To encourage all organisations, private and public to designate a member of senior management as "Chief Information Security Officer" (CISO) responsible for cyber efforts and initiatives.* The CISO would not only be responsible for coordinating all aspects of cyber security within the organisation but is also expected to act as a single point contact when dealing with the national nodal agency. While the NCSP talks of the role of the CISO, it hasn't made it mandatory for private companies to ensure its presence. This may be a shortcoming in the NCSP and must be amended. A suggested organisation for the structure of Information Security Department of CII is as under :-[8]

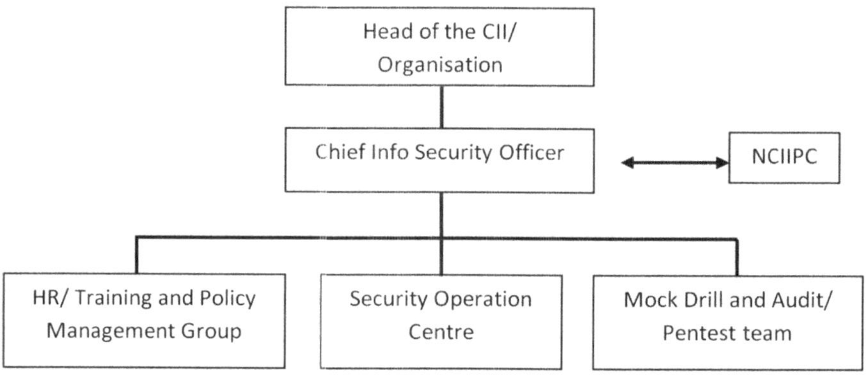

Figure 15: Information Security Organisation for CII

As recommended above, each CII must have the capability to audit its security preparedness as well as be able to carry out a penetration test of its networks and other ICT systems to determine their vulnerabilities.

3. *To encourage all organisations to develop information security policies duly integrated with their business plans and implement such policies as per international best practices. Such policies should include establishing standards and mechanisms for secure information flow, crisis management plan, proactive security posture assessment and forensically enabled information infrastructure.* In

8 Guidelines for Protection of National Critical Information Infrastructure Version 1.0 June 2013

other words, the flexibility of what kind of security policies an organisation wants to follow has been left to the organisation as long as the policy conforms to the global standards.

4. *To ensure that all organisations earmark a specific budget for implementing cyber security initiatives and for meeting emergency response arising out of cyber incidents.* Ensuring allocation of adequate dedicated budget for cyber security by a private organisation is a difficult task. Unless an organisation has been a victim of loss of information or money to cyberattacks, a business house will seldom understand the implications of a poorly implemented cyber security plan. India has an extremely large number of private business establishments using the cyberspace and this number is only going to grow. With such a large number of players involved, how the government proposes to ensure that each one of them earmark budgets for cyber security functions, has still not be spelt out.

5. *To provide fiscal schemes and incentives to encourage entities to install, strengthen and upgrade information infrastructure with respect to cyber security.* Although no such schemes have been announced till now, this appears to be a positive step towards encouraging private industry to invest in cyber security.

6. *To prevent occurrence and reoccurrence of cyber incidents by way of incentives for technology development, cyber security compliance and proactive actions.* Offence is the best form of defence in the cyberspace and hence it is essential to be proactive in the way one operates in it. India has a very large IT industry base. While not much hardware is produced in the country, but as far as the software industry is concerned, we are one of the world leaders. With such large pool of trained manpower in the country available, it should not be difficult for the Government to develop in-house technology and ensure compliance of global cyber security standards.

7. *To establish a mechanism for sharing information and for identifying and responding to cyber security incidents and for cooperation in restoration efforts.* Timely sharing of information about impending threats and also cyberattacks executed on an organisation are essential components of overall cyber security environment.

Effectual and timely flow of information will happen only when we create a well-structured organisation at the national level with its subsystems at regional levels with the sole responsibility of gathering and sharing such critical information. Presently we do not have any such coordinated effort in the country. Whatever is happening is unsystematic and unstructured. More efforts would be required to implement this strategy. National Cyber Coordination Centre is the first step towards achieving this.

8. *To encourage entities to adopt guidelines for procurement of trustworthy ICT products and provide for procurement of indigenously manufactured ICT product that have security implications.* This strategy is primarily meant to counter the threat of supply chain vulnerabilities. How the Government of India intends ensuring this remains a question mark. As on date, not many facilities exist in the country where electronic components and imported hardware could be tested for malware and trapdoors. Similarly, not much of electronic and IT hardware is being produced in India. This leaves us open to supply chain vulnerabilities. The Government on one hand encourages global competition in all projects including defence with the tender being allotted to the lowest bidder and in such a scenario we expect clean hardware to be installed in our CII. We today live in an environment where virtually everything is manufactured in China. Unless we ourselves manufacture trustworthy ICT products, it is impossible to keep cheap, malware infested ICT products from making their way into strategic networks and systems.

A critical analysis of the above eight strategies to establish a secure cyber ecosystem reveals that India is nowhere close to a functional secure cyber ecosystem. A lot of effort needs to be put in by all stake holders for establishing a cyber environment where our critical infrastructure can work with impunity without the fear of being knocked down by cyberattacks.

Does the above mean that our critical info-infrastructure would remain vulnerable in the absence of a secure cyber ecosystem? Perhaps not. Even a country like the USA has not been able to create such an ecosystem for their critical infrastructure. What therefore needs to be done is that each of the infrastructures that have a debilitating impact on India's national security needs to be correctly identified, fortified and protected against threats from the cyberspace. NCSP 2013 talks about protection of CII at length.

NCSP 2013 and CII Protection

NCSP 2013 specifically focuses on protection of CII from cyber attacks. As part of the overall strategy this includes designation of a national nodal agency to coordinate all matters related to cyber security and ensuring that each organisation whether private or public nominates a CISO. But specific to CII, NCSP 2013 also has laid down steps for its protection of CII.[9] These are as under:-

1. To develop a plan for protection of CII and its integration with business plan at the entity level and implement such plan. The plans shall include establishing mechanism for secure information flow (while in process, handling, storage and transit), guidelines and standards, crisis management plan, proactive security posture assessment and forensically enabled information infrastructure. The scope of this strategy is very large and diverse. It would once again involve coordination between a large number of government agencies and private sector undertakings. However, unless the aspects of cyber security are introduced at the entity level, the overall protection plan of the CII will never be successful.

2. To operate 24x7 National Critical Information Infrastructure Protection Centre (NCIIPC) to function as the nodal agency for CII protection in the country. NCIIPC has already been established and is operational under NTRO. In June 2013 NCIIPC for the first time came out with a comprehensive document titled "Guidelines for Protection of National Critical Information Infrastructure". The steps laid down by NCIIPS for CII protection will be discussed later.

3. To facilitate identification, prioritisation, assessment, remediation and protection of critical infrastructure and key resources based on the plan for protection of CII. This too involves wholehearted involvement of all key players and the NCIIPC.

9 National Cyber Security Policy 2013 p7, Para IV (G).

4. To mandate implementation of global security best practices, business continuity management and cyber crisis management plan by all critical sector entities to reduce the risk of disruption and improve the security posture.

5. To encourage and mandate as appropriate, the use of validated and certified IT products. Which organisation is going to validate and certify such IT products has however not been mentioned. Such a certification is a very essential part of the cyber security procedure and therefore we need to create this capability on priority.

6. To mandate security audit of CII on a periodic basis. Security audit is a very important facet of any cyber security policy. Not only does each organisation need to carry out a self audit of its cyber security preparedness, the Government too will have to establish an organisation with the sole mandate of carrying out regular cyber security audits and exercises to check for vulnerabilities and preparedness. CERT-in may not be the best suited organisation for such a task as it needs to put into place the action plan in response to cyberattacks.

7. To mandate certification for all security roles right from CISO/ CSO to those involved in operation of CII.

8. To mandate secure application/ software development process (from design through retirement) based on global best practices.

The eight step plan laid down by NCSP 2013 gives out the broad framework of protecting the CII in the country. It is now the task of the Nodal Agency created by the Government to implement each of these to ensure safety of CII from cyberspace. NCIIPC is one such agency raised by the Government of India. Let us therefore examine what this organisation has been able to achieve in the last two years.

NCIIPC came into being in 2013 with the vision "To facilitate safe, secure and resilient Information Infrastructure for critical sectors of the nation". Its mission is to initiate necessary measures to facilitate protection of CII from unauthorised access, modification, use, disclosure, disruption, incapacitation or destruction through coherent coordination, synergy and raising information security awareness amongst all stakeholders. How one organisation located in the capital of the Country is going to achieve all this yet remains to be seen. However, it certainly is a positive step in the right direction.

NCIIPC has identified 17 subsectors as critical and in phase I, has initiated actions for protection of seven as under:

1. **Air Traffic Management and Civil Aviation**: Aviation industry obviously is the most sensitive CII as hundreds and thousands of lives are at stake. Even today a lot of cyber pundits speculate that Malaysian Airlines flight MH 370 was lost due to cyberattack on the navigation systems of the Boeing 777-200ER.

2. **Power Grid**: The impact of cyberattacks on power sector has already been discussed in detail in the previous chapter.

3. **NSEI**: Stock Exchanges, Depositories and Clearing Corporations are systemically important market infrastructure institutions. As part of the operational risk management, they need to have robust cyber security framework to provide essential facilities and perform critical functions relating to trading, clearing and settlement in securities market.

4. **MTNL**: Impact of cyberattacks on telecom sector too has already been discussed in detail in the previous chapter.

5. **BSNL**.

6. **Railways**: Indian Railways carries over 13 million passengers and 1.3 million tonnes of freight everyday. It is modernising its safety processes and control systems. Such system could be targeted from the cyberspace. Hence it is truly a CII which needs to be secured in phase I.

7. **SBI**: State Bank of India is the largest government-owned corporation bank of the country which is an Indian multinational. It provides public sector banking and financial services. That is the reason why SBI has been included in phase I of the action plan.

The framework formed for protection of CII at the national level by NCIIPC is as follows:[10]

- **Prevention and Early Warning**: NCIIPC issues daily and monthly cyber alerts for the CII, based on the kind of cyber activity is notices in the cyberspace.
- **Detection**: NCIIPC carries out a malware analysis which poses a threat to the CII and tracks zombie and malware spreading IPs.
- **Mitigation**: NCIIPC is equipped to undertake all cyber forensic activities to detect a malware or threat to a CII that has been attacked and is capable of bringing the system back to a trustworthy state.
- **Response**: NCIIPC operates a 24X7 operations and helpdesk. In the eventuality of a cyberattack on any CII, it assists the CII to bounce back to a trustworthy state.
- **Recovery**: Recovery of the CII back to functional state post an attack.
- **Resilience**: NCIIPC facilitates CII owners in adoption of appropriate policies, standards, best practices for protection of CII. It holds annual CISO conference for critical sectors for better coordination amongst each other.

Regulatory Framework : Legal Aspects of CII Protection in India

For any policy to be effectively implemented in the right spirit, it is essential that the policy is backed by a strong and versatile regulatory framework. Before going any further into how the CII needs to be protected, it is essential to check what legal protection is available to the CII in India.

The Information Technology Act 2000 also known as the IT Act 2000 provides legal cover to a number of cyber related issues. The act was amended in 2008 and more teeth were added to various sections. Together they are a powerful tool to fight cybercrime in India and to ensure protection

10 National Critical Information Infrastructure Protection Centre (NCIIPC), A Presentation by Muktesh Chander IPS, as available at http://indiasmartgrid.org/en/Lists/Member/Attachments/19/ISGD%20Plenary%20III%20Muktesh%20Chander%20NCIIPC.pdf

of cyber assets. Section 70 of the IT Act 2000 deals with protected systems and reads as follows:

> Section 70: Protected System.
>
> (1) The appropriate Government may, by notification in the Official Gazette, declare that any computer, computer system or computer network to be a protected system.
>
> (2) The appropriate Government may, by order in writing, authorise the persons who are authorised to access protected systems notified under sub-section.
>
> (3) Any person who secures access or attempts to secure access to a protected system in contravention of the provisions of this section shall be punished with imprisonment of either description for a term which may extend to ten years and shall also be liable to fine.

Under the IT Act Amendment 2008, the term critical information infrastructure has been added to Subsection (1). The amended clause now reads as follows:

> The appropriate Government may, by notification in the Official Gazette, declare any computer resource which directly or indirectly affects the facility of Critical Information Infrastructure, to be a protected system.
>
> Explanation: For the purposes of this section, "Critical Information Infrastructure" means the computer resource, the incapacitation or destruction of which, shall have debilitating impact on national security, economy, public health or safety. (Substituted vide ITAA-2008)

Also clause 70(A) deals with data protection in India. Section 70(A) under the IT Act Amendment 2008 reads as follows:

> Section 70 (A) National Nodal Agency. (Inserted vide ITAA 2008):
>
> Subsection (1) The Central Government may, by notification published in the official Gazette, designate any organisation of the Government as the national nodal agency in respect of Critical Information Infrastructure Protection.

Subsection (2) The national nodal agency designated under sub-section (1) shall be responsible for all measures including Research and Development relating to protection of Critical Information Infrastructure.

Subsection (3) The manner of performing functions and duties of the agency referred to in sub-section

The amendments in the IT Act clearly indicate that the Government of India realises the importance of CII and has ensured legal cover for its protection. How far has the government succeeded in doing so remains something to be seen. Here is an example of how callous are we in our approach towards protection of CII. In May 2012, an RTI was filed by an organisation called 'Bidirectional Access Promotion Society' which enquired from the Department of Electronics and Information Technology, "Which agency has been notified under section 70(A) of the IT Act 2000/ Amendment 2008 as national nodal agency in respect of Critical Information Infrastructure Protection".[11] The RTI also demanded for a list of every computer resource declared to be a protected system by notification in the Official Gazette. In response to the RTI, this is what the Department of Electronics and Information Technology had to say:

Government has not yet notified any agency under Section 70(A) of the Information Technology (IT) Act 2000 as national nodal agency in respect of Critical Information Infrastructure Protection.

Only the TETRA Secure Communication System Network, its infrastructure and software installed at some locations in Delhi have been notified to be Protected Systems under Section 70 of the Information Technology Act 2000.

This clearly indicates that the Government of India, till 2012, had not even identified what infrastructure should constitute towards CII so that legal cover could be granted to such critical infrastructure. Till as late as 2013, the Government of India had not notified NCIIPC as the nodal agency for this task, although the centre had started to function under NTRO. Yet despite the gazette notification not having being published, NCIIPC is an operational organisation and has released an important

11 No investigation on Chinese hacking of sensitive Indian government computers, as available at http://www.bapsi.org/press-releases/28-may-2012

document "Guidelines for protection of national CII", version 1.0 in June 2013. Details of this will be discussed later.

Mr. Pukhraj Singh, a cyber-warfare specialist and Officer on Special Duty (OSD) at NTRO has this to say about aspect of cyber security preparedness in the country, "*An inter-ministerial task force on cyber-security has been established and reports on cyber-attacks have started trickling to the top echelon of the establishment. Like any other institution, the progress is extremely slow but it is happening. We are very vulnerable, a lot of damage has been done to our national security but the Government has now taken notice. How quickly or efficiently we can put corrective systems in place remains to be seen*"[12].

India faces a different reality than most of the developed world, being a high tech country in a volatile environment. A large part of our nation is coping with problems of terrorism, left wing extremism and communal violence. If these radical elements take the cyber route to spread terror, they could cause grave damage to the country which could impact our national security. We are very vulnerable in the cyberspace and a lot of damage has been done to our national security. But the good part is that Government has now taken notice. How quickly or efficiently we can put corrective systems in place remains to be seen.

Relationship Between CII Protection and Cyber Security

It has been well established beyond doubt that CII in the country needs to be secured and protected from attacks propagated through the cyberspace. We have also seen the legal provisions and the strategy at the national level to create a secure cyber ecosystem. But how does a CII go about protecting itself in the cyberspace? What are the various steps that an organisation can take to ensure that its infrastructure does not become a victim of cyberattacks? Is isolating your network from the internet enough to ensure its protection from cyber threats? A lot of such questions now need to be answered. We need to clearly establish what cyber security refers to as far as CII is concerned.

Let us therefore first look at what are the international standards available for CII protection and cyber security. ISO 27000 series of standards

12 India Hacked, Part II: Cyber Warfare – The New Battlefield as available at http://www.theindiasite.com/india-hacked-part-ii-cyber-warfare-the-new-battlefield/

deal with various aspects of cyber security. At present, twenty-three of the standards in the series are published and available, while several more are still under development. The most comprehensive policy and guidelines are perhaps laid down by ISO 27001, 27002, 27032. ISO/IEC 27032:2012 provides guidance for improving the state of cyber security, drawing out the unique aspects of that activity and its dependencies on other security domains, in particular:

(a) Information security,

(b) Network security,

(c) Internet security, and

(d) Critical information infrastructure protection (CIIP).

ISO 27032 deals with cyber security issues which concentrate on bridging the gaps between different security domains in the cyberspace. The figure below is an adaption of ISO 27032 "Information Technology – Security Techniques – Guidelines or Cyber Security".[13] Some of the key components of the policy framework are as under:-

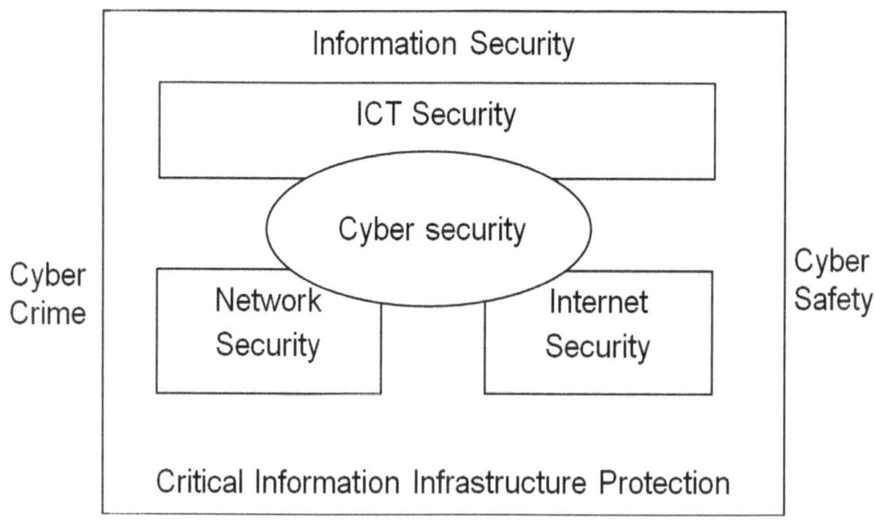

Figure 16: Key Components of Securing Cyberspace

13 National Cyber Security Framework Manual, Edited by Alexander Klimburg P10

Information Security: It is the practice of defending information from unauthorised access, use, disclosure, disruption, modification, perusal, inspection, recording or destruction. Information security is a general term that can be used regardless of the form the data may take. It is concerned with the protection of confidentiality, integrity and availability of information in general, to serve the needs of the applicable user. It has been placed right at the top of the figure as information rides on the ICT systems, networks and internet.

ICT Security/ Application Security: ICT is an umbrella term that includes any communication device or application, encompassing: radio, television, cellular phones, computer and network hardware and software, satellite systems and so on, as well as the various services and applications associated with them. In general ICT security is associated with technical origins of computer security and is directly related to information security principles. It extends beyond devices that are connected to the internet to include computer systems that are not connected to the internet.

Network Security: It is concerned with the design, implementation, and operation of networks for achieving the purposes of information security on networks within organisations, between organisations, and between organisations and users. What makes it foolproof is when the security architecture is inbuilt as part of the network and not implemented as an overlay to the networks.

Internet Security: It is concerned with protecting internet-related services and related ICT systems and networks as an extension of network security in organisations and at home, to achieve the purpose of security. Internet Security also ensures the availability and reliability of Internet services.

CIIP: CIIP is concerned with protecting the systems that are provided or operated by critical infrastructure providers, such as energy, telecommunication, and water departments. CIIP ensures that those systems and networks are protected and resilient against information security risks, network security risks, internet security risks, as well as Cyber security risks. It also includes ICT security.

Cyber Security or Cyberspace Security has been defined as the 'preservation of confidentiality, integrity and availability of information in the Cyberspace'. However, it has also been noted that in addition, other properties such as authenticity, accountability, non-repudiation and reliability can also be involved in cyber security

As can be seen from the explanation above, CII protection is a blend of ICT security, information security, network security, internet security and cyber security. Since it has all the ingredients, it is bound to be the most difficult task in the cyberspace. In the Indian context, ICT security is the most important aspect of CIIP as hardware and software being used in SCADA and industrial control systems are both not produced in the country and hence are vulnerable to supply chain attacks.

ICT Security

While a lot is said and written about most aspects of the above security framework, very little is discussed about ICT security which has a direct bearing on CIIP. Use of the term 'ICT security' usually includes the term 'supply chain security'. India along with the US, Russia and many other countries has increasingly been voicing concerns that the introduction of counterfeit, malicious or untrustworthy ICT could disrupt the performance of sensitive national security systems, and compromise essential government services.

The ICT supply chain consists of many phases, to include design, manufacture, and integration into the overall system, distribute, install. Post installations operate, maintain and decommission. To ensure foolproof security, there is a need to address each phase of the lifecycle. Protection measures must be therefore developed across the product lifecycle and be reinforced through both acquisition processes and effective implementation of government/enterprise security practices. For example, the highest risk factors in the supply chain are 'after build' (e.g., during the install and operate and retire phases) because this is where multiple vendors participate in the process (e.g., integrate products with other systems, patch/update, etc.) and there are few measures to monitor and assure integrity throughout the entire process. This is a problem for all countries: the evolution of the ICT industry means that many countries and global corporations now play a role in the ICT supply chain, and no country can source all components from totally 'trusted providers'.

The life cycle concept for ensuring infrastructure hardware and software remains free of any malicious codes and a trapdoor is perhaps the only method to ensure foolproof cyber security. National Institute of Standards and Technology in the US lays downs six steps for all the five phases of any hardware or software as shown below:[14]

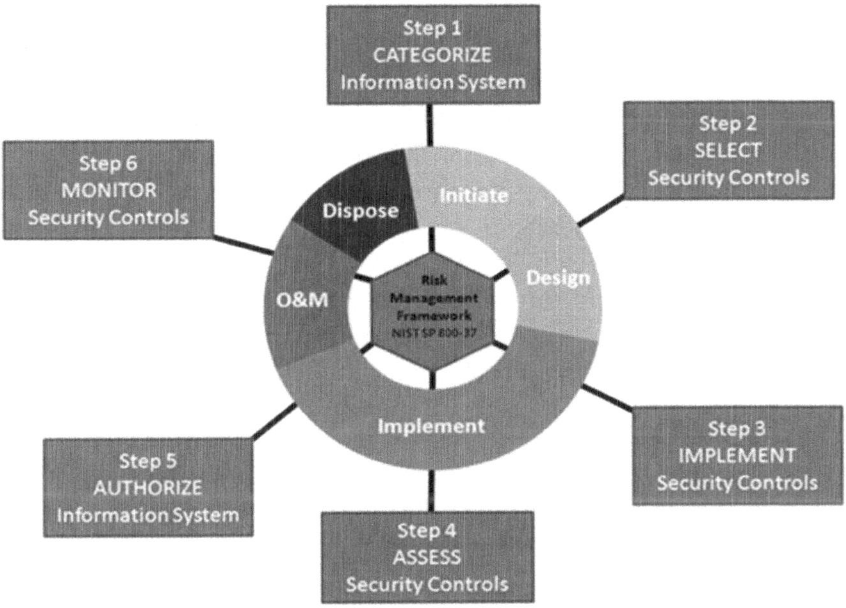

Figure 17: Risk Management Framework and Life Cycle Concept

All six steps i.e. Categorisation of systems, selection of security controls, implementation of security controls, assessment of security control, authorisation to information systems and monitoring of security controls need to be implimented for the entire life cycle of any information system. Unfortunately, we tend to implement these six steps only in the operation and maintenance (O&M) stage and tend to ignore the other phases of the lifecycle of the systems installed as part of the CII. Each phase of the infrastructure starting from "Initiate" – when the concept of infrastructure is conceived and along with it the concept of the information systems are conceived to "Disposal", are equally important in the cyber security chain. The apex national nodal agency responsible for CII protection needs to,

14 Security Architectures: Risk Management Framework as available at http://is355.wikidot.com/security-architectures

therefore, implement something similar for all our forthcoming projects which could be critical for our national security.

To reduce the threat of supply chain vulnerabilities of our ICT products, Government of India in 2013 approved setting up of two Semiconductor Wafer Fabrication (FAB) manufacturing facilities in the country at a cost of Rs. 63,410 Crores.[15] As per a press release of 13 Sep 2013 given by Ministry of Communication and Information Technology, these FAB facilities are expected to provide big boost to the Electronics System Design and Manufacturing eco-system in the country. Once again both these FABs are being put up with foreign collaboration. So how far do we succeed in countering the threats originating from supply chain vulnerabilities remains to be seen.

Organising the Nation for CII Protection

While the Government can lay down policies with a broad framework of establishing a secure cyber ecosystem, create organisations to tackle the issue and provide a legal framework for the implementation of such policies, the job is far from over. The private sector has made big inroads into CII and hence, it is the responsibility of every such organisation which has a stake in CII to implement these guidelines in their organisation to make their infrastructure safe and secure against cyberattacks. CII protection therefore has to follow a multi stakeholder approach with both government and nongovernment sector playing an equally important role. After all, the weakest link in the chain of cyber security decides how strong the protection system is.

Department of Homeland Security (DHS) in the USA follows the model of Public – Private Partnership Councils as part of the National Infrastructure Protection Plan. The Office of Infrastructure Protection under the DHS has established a critical infrastructure protection and resilience programme that is grounded in unprecedented public-private partnerships, coordination, and collaboration. The programme is organised as under:-[16]

---

15 India approves setting up of fab units at Yamuna Expressway and Prantij, Gujarat as available at http://gadgets.ndtv.com/others/news/india-approves-setting-up-of-fab-units-at-yamuna-expressway-and-prantij-gujarat-483854

16 Office of Infrastructure Protection as available at http://www.dhs.gov/office-infrastructure-protection referred on 31 Oct 2014.

Infrastructure Information Collection Division (IICD). The IICD leads the Department's efforts to gather and manage vital information regarding the nation's critical infrastructure. Accurate critical infrastructure data is essential to developing and executing infrastructure protection programs at all levels of government. IICD helps ensure that the necessary infrastructure data is available to homeland security partners by identifying information sources and developing applications to use and analyse the data.

Infrastructure Security Compliance Division (ISCD). The Infrastructure Security Compliance Division is responsible for implementing the Chemical Facility Anti-Terrorism Standards (CFATS), the US program to regulate security at high-risk chemical facilities, and a proposed Ammonium Nitrate Security Program.

National Infrastructure Coordinating Center (NICC). The NICC is the dedicated 24x7 coordination and information sharing operations center that maintains situational awareness of the nation's critical infrastructure for the federal government. When an incident or event affecting critical infrastructure occurs and requires coordination between the Department of Homeland Security and the owners and operators of the nation's infrastructure,the NICC serves as that information sharing hub to support the security and resilience of these vital assets.

Protective Security Coordination Division (PSCD). The PSCD is a division that provides programs and initiatives to enhance the protection and resilience of the nation's critical infrastructure with respect to all-hazards incidents.

Sector Outreach and Programs Division (SOPD). The SOPD builds stakeholder capacity and enhances critical infrastructure security and resilience through voluntary partnerships that provide key tools, resources, and partnerships. The division operates the council and stakeholder engagement mechanisms for the critical infrastructure security and resilience community. The division also serves as the sector-specific agency for 6 of the 16 critical infrastructure sectors and collaborates with the other 10.

The National Infrastructure Protection Plan establishes a partnership framework that enables federal, state, regional, local, tribal, territorial, and international governments to work with each other and their private sector partners. The Critical Infrastructure Partnership Advisory Council (CIPAC) supports a legal framework for their collaboration as under:-[17]

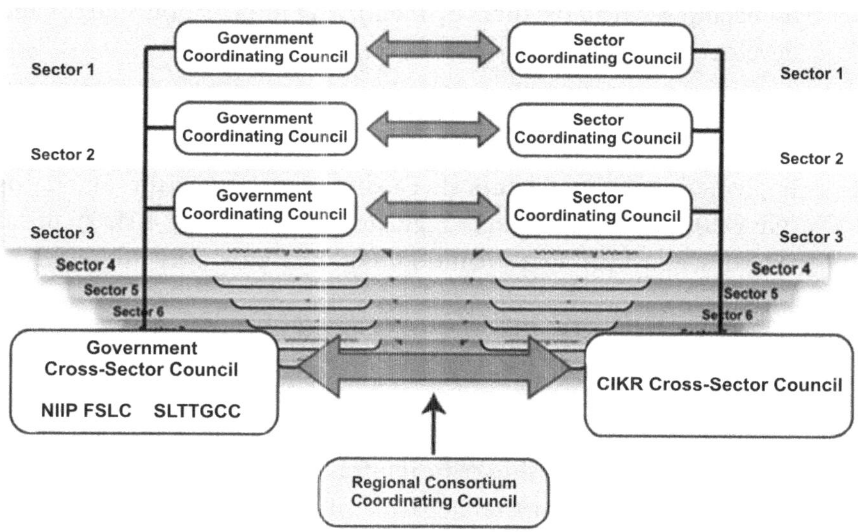

Figure 18: Critical Infrastructure Partnership Advisory Council

Partnership engagement enhances communication, planning, risk assessment, program implementation, and operational activities, including incident response and recovery. A networked alliance of critical infrastructure partnership councils helps implement protection and resilience activities across the nation:

(a) Sector Coordinating Councils (SCCs) are self-organised and governed entities of private sector critical infrastructure owners and operators. SCCs serve as the federal government's principal point of entry into 16 of the 18 critical infrastructure sectors (In the US, only two sectors are government owned and led and have only Government Coordinating Councils).

17 Critical Infrastructure Protection Partnerships and Information Sharing as available on http://www.dhs.gov/critical-infrastructure-protection-partnerships-and-information-sharing#2 viewed on 31 Oct 2014

(b) Government Coordinating Councils (GCCs) serve as the government counterpart to the SCCs and focus on maximising interagency coordination and information sharing.

(c) Cross-Sector Councils promote coordination, communication, and best practices across the critical sectors and regionally in order to identify commonalities and address

Something similar needs to be established in India too for protection of our critical infrastructure. While the critical infrastructure in India may not be as networked as the infrastructure in USA or other developed nations, yet, it is a matter of time before we too achieved that state. The organisation so created, therefore, should be dedicated to strengthening and expanding critical infrastructure expertise within and across regions of India. Hence, the Government needs to involve all stakeholders and establish such an organisation in the country. Whatever be the structure of the organisation, it should be able to perform the following three crucial tasks:

(a) Strategic planning and investment to inform effective risk management decisions. Risk assessment and management is perhaps one of the most important facets of CII protection. We shall examine this aspect in more detail later in this chapter.

(b) Situational awareness in steady state (normal) operations and during a crisis or event, including suspicious activity reporting, incident analysis, and recommended protective actions;

(c) Operational and tactical planning to counter the threat of cyberattacks and execution of the plan so evolved.

Another important facet of protecting critical info-infrastructure from cyberattacks in a multi stakeholder environment would be information sharing. Information shared within a structured and secure information sharing environment helps critical infrastructure owners and operators guide investments, implement protective programs, and ensure effective response to infrastructure threats as they arise. Presently NCIIPC has been tasked with this responsibility. NCIIPC is driven by the mission "To take all necessary measures to facilitate protection of Critical Information Infrastructure from unauthorised access, modification, use, disclosure, disruption, incapacitation or destruction through coherent coordination, synergy and raising information security awareness among all stakeholders" and with a vision "to facilitate safe, secure and resilient Information Infrastructure for Critical Sectors of the nation".

Following are the guiding principles for NCIIPC to achieve its mission and vision[18]:

(a) Develop mechanism to facilitate identification of CII, protection of CII through risk management and ensuring compliance of NCIIPC policies, guidelines, advisories/ alerts etc. by CIIs. As brought out earlier, NCIIPC has identified seventeen such critical infrastructures which can be graded as CII.

(b) Lead and coordinate national programs and policies on Critical Information Infrastructure. While the government will lay down broad framework of CII protection, it would be the task of NCIIPC to frame policies for specific infrastructures.

(c) Establish national and international linkages / initiatives for the protection of CII including R&D. As much as coordination between various sectors within the country is essential for effective cyber defence of CII, international cooperation is equally important too. Cyberspace being a seamless domain, international cooperation especially R&D cooperation would prove to be very beneficial for India.

(d) Promote Indigenous R&D relating to protection of CII including Modelling and Simulation of Complex CII, development of CIIP tools and Threat Scenarios.

(e) Develop mechanism to facilitate sharing of information on Information Security breaches, incidents, cyber attacks, espionage etc. among CII stake holders as well as with NCIIPC.

(f) Facilitate thematic workshops and Information Security Awareness and Training Programme through PPP.

(g) Facilitate capacity building towards creation of highly skilled manpower through engaging premier institutes like IISc, NITs etc. as well as private/non government partners working on CIIP.

18 Guidelines for Protection of National Critical Information Infrastructure Version 1.0 June 2013

(h) Develop capability for real time warning system and facilitate sharing of information on emerging threats, cyber attacks, vulnerabilities etc. with CIIs.

(i) Establish Sectoral CERTs to deal with critical sector specific issues.

With the broad framework having been established, NCIIPC now would have to get down to the task of implementing the above vision statement. In a country like India, this would be an herculean task considering the number of diverse organisations that will be required to coordinate and cooperate.

Some Important Control Measures for CII Protection

So far we have seen the variety of policies, legal framework and organisations that are available across the world as well as India to guard our critical assets against cyber threats. Let us now examine the control measures that an organisation or a business house would need to adopt to prevent cyber-attacks from taking place on their critical infrastructure. The list of such measures would be rather long starting from physical security of the infrastructure to counter measures against Advance Persistent Threats. Hence only a few important control measures are being discussed.

Critical Infrastructure Protection and Data Loss. As per a survey carried out by a private US company involved in computer security business, almost three quarters of companies responsible for global critical infrastructure have been the subject of a security breach with confidential information about the system lost. More such attacks on the CII are expected in future. Loss of critical data about the infrastructure can render the infrastructure vulnerable to cyberattacks. The information here refers to both technical information about the ICT systems being used by the CII as well as information about humans manning these systems. Details of what kind of control systems or SCADA systems or even information like what kind of protocols and operating system or firewalls is the organisation using can prove to be critical for the infrastructure. Hence protection of data about the infrastructure is a very vital aspect and can be a leading issue in the protection of the CIIs. This data can not only be lost from the CII information banks but also from agencies/ vendors involved in operation and upkeep of such critical infrastructure. This is the reason that the defence contractors in the US are among the most attacked communities through which a large amount of sensitive data has been lost. While it may be a little difficult to target the CII directly, information gathered from such contractors can make the job of the attacker much simpler. This would become even more complex when such organisations and individuals are located on foreign soils. Even if the local government wanted to protect its data in full earnest, issues of jurisdiction may prevent it from doing so. We in India need to particularly guard against this as more often than not, organisations involved in establishing CII may not be based in India. This makes our CII even more vulnerable.

A big reason for data loss is the insider threat which can be attributed to understand the true threat against/ from the employees, suppliers and ultimately, their data. One of the greatest challenges that IT professionals working for CII face is the omnipresence of insider threats. Employees leak data verbally, physically, and over the network. The CII operators therefore need to lay down clear and strict data loss prevention strategy for the organisation. Data loss prevention is a strategy for making sure that end users do not send sensitive or critical information outside the corporate network. Adoption of DLP is being driven by insider threats. To counter the threat of data loss from the CII it is essential to foster a security aware culture in which protecting data is a normal and natural part of every employee's job, and not an additional task that is perceived as a burden or contrary to other goals.

Leadership plays a very important role in prevention of critical data. Each CII must provide clear leadership through executive commitment and visibility, so employees understand that executives are engaged and accountable. Also, the leadership needs to create, communicate and enforce sensible security policies. The leadership must address the insider threats with the same energy as attacks from outside the company. Unless such a culture is evolved in the nation, critical data will continue being lost to nations which can then exploit our CII.

Risk Assessment and Management. In order to determine how well a system is protected, it is important to know its vulnerabilities. Technically, the vulnerability of a system is an aspect of the system that heightens the probability of malfunction due to specific incidents. Depending on the severity of the malfunction, ranging from the complete loss of control/ destruction of the system to mere errors, the vulnerability may impose a threat to the systems security.

Risk Management in simple words is to look at what could go wrong and then decide on ways to prevent such events which could go wrong or minimise these potential problems. It encompasses three processes—risk assessment, risk mitigation and evaluation. Risk assessment and management provide a decision making help to the management of any CII for preparing policies and plans for risk identification, categorisation, evaluation and its pro-active prevention. ISO 27032 describes the process of Risk Management as under:[19]

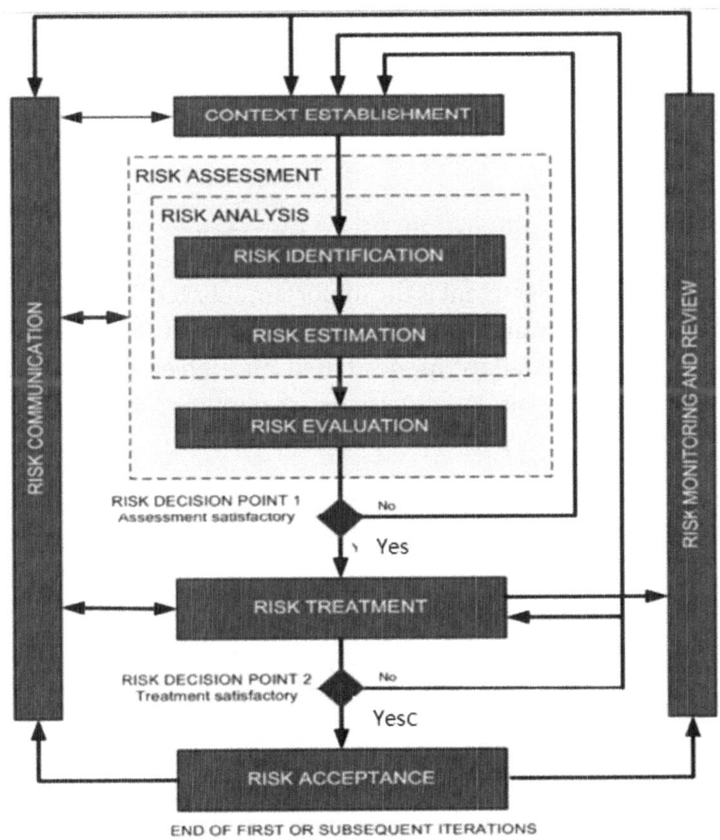

Figure 19: Process of Risk Management

The above flow clearly describes how cyber risks can be managed effectively by organisations operating critical infrastructure. The entire process involves identification of the threats, identification of vulnerabilities

19 National Cyber Security Framework Manual, Edited by Alexander Klimburg P10

of the system, evaluating the risks based on vulnerability identification and analysing the implications of such attacks on the system. Based on the above analysis, a risk prevention and recovery methodology is then evolved.

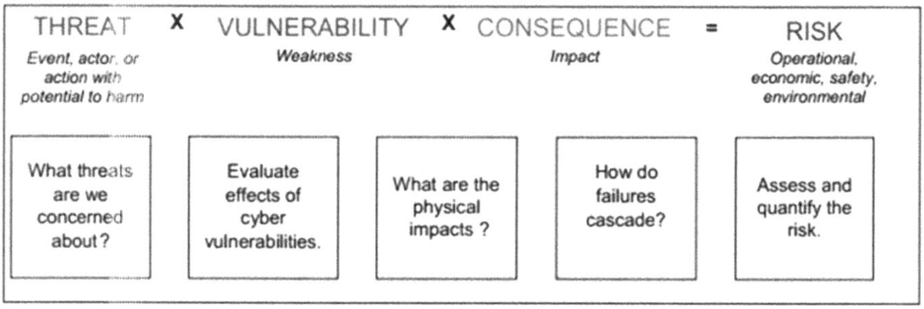

Figure 20: Risk Assessment

Vulnerability assessment is the important subset of the risk assessment process. Vulnerability assessment involves looking at the system elements and layout and their failure modes based on a given set of threats. The vulnerability assessment answers the basic question, what can go wrong should the system be exposed to threats and hazards?

Risk management is the ongoing process of identifying, assessing, and responding to risk. To manage risk, organisations need to understand the likelihood that an event will occur and then analyse how it will be managed. Also, determine the acceptable level of risk for delivery of services i.e. risks tolerance. With an understanding of risk tolerance, organizations can prioritise cyber security activities

Incidence Response. Cyber incident response is the way in which an organisation operating CII responds to a perceived cyber-related incident. An incorrect response may result in chaotic and reactionary actions that are ineffective or may even increase the damage. A cyber incident response capability includes some elements that are proactive in nature to prevent an incident or better allow the organisation to respond when one occurs. These elements are shown in the top row in the figure below and include planning, incident prevention, and post-incident analysis/forensics. Other elements center on detecting and managing an incident once it occurs. These are reactive in nature and are typically carried out under severe time constraints and great visibility. These elements are shown in the bottom row of the figure and include detection, containment, remediation, and recovery and restoration.

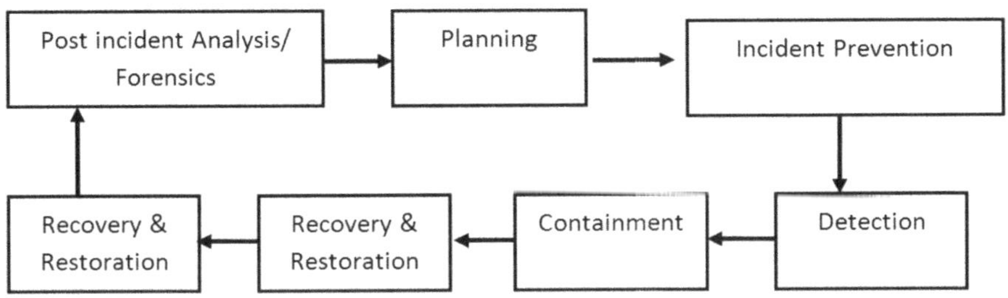

Figure 21: Cyber Incidence Response Cycle

If cyber incident response teams are not in place, the extent of damage caused to the CII post incident can be enormous and recovery time from the incident may also increase significantly. Hence it is essential to develop an incident response plan with clear roles and responsibilities for these teams for timely detection and thwarting the same. The US Department of Homeland Security's Control Systems Security Program (CSSP) has developed the Industrial Control Systems-Cyber Emergency Response Team (ICS-CERT), which is chartered to reduce control system cyber-security risks within and across all critical infrastructure sectors. Something very similar needs to be put in place in India too. The NCIIPC calls it "Mock Drill and Audit/ Penetration Testing Team" working under the CISO of the organisation. Whatever the response team may be named, it will have to be mandated with the following tasks:

(a) Acting as an expert resource on cyber-security threats and vulnerabilities.

(b) Serving as a clearing house for incident prevention, information, and analysis.

(c) Developing organisational policies and procedures related to incident response.

(d) Understanding safeguards on the ICS.

(e) Identifying operational impacts to the organisation in the event of an incident.

(f) Creating and testing the incident response plan.

(g) Acting as a single point of contact for all internally reported incidents or suspected incidents.

(h) Responding to the incident when one occurs.

(i) Reporting to key stakeholders and external agencies after the incident such as NCIIPC, CERT-in and law enforcement agencies in the country.

(j) Gathering forensic information to support analysis and any legal actions.

(k) Implementing safeguards to prevent a recurrence of the incident.

(l) Remediating the ICS after the incident.

While CERT-in and sectoral CERT are functional in the country, some effort still needs to go into coordinating their efforts as one homogenous body.

Asset and Inventory Management. Asset and inventory management is an important step in the critical assets management and security. It correlates all the physical and virtual critical assets owned by the CIIs. Asset inventory provides information that is important for routine system management, CIIs asset tracking, and security incident response. An asset inventory is also important for managing maintenance, servicing, theft prevention, controlling system builds, performing regular audits/reviews, replacing faulty systems and discarding/ destroying/ auctioning older/ faulty systems. Absence of this control can lead to theft of the assets. The most difficult aspect of inventory management is to track the older systems which might need urgent attention in terms of servicing or replacement. The concept of asset and inventory management is summarised as under:-[20]

20 Guidelines for Protection of National Critical Information Infrastructure Version 1.0 June 2013 P 44

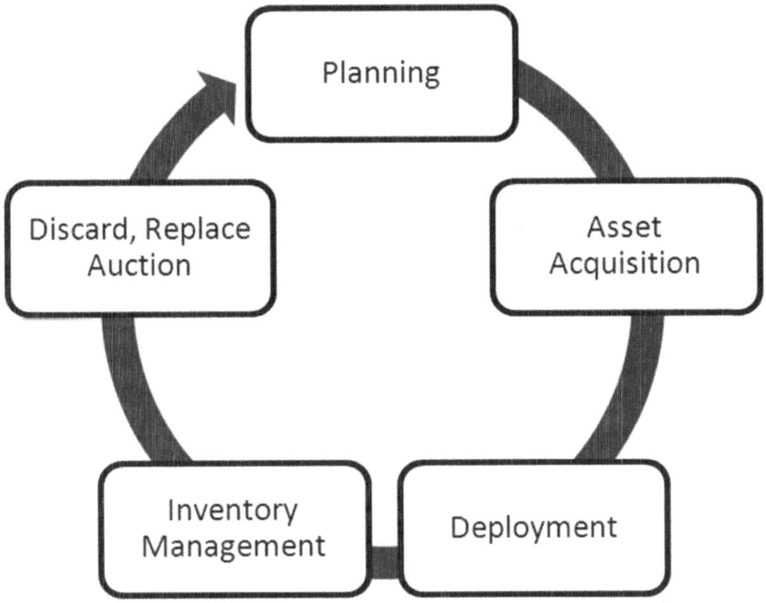

Figure 22: Cyber Asset and Inventory Management

Implementation of information security policies and security controls will be difficult in the absence of proper inventory management. Periodic audit of the asset and inventory management system need to be conducted so as to unravel any flaws in the implementation of the asset and inventory management control.

Contingency Planning. Contingency planning refers to visionary approach nurtured through proper assessment, policies, plans, procedures and technology involvement aimed for dealing with the adversaries or disruptions due to any disaster or major CII attack. There can be great deal of implications if the contingency planning of any CII is not in place or is not implemented properly keeping in view the real threats and challenges. If the disaster or any major attack on CII is reported for which the contingency plan is to be utilised, losses are bound to happen. Through contingency planning we can reduce the impact of losses and can do the early recovery of the functioning of CII. Contingency planning statement of the CII should be conceptualized, formalised and implemented as soon as possible at the early stages of the formation of the organisation.[21] For existing CII, every time there is a change in the hardware or the software,

21 ibid

the contingency plan must be revisited. Also, it is very essential that a contingency plan is actually tested out during the external audits of the infrastructure. Conducting regular exercises to check the protection standards and contingency planning is a must and should be carried out at the national level. DHS conducts such exercises regularly to check the preparedness of national critical infrastructure in the USA. Cyber Guard 2014 conducted in June 2014 saw Maryland Guardsmen from the Air's 175th Network Warfare Squadron, the Army's 110th Information Operations Battalion, and the Maryland Defense Force participate in a two-week exercise, as one joint team to prepare the state to defend from a cyber attack.[22]

NCIIPC in the document Guidelines for Protection of National Critical Information Infrastructure Version 1.0 released in Jun 2013 lists out forty control measures which any organisation responsible to manage/ operate a CII needs to follow. Once again how the government will implement these guidelines both in the public as well as private sector undertakings remains to be seen. While the task of automating and upgrading of most of the infrastructure is being carried out at a rapid pace, the measures to counter the threat are not being put in place. This becomes more relevant especially when CII subsystems are shedding customised software and protocols for cost cutting and are relying more and more on commercial products.

While intrusion detection and intrusion prevention firewalls are being installed, these can be easily bypassed. What is required is a holistic assessment of the threat the CII faces from the cyber domain. It needs to be done in a similar manner a military man would carry out threat analyses of the enemy in any conventional operation. Risk Analysis is the buzz word in the industry today. However, the Government does not have any policy which will make it necessary for all CII stakeholders to periodically analyse the risk they face from the cyberspace. This is more important as a large part of the CII is with the private sector. A nodal agency in the county needs to be created whose task would be to carry out regular audits of the vulnerabilities of the CII and its cyber preparedness.

The basic functions for ensuring cyber security for any organisation operating a critical info-infrastructure will be as under:

22 Cyber Guard 2014: Maryland Guard Forms a Joint Cyber Team as available on http://www.md.ngb.army.mil/absolutenm/templates/?a=1447 referred on 05 Nov 2014

Function	Action
Identify	Develop the organisational understanding to manage cyber security risk to systems, assets, data, and capabilities
Protect	Develop and implement the appropriate safeguards to ensure delivery of critical infrastructure services.
Detect	Develop and implement the appropriate activities to identify the occurrence of a cyber security event.
Respond	Develop and implement the appropriate activities to take action regarding a detected cyber security event.
Recover	Develop and implement the appropriate activities to maintain plans for resilience and to restore any capabilities or services that were impaired due to a cyber security event.

Table 14: Basic Functions of Cyber Security

The above mentioned functions summarise what an organisation needs to do to protect its assets from threats from the cyber space.

Conclusion

India is witnessing extremely challenging and all-encompassing times. The new millennium is likely to sustain more transformational, innovative and challenging trends than any other century in the past. While at one hand we continue with our endeavor to become a global economic power, we are also constantly faced with a large number of external and internal challenges. In today's time, the concept of security is being enlarged to encompass military as well as non-military, conventional as well as non-conventional threats and challenges to the state and society. Security is increasingly being revamped as "Security of the people, not just territory; security through development, not arms, security of all everywhere, in their homes, on their jobs; in their streets, in their communities, and in their environment". The concept of Cyber warfare has brought about additional security challenges to our nation. Protection of CII against attacks from the cyber space today assumes great relevance in the overall national security environment. As and when a National Security Policy is issued by the Government of India, the aspect of protection of CII from cyber-attacks and creating a secure cyber ecosystem for the country will certainly form a part of it.

Cyberspace is an arena for positive and stabilising impulses that help in sustaining India's identity. But it can also be a battlefield in which threats from outside and within jeopardize our nation's security. The challenge of securing cyberspace and protecting the CIIs against threats emanating from the cyber space is daunting, but not insurmountable. Given that the private sector in India today owns approximately 50 to 60 percent of the nation's CII, the private sector has placed itself "on the front line of India's national security". Hence, any strategy to defeat the cyber threat and protect India's CII base has to be a multi-stakeholder approach backed by flexible legislation that defines government's role and authority while balancing national security imperatives with personal privacy.

Today a large number of nations, including our potential adversaries, have acquired cyber warfare capabilities. In such a scenario, a strike against CII both during war as well as peace is a highly likely scenario. Hence, the time has come to ensure that whatever is critical to the nation both for its sustained growth as well as ensuring sovereignty of our territorial boundaries, is protected from attacks through the cyber domain.

5 Cyber War Model

The nature of warfare never changes, only its superficial manifestations

– Peters, Ralph : Expanding America's Global Supremacy

The armed forces need to incorporate "new thinking" and keep pace with a changing world where domination of cyberspace will become important and full scale wars may become rare

– Prime Minister Narendra Modi

In Aug 2012, just around the time when India had finished celebrating its 66th Independence Day, thousands of citizens from the Northeastern part of the country, especially those from Assam living in southern cities of Bangalore, Chennai and Pune began heading to railway stations to go back to their homes. The reason – many had received text messages warning them that they would be attacked because of the violence that flared between the mostly Hindu Bodo tribe and Bangladeshi Muslim immigrants. Threatening text messages sent in bulk were the main vehicle of these rumours driving panic into the hearts of the tens of thousands of people. The Government of India reacted immediately and banned bulk text messages for a fortnight to prevent rumours from spreading. The second wave of rumour mongering happened through Facebook and Twitter. Investigations by the Home Ministry revealed that by the end of a week, over 10,000 panic-stricken innocent citizens had fled these three cities. The Government of the day blamed Pakistan-based elements for uploading provocative and offensive content on the Internet and spreading it through social networking sites to create a scare among people of northeastern regions.

Was this the beginning of a new era? An era, where panic and terror could be spread from across the border through the cyberspace to destabilise a growing economy like India; where a virtual war can be triggered through the Internet causing widespread communal clashes leading to loss of life and property not only during peace but also during a conflict situation; where actions in the virtual world by our neighbours could have serious implications on public safety and national security? It is time to check what kind of impact the virtual world has on our preparedness for defending our nation against external aggression and internal disorders.

The above was a scenario where cyber domain triggered an incidence related to internal security. We also need to determine how operations in the cyberspace can be a tool that can be effectively employed for a field force commander during war. Can actions undertaken through the cyberspace contribute to deciding the outcome of a war? If that is possible, we need to determine what kind of capability India needs to develop to undertake cyberspace operations.

In Chapter One, cyber warfare was very briefly discussed. This Chapter will focus in detail how defensive and offensive cyber warfare is carried out both at strategic and operational levels and what kinds of capabilities do we, as a nation, need to develop for undertaking cyberspace operations.

Objectives of War

Before analysing how cyberwar can be undertaken at strategic and operational level, let us first examine what are the objectives of a war and can a campaign launched through cyberspace help the Government and the armed forces in achieving these objectives? Clausewitz was amongst the first military thinkers who defined war and its objectives in the modern times. In his book 'On War', Clausewitz states his most famous line that "*War is merely the continuation of policy by other means*".[1] He further states "*The political object is the goal, war is the means of reaching it, and means can never be considered in isolation from their purpose*". Though times may have changed and technology may have revolutionalised the way wars are fought today, yet the objectives of war have not undergone much change. The figure below describes the various political objectives of a war as

1 On War by General Carl von Clausewitz Translated by Colonel J J Graham P 18 as available at https://edcat.uni-muenster.de/.../Clausewitz%20%22On%20War%22.pdf

applicable today :-[2]

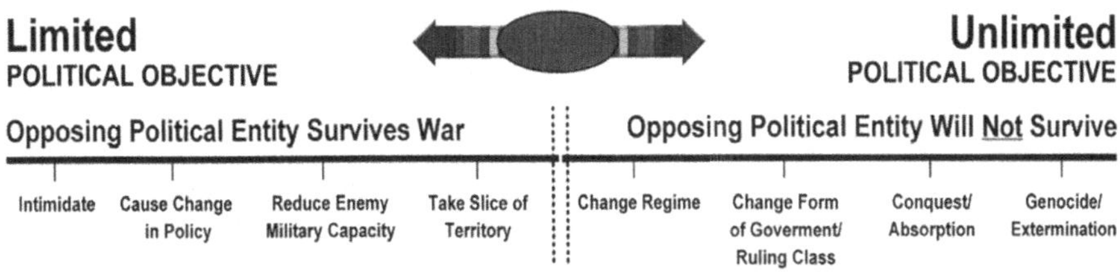

Figure 23: Objectives of War

The political objectives of any war may vary from intimidating the opposing nation to completely destroying it (easier said than done objective). The spectrum is rather large. Whatever be the political or military objectives of a war, destruction/ neutralisation of the war waging potential of the opposing nation will be the aim plus of any war. This can be achieved by launching a series of campaigns through land, air and sea and perhaps through space also now. Complete might of a nation needs to be targeted through these campaigns. Depending on the amount of destruction/ neutralisation that has been achieved, any future war can be prevented.

Cyberattacks are proving themselves to be a potent tool of sabotage. Today such attack capabilities are available with nations and can be employed by military commanders in a conflict to help them achieve the aim of destruction/ neutralisation of the enemy's war waging potential. Operations launched through cyberspace can impact the outcome of a future battle. Let us therefore examine how this can be achieved.

Understanding Cyber Warfare

Each era brings with it new techniques and methods of waging war. The Romans perfected the art of infantry field combat. Staffing norms developed during the Napoleonic era and the concept of use of artillery in conjunction with tactical deployment of infantry and cavalry are still relevant. World War I saw the introduction of poison gas attacks and use of tanks for the first time. Deployment of air power, missiles and rockets in the battle field

2 The Relationship Between Political and Military Objectives in War by C. Bassford/B.A. Andrews as available at www.clausewitz.com/readings/Bassford/PolMilObjModelLGX05.pps

took the centre stage during World War II. The world was suspended in an uneasy equilibrium when the threat of nuclear weapons was introduced at the beginning of the cold war. Operations in Sri Lanka and Vietnam were examples of the use of the guerrilla warfare to subdue a superior force and technology. The terror wars in Jammu and Kashmir and the northeastern parts of India and many other parts of the world have seen use of suicide bombers and IED's as effective weapons. 9/11 and Mumbai attacks gave the meaning of low intensity conflicts another dimension. With networks and information technology having made such an impact on war fighting, it is but natural that ways and means are developed to negate the advantages accrued by them. When nations started to depend on internet and other such technologies, foundation of cyberwarfare was laid.

Cyber war has been going on in some form or the other for a while on the Internet. We have seen hackers, non-state actors and even nation states indulging in acts like defacing of websites and breaking into public and private networks. This though may not be classified as all out cyberwarfare, yet it is certainly part of the overall game plan as was clearly demonstrated by the cyberattacks on Estonia in 2007 and Georgia in 2008. It is apparent that networks, which have an immense bearing on the communication, control of infrastructure, commerce and social interaction and many other important aspects, need to be targeted as overall strategy in waging any future war. Attack on and across the networks are poised to become the defining innovations of 21st century.

Before delving into how cyberwarfare is undertaken let us once again reexamine some to the definitions of cyber warfare and analyse them in detail. As brought out in Chapter 1, one of the initial definitions of cyberwarfare was constituted by United Nations Integrated Crime and Justice Research Institute (UNICRI). According to them, Cyberwarfare can consist of following threats :-[3]

(a) **Online acts of espionage and security breaches** – This is done to obtain material and information of a sensitive or classified nature through the exploitation of the internet (e.g. exploitation of network flaws through malicious software).

(b) **Sabotage** – the use of the internet by one nation state to disrupt

3 Cyberwarfare as available on http://www.unicri.it/special_topics/cyber_threats/cyber_crime/ explanations/ cyberwarfare/

online communications systems of another (e.g. military communication networks) with the intent to cause damage and disadvantage.

(c) **Attacks on SCADA networks and National Critical Infrastructures.**

The above encompasses some key issues. Each of these needs to be analysed to understand nuances of cyberwarfare. These issues are:

Acts of Espionage Forms Part of Cyberwarfare. The first aspect that the UNICRI talks of is cyber espionage. Espionage and surveillance have been a part of all forms of warfare for centuries. Therefore it is but obvious that cyber espionage too will be an important part of this new form of warfare, i.e. cyberwarfare.

Cyber espionage is the act or practice of obtaining secrets without the permission of the holder of the information (personal, sensitive, proprietary or of classified nature), from individuals, competitors, rivals, groups, governments and enemies for personal, economic, political or military through the Internet, networks or individual computers by using cracking techniques and malicious software. The global surveillance industry today is estimated to be growing at over US $ 5 billion a year. Cyber surveillance and espionage techniques range from malware (which infects a target computer to record every keystroke), to systems for tapping undersea fibre optic cables in order to monitor the communications of entire population. Some of the common techniques being used to gather information from the cyberspace are as under:-

(a) **Network Surveillance.** Majority of computer surveillance involves monitoring of data traffic while it is moving on the network. This includes both the Internet as well as standalone discrete networks. As far as internet is concerned, we are aware of the infamous PRISM project clandestinely run by the NSA in the US. PRISM findings indicated that the internet service provider companies in the US, whom the world trusted with their most private data, were handing over the data travelling over their networks to the NSA as if they too were a part of the entire clandestine operation.

(b) **Packet Capture.** Packet capture or packet sniffing is monitoring of data traffic on a computer network. Deep packet inspection (DPI) is the leading method of such surveillance. DPI technologies are capable of analysing the actual content of the traffic that is flowing. DPI allows network operators to scan the payload of IP packets as well as the header. This technique is often employed by law enforcement agencies and security forces trying to identify cyber criminals and cyber terrorists over the internet.

(c) **Malicious Software.** Use of computer viruses, worms and Trojans is an effective method to monitor or steal data stored on a computer's hard drive, other storage devices and even cloud perhaps. Malicious software can be employed to even monitor activities of a person using the computer. The entire digital life of a person or an organisation can be mapped using malicious tools. Malicious software is perhaps the most important cyber espionage tools.

(d) **Hardware Monitoring.** Today techniques exist through which network or computer transmissions can be monitored using the hardware installed in the system. This technique is especially applicable for air gapped computers and networks not directly connected to any enterprise network. Some of these monitoring techniques are:-

- Monitoring by detecting the radiations emitted by the CRT monitor. This could be both by picking up transmissions using a malware or monitoring of spurious transmissions which the hardware unintentionally radiates. In the US, surveillance using spurious transmissions being emitted by hardware is termed as TEMPEST.

- Using the transmissions between a computer and a presentation device such as a projection system.

- Picking up the noise of the key board clicking. Research shows that each key has a distinct noise which can be picked up using an audio surveillance device and the message can be deciphered.

- Use of the audio speakers connected to the system for picking up and transmitting information from a computer.

- Radio Pathways - Tiny trans-receivers are built into USB plugs and inserted into target computers which then communicate with a hidden relay station up to 12 kms away. This method is most effectively used for machines isolated from the internet.[4]

Supply Chain Vulnerability. As discussed in the previous chapters, a supply chain attack is through subversion of hardware or software supply chain. A product, typically a device that performs encryption or secures transactions is tampered with during manufacture or while it is still in the supply chain by persons with physical access. The tampering may, for example, install a rootkit or hardware-based spying components. The aim is to first gather information from the place where this hardware or software is installed and then to execute a cyberattack. Countries like India where most of the civil as well military hardware and software is ex-import remain vulnerable to supply chain surveillance and attacks. Although National Cyber Security Policy 2013 does talk of undertaking R&D programs by the government for addressing all aspects including development of trustworthy systems, their testing, development and maintenance throughout their life cycle, it is still a farfetched dream. It is unlikely that we will ever be able to completely sanitise the hardware and software being used in the country. But even if we are able to sanitise the critical components being installed in the national info-infrastructure, we would be able to save ourselves from loss of critical information and Stuxnet kind of cyberattacks

Most of the world is ill prepared to defend against these new types of surveillance and espionage techniques which have emerged in the last two decades. In 2013, Edward Snowden, a former employee of the CIA and then a contractor working for the National Security Agency, revealed the scale of America's secret mass cyber surveillance programme at the transnational level, codenamed "PRISM". (Interestingly Snowden is said to have learnt his hacking skills at an ethical hacking institute in India). Snowden's leaked documents uncovered the existence of a large number of global surveillance programmes, many of them run officially by the US. Similarly China and other countries are also known to be running such clandestine operations for gathering critical information. Governments, business, organisations, individual owners and users of cyberspace therefore need to assume responsibility and take steps to enhance the security of the

4 NSA uses secret radio pathways to spy on offline PC's, Times of India, 16 January 2014

information technologies against such malicious cyber activities.

Cyber surveillance has existed ever since cyberspace came into being. And why not? After all so much of data passes silently through this domain that it is impossible for it to remain untouched to snooping. Take for example the hacking of Controller of Defence Accounts, Pune website in March 2015.[5] In this case the hacker, who in all probability was based in Pakistan, with one master stroke, was able to gather data of all Indian Army officers. According to a report published by a cyber security firm FireEye on 13 April 2015, Chinese Government is probably behind an anonymous group 'APT30' that has been cyber spying on Indian companies and officials for close to a decade now.[6] As per the FireEye report, the malware when studied revealed a decade long operation focused on targets - government and commercial that hold key political, economic, and military information about the region.

Cyberwarfare is Undertaken by a Nation State Against Another for Sabotage. The second facet of the UNICRI definition of cyberwarfare is sabotage. Thomas Rid too in his book "*Cyberwar Will Not Take Place*" highlights that malicious software and cyberattacks are ideal instruments of sabotage.[7] In the previous two chapters we have analysed in detail how the CII of a nation can be attacked through the cyberspace and what needs to be done to protect CII from such attacks. But is it only a nation state which will indulge in the act of sabotage though the cyberspace? Unlikely! In fact in a situation like India and Pakistan, where the two nations are not in a state of war and the relationship between the two countries are strained, it is the non-state actors acting on behalf of Pakistan who may be the bigger players in the cyberspace than the government of Pakistan. The very nature of cyberspace makes non-state actors a potent force that will play a pivotal role in any future cyberwar.

So who are these non-state actors operating in the cyberspace? They

---

5 Armed Forces need to learn from the CDA (o) hack and protect their critical information by Sanjeev Relia as available at http://usiblog.in/2015/04/armed-forces-need-to-learn-from-the-cdao-hack-and-protect-their-critical-information/

6 Beijing May Have Been Spying on India's Defense Industry for a Decade by Manu Balachandran as available at http://www.defenseone.com/ideas/2015/04/beijing-may-have-been-spying-indias-defense-industry-decade/109993/?oref=defenseone_today_nl#

7 Thomas Rid, Cyberwar Will Not Take Place, P56

could be anyone - an ordinary citizen, a patriotic hacker, a cybercriminal, cyber terrorist or even cyber militia. Anonymity is a characteristic of cyber domain. The state machinery can therefore easily hide behind non-state actors with little or no risk of attribution and deny any involvement in perpetrating devastating cyber-attacks. In fact, the ease with which cyber militia can operate and carryout cyberattacks, make them a better choice than establishing a full-fledged cyber wing as part of the armed forces. Non-state actors or cyber militia are a group of volunteers who are willing and able to use cyber-attacks or other forms of disruptive cyber actions in order to achieve a political goal.[8] They are persons, not in uniform but motivated enough to be employed in covert government-orchestrated campaigns with the purpose to further the strategic political or military objective of the instigating state.

It is believed that China has established PLA Unit 61398 based at Shanghai, staffed by thousands of computer professionals as "Cyber Troops" acting on direct orders of PLA.[9] Unit 61398 is believed to be responsible for all major cyber-attacks on the US and other countries. China, however, completely denies the existence of any such unit, leave alone its involvement or connection with any other state machinery. But if reports in the Western media are to be believed and also if Snowden revelations are correct, then China does have a potent group of non-state actors organised in the form of Unit 61398, acting completely under the control of PLA.

Employing such cyber militia has tremendous advantages. Some of these are:-

(a) **Counterstrike**. Although employing non-state actors to carry out cyberattacks might raise suspicion in the international community, the lack of any hard evidence will protect the attacker of any political ramifications. Thus, the threat of a counterstrike is negligible. In 2007 while all evidence showed that the DDoS attacks on Estonia originated from Russia, Estonia or the NATO could not retaliate due to lack of attribution. While Russia completely denied

8 Ottis, R., "Proactive Defense Tactics Against On-Line Cyber Militia," in the proceedings of the 9th European Conference on Information Warfare and Security (ECIW 2010), Thessaloniki, Greece, Jul. 2010.

9 China hacking charges: the Chinese army's Unit 61398 as available at http://www.telegraph.co.uk/news/worldnews/asia/china/10842093/China-hacking-charges-the-Chinese-armys-Unit-61398.html

of any involvement, the execution may have been carried out by patriotic cyber militia on behest of the Russian Government.

(b) **Cost Factor**. To raise a well organised cyber wing as part of the government or the defence forces would cost a lot of money as such a force will have to be funded and manned by uniformed personnel. By recruiting suitably motivated and technically competent non-state actors, the same task can be achieved at little or no cost. Small nation states today by sponsoring such cyber militia at negligible costs can threaten the critical infrastructure of much bigger and stronger nations.

(c) **Sponsor Cyberwar**. Non state actors with the backing of state machinery can form unholy alliances, where state provides advanced capabilities whether money or actual intrusion tools to non-state actors who can then pass them on to another state or its non-state actors which wants to build cyberwar capability. As on date there are no international laws or treaties banning such actions. Hence, sponsoring cyberwar through transfer of such technologies *via* non-state actors is perfectly legal.

(d) **Freedom to Attack from Anywhere**. Non state actors need not be based in the same country which is sponsoring them. Cyberspace knows no boundaries. Hence, the attack can be carried out with the same precision and impact with the attacker based in a neutral country. This makes the task of the attacking nation even easier as attribution becomes even more difficult in such cases.

(e) **Laws of War**. Even if an indisputable link is established between a non-state proxy and a nation-state, no laws of war apply to these cyber militias. This is because status of such non-state actors cannot legally be considered to be that of combatants. Also, in some cases, no physical damage may have been caused by these cyberattacks; hence laws of armed conflict do not apply to them. Therefore such non-state actors in the cyberspace may get away from being tried for war crimes despite the attacks having the same devastating impact as physical attacks.

Raising and employment of such cyber militia forces may have a flip side too. Like there are no good terrorists, similarly, there are no good or bad hackers. Armed with adequate knowledge and skills, the same attacker may turn against the state and threaten own infrastructure. They may even blackmail the government in order not to disclose sensitive details. Contracted cyber espionage agents might defect to the opposing nation if offered political asylum and cause damage, like it happened in the case of Edward Snowden. Yet, the advantages of using such non state actors outweigh the drawbacks. This is the reason that a number of nations are preferring employment of such hackers instead of employing regular troops to attack the opponents.

Attacks on SCADA Networks and National Critical Infrastructures. The third aspect of the definition talks about attack on CII. This aspect has been dealt with in great detail in Chapter 3 and 4 and it has clearly emerged that cyberattacks can be effectively used as a tool of war to target critical infrastructure of a nation. Though such attacks may not permanently damage the facility being provided by the CII, yet even if the cyberattack degrades the performance of such critical infrastructure at critical junctures, the objective of the attack would have been met to a great extent.

Let us examine how cyberwarfare is conducted both at the strategic as well at operational levels.

Strategic Cyber Warfare

As defined in Chapter 1, cyberattacks launched by one entity against a state and its society, primarily but not exclusively for the purpose of affecting the target state's behaviour, would be strategic cyberwar. [10] The attacking entity could be a state or as discussed above a non-state actor acting on behalf of the state. The definition does not imply at all that strategic cyber warfare is only a wartime activity. This implies that such a form of warfare can be undertaken at any time, without the two nations being in a state of war. Even when no hostilities exist between two nations, they could be in a state of cyberwar! While airspace or territorial water violations may be seen as acts of aggression; violation of cyberspace is still not an act of aggression. Of course, when hostilities between two countries become imminent, strategic cyberattacks can commence much before physical hostilities break out and yet the two states will not be blamed for waging a war against each other.

10 Cyberdeterrence and Cyberwar, Rand Corporation monograph by Martin C. Libicki, P 117 Published 2009 by the RAND Corporation

What kind of targets could a state or its society present for cyberattacks? The most obvious ones are CII of the opposing state. The impact of cyberattacks on CII has already been analysed in detail. Highly asymmetric outcomes of such attacks are possible. Targets may well fail due to such attacks and the effects may be highly public and consequential.

India could find itself as a victim of strategic cyberwar in any of the following two ways: through deliberate provocation by our adversaries or through escalation of cyberwar started by our adversaries. Provocation need not necessarily come from the cyberspace. Consider this; India could well decide to react to Pakistan sponsored terrorism in Jammu and Kashmir by undertaking strategic cyberattacks against Pakistan's CII. Though this may not deter Pakistan from sponsoring terrorist activities on Indian soil, it can certainly make them cautious that India too can react to their nefarious activities in an aggressive manner. Provocation could be carried out even in a scenario in which the attacking state knowingly and even overtly carries out attacks on the other in cyberspace to provocate but refrains from physical violence. A recent example of provocation was the case of Sony Pictures Entertainment hacking in November /December 2014. In which a hacker group going under the nickname "Guardians of Peace" (GoP) based in North Korea was involved. In response to the North Korea cyberattacks and consequent cyber threats, President Obama said that the US would respond proportionately against these cyberattacks. Though the cyberattacks from GoP cannot be termed as strategic cyberwar, yet they are a good example to provocating an advisory in starting a cyberwar, though in this case it did not happen.

As we get more networked, our adversaries may believe they can gain advantage over us by disrupting or damaging our infrastructure through cyberattacks. In such a scenario, a cyberwar might start. The tendency for escalation and counter-escalation to descend into cyberwar may be related to the motive for the original attack.

Strategic cyberattack campaigns can be undertaken by our adversaries just before a war breaks out in the form of preemptive cyber strikes. CII, civilian networks and communication infrastructure could be some of the targets of such a campaign. Imagine a scenario where the Indian Armed Forces are being mobilised to an imminent threat of outbreak of hostilities on the Western front. While the mobilisation is on, a spate of cyberattacks launched by our adversary starts routinely tripping the national power grid resulting in long blackouts in important cities including the national capital. An important nuclear power plant shuts down due to overheating and presents a threat of nuclear fallout from the reactor. Banking networks constantly malfunction resulting in chaos in the financial sector. Private cellular networks constantly wrong route the calls or are not able to provide services to the general public for long durations because of breakdown of their networks. The speed with which these attacks could be launched can numb the state machinery in no time. Though all this may not directly impact the mobilisation of the armed forces, but would certainly preoccupy the government machinery in dealing with such attacks and the public anger that may generate due to the prevailing chaotic situation. Even before commencement of war, our adversary would have achieved the aim of causing confusion and saddling the government and other state mechanism with chaotic situation while the threat of war is looming on the country.

Cyberwar at strategic level lends itself to an incremental approach because it presents such a broad range of options for contemplation. Attacks may range from introducing modest but inexplicable changes in the enemy's information systems, to wholesale attempts to collapse all the adversary's infrastructures at once. Strategic cyberwar can also be used to put the adversary on notice that their systems are not as reliable as they consider them to be and that they cannot afford to engage in such a fight. Some targets may be too risky to be good targets. The risky targets include nuclear command-and-control systems and space systems. There may be good reason to leave such targets alone and the restraint shown may persuade the other side to do likewise, thereby limiting mutual destruction.

War strategies are ultimately about war termination when an advantageous situation has been reached. While this may apply for wars being waged in the other four domains, it does not apply to the cyberspace. Cyberwar is unlikely to be terminated because the adversary has been disarmed by force. Additionally cyberwar presents a compelling challenge: How can one tell that the other side has, in fact, stopped its attacks and has declared truce?

Operational Cyber Warfare

New tools and processes of waging war like information warfare, network-centric warfare (NCW), integrated Command and Control (C4ISR), all powered by information technology, have led to the revolution in military affairs (RMA). Today the advent of new forms of communication and imaging technology, incorporated into systems such as "smart" weaponry and digitised battlefield networks have led to the rethinking of war making and strategy conceptualisation over the ages. As technology has developed, new methods of collecting information have also emerged.[11] These new methods have vastly improved the battlefield transparency and situational awareness of our commanders and soldiers. Now we live and fight in an era where some nations talk of achieving information superiority and even information supremacy (though contested by most scholars that there is nothing called as information supremacy) in future conflicts. These are terms that were never even heard of a few decades back. Indian Army too is in the process of introducing a large number of such systems to improve our battle awareness and war fighting abilities. But as more and more systems in the battlefield get digitised and networked, do they also become an easy target for enemy's cyberwarfare capabilities and other asymmetric warfare means? Can systems and networks, being employed in the battlefield, not connected to the internet be targeted by cyber weapons? Prime Minister Shri Narendra Modi feels so. While addressing the top military commanders in October 2014 he said, "*Threats may be known, but the enemy may be invisible. Domination of cyberspace will become increasingly important*".[12] He added that control of cyberspace may become as critical as that of land, air and sea. To summarise, the Prime Minister of India cautioned the Armed Forces to prepare for operational cyberwarfare in the times to come.

So what is operational cyberwarfare? According to Martin Libicki, operational cyberwar consists of wartime cyberattacks against military targets and military-related civilian targets. Even if this does not constitute raw power, it can be a decisive force multiplier if employed carefully, discriminately, and at precisely the right time.[13] In the above definition there are two key elements of operational cyberwar. The first is that, unlike strategic cyberwarfare, this is a wartime activity. Operational cyberattacks

---

11 Revolution in Military Affairs (RMA) by Sharjeel Rizwan as available at http://www.defencejournal.com/2000/sept/military.htm

12 Brace Up to Battle Invisible Enemy in Changing World: PM, By Pradip R Sagar Published: 18th October 2014 in the Indian Express.

13 Cyberdeterrence and Cyberwar, Rand Corporation monograph by Martin C. Libicki, P 139 Published 2009 by the RAND Corporation

are carried out during a conflict and hence are a tool available to the military commanders like other means of waging a war. If they are such tools then they should be able to have an overbearing impact on the outcome of a battle. This aspect of cyberattacks being used as a "*Cyber Weapon*" needs to be analysed in detail. The second and the more important aspect is "*Military Target*" and military related civilian targets. While till now we have seen the impact of ICT and networking on critical infrastructure, we still have not analysed the impact of technology on modernisation of armed forces and how technology savvy armies are vulnerable to cyberattacks. Let us therefore examine both these aspects in detail.

Cyber Weapons. When we talk of a weapon, a distinct shape of the weapon system emerges in the mind. Whatever may be the weapon system, IHS Jane's Defence Weekly would clearly spell out the destructive powers of each of the systems with a few glossy pictures leaving little doubt in the mind what the weapon platform or system can do. But as the concept of cyber weapon is abstract, these weapons find no such mention in any of the glossy journals. A cyber-weapon is designed to have an indirect kinetic outcome which may, or may not, result in inflicting damage or harm to living beings, structures, or systems. Large numbers of scholars argue if there is anything such as a cyber weapon.

To define a cyber weapon in the specific context of conflicts, it is necessary to differentiate it from a malware, typically used for criminal purposes or an information tool used to perform espionage in the cyber space. To reach a definition of cyber-weapon, it is therefore necessary to focus on three essential elements :-[14]

- **The Context.** This concept may be defined as a conflict among actors, both national and non-national, characterised by the use of technological information systems, with the purpose of achieving, keeping or defending a condition of strategic, operative and/or tactical advantage.
- **The Purpose:** It must cause, even indirectly, physical damage to equipment or people, or rather sabotaging or damaging in a direct way the information systems of a sensitive target of the attacked subject.

14 Stefano Mele, Cyber Weapons: legal and strategic aspects Version 2.0, June 2013.

- **The Mean/Tool:** It is an attack performed through the use of technological information systems, including the Internet.

Based on the above, Stefano Mele defines a cyber-weapon as, "*A part of equipment, a device or any set of computer instructions used in a conflict among actors, both national and non-national, with the purpose of causing, even indirectly, a physical damage to equipment or people, or rather of sabotaging or damaging in a direct way the information systems of a sensitive target of the attacked subject.*"

Cyber weapons, therefore, too are built with lethal intent, although the aspect of their lethality cannot be quantified like a conventional or a nuclear weapon. How lethal is a cyber weapon, depends on its ability to cause the following to a network:

(a) Disruption of the network services.

(b) Denial of services of the network to its users.

(c) Degradation of the performance of the network, thereby degrading the efficiency/ performance of the overall system.

(d) Destruction of critical components of the network thus rendering the entire system useless.

(e) Complete destruction of the system.

Lethality of a cyber weapon could be checked by carrying out a live test fire, like an underground nuclear test for a nuclear weapon. However no such tests of these weapons are possible on actual networks as the damage caused may result in loss of property and revenue and also may be seen as an act of aggression. To establish the lethality and destructive power of cyber weapons and the network security aspects against such attacks, the US Defence Advanced Research Projects Agency (DARPA) is developing the National Cyber Range (NCR) to provide realistic, quantifiable assessments of the Nation's cyber research and development technologies.[15] The NCR will provide fully automated range management and test management suites to test and validate leap-ahead cyber research technologies and systems. We do not have any such test facility in India

15 The National Cyber Range: A National Test bed for Critical Security Research as available at http://www.whitehouse.gov/files/documents/cyber/DARPA%20-%20NationalCyberRange_FactSheet.pdf

where we could test our offensive cyber capabilities.

Cyber weapons can have varied effects on the target. Not only can they impact the physical domain, but also can target the cognitive domain. Various effects of cyber weapons on a network has been summarised by Dr Ronald Heickerö as shown below in a matrix :-[16]

	Physical arena (land, air, maritime, space)	Information Arena	Cognitive domain (cognition, perception, emotion)
Physical Effects	Interruption, destroy electronics and sensors, affect transmissions and access links, derive robots, system failure	Interrupted communication, denial of services; DOS	Fragmented communication, decreased amount of information, reduced analysis capability
Syntax Effects	Hacking, cracking virus, Mistrust against system Trojans, spam, interception, exploit, bugging illegal misuse of information system	Attack logic of systems, delay and distortion of information	Mistrust against system
Semantic Effects	Mass media manoeuvres, planted information, mutilation of sensor data	Deception and manipulation of information (disinformation)	Changed situation awareness, mistrust against and questioned of information, inability for decision making

Table 15: Effects of Cyber Weapons

A single cyber weapon may not be able to impact the physical arena, information arena and the cognitive domain and hence multi-pronged cyberattacks may be necessary if all the three spheres are to be addressed simultaneously. Key for success in cyber space is to understand prerequisites for conducting operations in the info arena and cognitive domain of the enemy.

Another important aspect of cyber weapons is that they do not create the same spectacular visual effect that a nuclear or even conventional missile does, which makes them weapons of stealth. Also before being hit, a network is unlikely to get any advance warning of an incoming cyber-attack. Not knowing what the next attack is going to be or when it will

16 Some Aspects on Cyber War Faring in Information Arena and Cognitive Domain http://www.dodccrp.org/events/11th_ICCRTS/html/presentations/157.pdf

happen has a profound effect on the victim and makes cyber weapons unique amongst all possible coercive systems. This makes them a weapon of choice for small states with minimal defense budgets to inflict serious harm on a vastly stronger foe at extreme ranges.

The US Air Force has designated six cyber tools as weapons to help normalise military cyber operations and keep up with rapidly changing threats in this most recent theatre of war.[17] This clearly indicates that time has now come that the Armed Forces around the world gear up to employ as well as defend against cyber weapons. When employed in conjunction with conventional operations, cyber weapons increase the cost of conflict for adversaries as he has to now protect the National Critical Infrastructure as well as military targets against cyber weapons.

Military Targets. The most significant war fighting model evolved by the western armies, which is based around the information domain is the concept of Network Centric Warfare (NCW). Gone are the days when a field force commander had to impatiently wait for intelligence. Today, information about the enemy is gathered on the battlefield in real time. The computing power available to commanders can process this information at unbelievably high speeds. Special networks created both at the strategic level as well as in the Tactical Battle Area (TBA) can disseminate information in near real time at the point of decision. NCW is about the increased combat power that can be generated by a well networked force. The power of NCW is derived from the effective networking of knowledgeable entities that are geographically or hierarchically dispersed. The networking of knowledgeable entities enables them to share information and collaborate to develop shared awareness, and also to collaborate with one another to achieve a degree of self-synchronisation. The net result is increased combat power.[18] So, if the power of networking is being leveraged to derive combat power, then such networking would be an obvious target for the enemy. If the enemy is able to bring down the networks in the TBA, he will be able to negatively affect combat effectiveness of such network centric forces.

The term Network Centricity comprises of two key elements. The first is the communication networks which carry the information and the

17 US Air Force designates cyber weapons Apr 10, 2013. http://www.itnews.com.au/News/339234,us-air-force-designates-cyber-weapons.aspx

18 NETWORK CENTRIC WARFARE: Developing and Leveraging Information Superiority by David S. Alberts, John J. Garstka and Frederick P. Stein, P7

second is the warfare or operations which are the focus point of NCW. Networks are merely a means to an end; they convey "information" from one place to another and they are the purview of technologists. NCW does not focus on network-centric computing and communications, but rather focuses on information flows, the nature and characteristics of battlespace entities, and how they need to interact. NCW is all about deriving combat power from distributed interacting entities with significantly improved access to information.

If Network Centric Operations can enhance the combat potential of networked armies, then surely, disruption of such capabilities will have debilitating impact on the war fighting capabilities. Therefore, it's time to examine various components of a networked centric force so that the impact of cyberattacks on these elements can be analysed. NCW has been defined by many scholars in a number of ways. The common aspects of all these descriptions are – Sensor Networks, Command and Control Elements and the Shooter or the Weapon systems. Both these elements - timely passage of information and effective decision making - rely on data and voice networks.

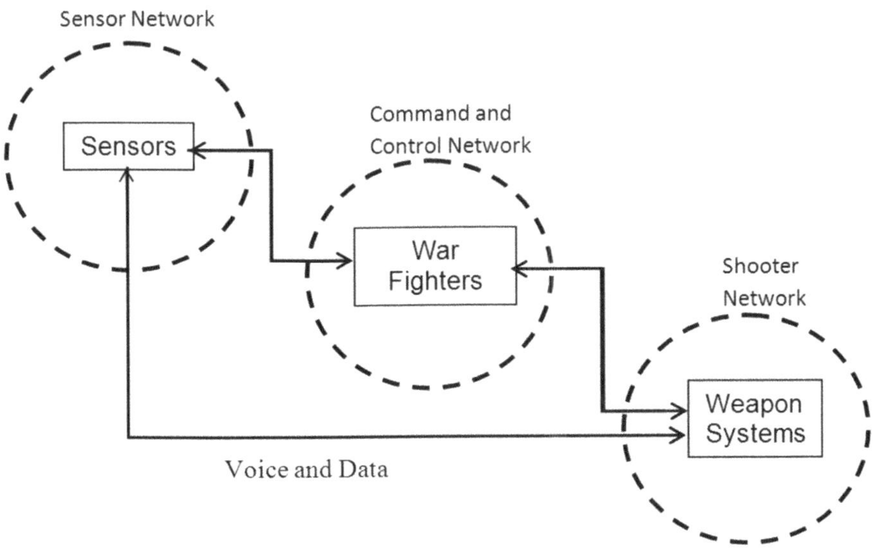

Figure 24: Components of a Networked Centric Force

The figure above is a basic representation of a NCW environment. In NCW, capabilities for sensing, commanding, controlling, and engaging are robustly networked via digital data links. The source of the increased power in a network-centric operation is derived, in part from the increased content, quality, and timeliness of information flowing between the nodes in the network. This increased information flow is the key to enabling shared battlespace awareness, and increasing the accuracy of the information

Any force which is networked as above has two key elements which are the pillars of the net centricity. The first is the Voice and Data links and the second is the power of gathering data, processing it and acting on it. Both these elements can fall victims to cyberattacks.

In a manoeuver battle, especially on land, one thing that is constantly changing is the location of own and opposing forces. Manoeuver and speed of operations are two critical elements of any mechanised warfare. In such a battlefield environment, to ensure that each element of the force is constantly connected to the network, extensive amount of communication resources for provisioning of voice and data networks are deployed and redeployed as a grid. The basic concept is that network is omnipresent in the battlespace whereas, fighting entities hook and unhook to the nearest node. To ensure such a kind of presence in large battlefield, the network elements will use land, air and space for deployment of nodes. A typical manoeuver battlefield network will look like the figure below :- [19]

19 Picture courtesy Cognitive Tactical Communication Networks as available at http://www.elektrobit.com/whats_new/newsletters/eb_defense_newsletter/2013/issue_02/cognitive_tactical_communication_networks

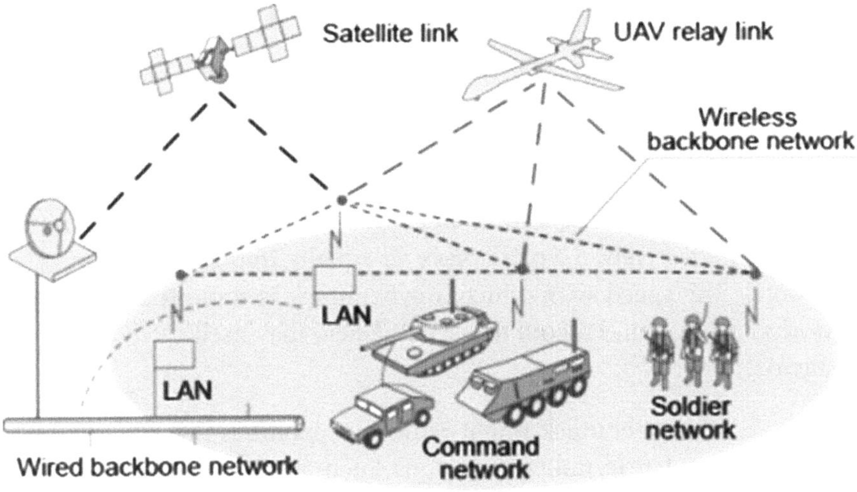

Figure 25: Typical Layout of Tactical Communication Network

In a manoeuver battlefield, several command and control functions such as air defense, fire support, maneuver control, intelligence, electronic warfare, and logistics support need to be executed simultaneously through rapid and reliable exchange of information. As can be seen above, the network for such exchange of information is formed by a large number of radiating and non-radiating media. The system architecture of such a network will typically consist of three interconnected subsystems; the Wide Area Subsystem, Local Area Subsystem and the Mobile Subsystem. While the backbone network may use wired media, mobile forces will heavily rely on various types of radiating media from satellite to Unmanned Aerial Vehicles (UAV) and UHF/ VHF broadband radio. A network like this will be based on full IP solution and will incorporate IP, ATM and ISDN switching technologies together.

In an NCW environment, where networks play a predominant role in exchange of massive amount of data, Cyberwar can play three key roles :[20]

(a) Surprise the enemy.

(b) Provide temporary but decisive military advantage to own forces.

(c) Prevent the enemy from using his systems confidently in future.

20 Cyberdeterrence and Cyberwar, Rand Corporation monograph by Martin C. Libicki, P 142 Published 2009 by the RAND Corporation

Let us examine each of the above elements in more detail.

Cyberattacks might cripple adversary's capabilities quickly, if the adversary is caught by surprise. Surprise is a war winning factor. If the enemy is caught by surprise, defeat is inevitable. Surprise means striking the enemy at a time, place or in a manner for which he is not prepared. It is not that the enemy is caught unaware, but only that he becomes aware too late to react effectively. Surprise plays an equally important role in cyber operations. The speed with which a cyberattack is mounted on enemy's networks and systems laid out in the battle field may itself catch the enemy by surprise.

A surprise cyberattack might remove capabilities that the adversary relied on to complete its military missions. Such capabilities can be defensive - perhaps a surface to air missile failed to engage its target correctly or the surveillance network designed to keep a constant watch on the enemy's movement is rendered ineffective. A perfect example of this is the 2007 bombing of the Syrian nuclear facility by Israeli fighters. While the Syrians had spent billions of dollars on their air defence system and the airspace was constantly being watched, not a single Israeli aircraft appeared on the screen of the AD radars on 06 Sep 2007. As the raid was being mounted, the skies over Syria seemed safe and empty of any enemy activity. How was this achieved? It was a result of a flawlessly planned and executed cyber assault by the Israelis. Richard A Clark, in his book '*Cyberwar*', explains three likelihoods of how cyberattack was the reason for success of this air raid. Though the Russians, whose Air Defence systems the Syrian army was using, till date remain silent on this issue, it is quite likely that one of the three options was actually employed by the Israeli air force. Operation Orchard, as the air raid was called, was a complete success. The suspected nuclear reactor in the Deir ez-Zor region of Syria was completely destroyed without facing any opposition from the enemy. It is pertinent to note that Indian Air Defence systems are also based on similar Russian technology. If a cyberattack could cripple the Syrian AD system, can a similar attack by our adversaries during the initial stages of war, where preemptive air strikes play a key role in shaping of the battlefield, bring down our national air defence system thereby making our skies vulnerable? After all, the PLA cyber warfare capabilities are no less than those of Israel. If this was to happen, the PLAF or Pakistan Airforce will be able to operate with quite impunity during the critical stages of the war.

Cyberattacks can also impact the offensive capabilities of the enemy. A surprise cyberattack can perhaps bring down the command and control elements required to synchronise a mechanised combat command moving in for an offensive, leaving a very potent force crippled by a consequent loss of efficiency, hampering synchronisation and coordination. Success requires that the adversary be surprised by an exploit targeting vulnerability it did not realise it had or did not think anyone could utilise. However, the effects of any attack may be enhanced if the possibility of an attack is also a surprise.[21]

It can be used as a rapier in limited situations, thereby affording a temporary but potentially decisive military advantage. This can be achieved by targeting the command, control, communications, computers, intelligence, surveillance and reconnaissance (C4ISR) systems of the enemy. Advance armies in the world such as the US Army, Navy and the Airforce have completely integrated cyber-based C4ISR into its full spectrum of operations. These systems support everything from command and control of combat forces (conventional and nuclear) to logistics (i.e., ordering, distributing, tracking of munitions, medical supplies, spare parts, etc.) and administration (i.e., military pay/medical records). Land, sea, air, and space-based C4ISR assets collect, store, and transmit data for operations throughout the globe. In countries like India, we are in the process of implementing such technologies. If the C4ISR system of the enemy can be put down in the critical phases of the battle through discreet cyberattacks, the force launching such attacks can gain a decisive military advantage over the adversary till such time the systems are down.

It can also inhibit the adversary from using its systems confidently. Once a system or network of the enemy has been attacked and its performance degraded, it is but obvious that the enemy will now use such networks or systems with caution. On 04 Dec 2011, the Iranian FARS news agency announced that the electronic warfare group of the Iranian military took over the operations of a very sophisticated, un-manned RQ170 Stealth Sentinel drone nicknamed "The Beast of Kandahar" along the border between Afghanistan and Iran. The drone was not shot down, as previously reported by the American news. It was brought down through an Iranian cyberattack which disabled its communications system.[22] The loss of one

21 ibid

22 Israeli Intelligence Report: US Drone downed by Iran Cyber Attack, Global Research,

RQ170 Stealth drone immediately slowed down the rapidity with which they were being used over Iran. Extensive investigations followed to determine which system of the drone was subjected to a cyberattacks that resulted in such a loss. No one will know for sure if Iran successfully launched a cyber attack against "The Beast of Kandahar" unless Iran presents proof, but its intent to do so was real, the theft of related technology was real, the lapse in cyber-security at Creech AFB from where the drone was being piloted was very real.

Another example involving a similar aerial vehicle of the US armed forces was actually reported before the RQ170 incidence. In 2009, the Wall Street Journal reported that militants in Iraq as well as Afghanistan had used COTS software worth US $ 26.00 to hack into the live video feeds from US Predator drones.[23] The report mentioned that militants used software programs such as SkyGrabber -- available for as little as US $ 25.95 on the Internet to regularly capture drone video feeds, thereby removing the battlefield advantage that is gained by the element of surprise. The vulnerability lay in an unencrypted downlink between the unmanned Predator drone and the ground control station.

The above two examples show how battle field technology and systems can be victims of cyberattacks. Though no official logs are available in the public domain, if the drone operators who lost the "The Beast of Kandahar" to Iran or the ones who were operating the Predator on a routine basis were to be asked, they would certainly confirm, that reports of their equipment being hacked by the enemy impacted their operations and the integrity of information gathered by these aerial missions.

Since a typical Network Centric Warfare framework uses the TCP/ IP suite of protocols as its backbone it is therefore automatically susceptible to most of the threats and vulnerabilities relevant to the Internet. In addition to common threats, the NCW framework is also susceptible to attacks aimed at destroying the operational capability of critical infrastructure and espionage. Major threats and vulnerabilities are summarised in the figure below:

December 08, 2011 s available at http://www.globalresearch.ca/israeli-intelligence-report-us-drone-downed-by-iran-cyber-attack/28114

23 Insurgents Hack U.S. Drones, The Wall Street Journal 17 Dec 2009 as available at http://online.wsj.com/article/SB126102247889095011.html

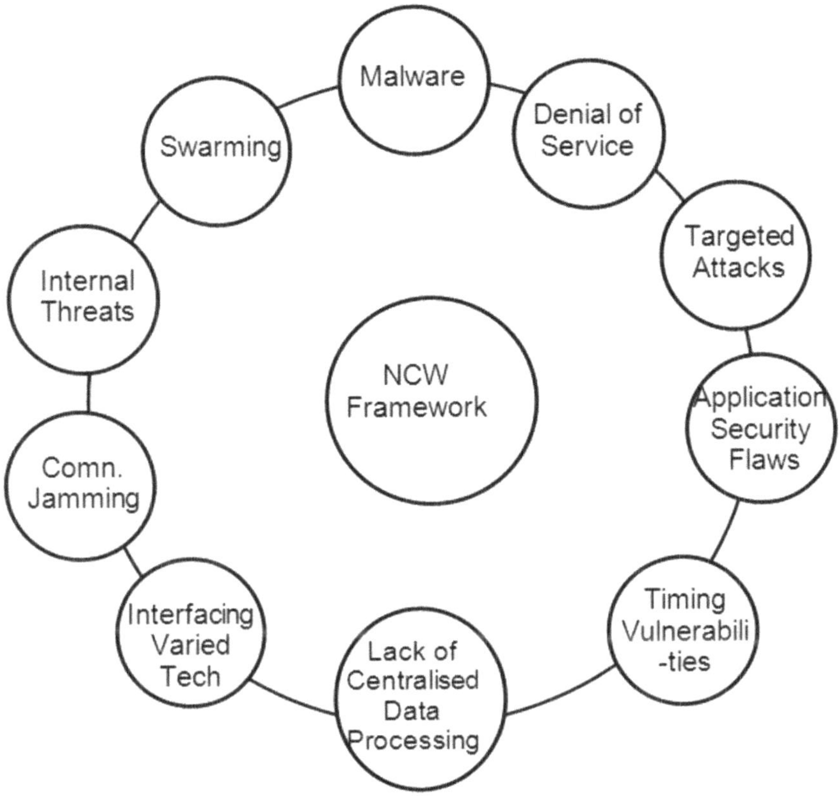

Figure 26: NCW Framework

Since NCW seeks to integrate diverse systems and each system has its own data processing control standards and procedures, vulnerabilities are bound to creep in, that can be exploited by sophisticated users. Such vulnerabilities can be termed as Lack of Centralised Data Processing. Also, most weapon systems and sensors that are interfaced for achieving NCW advantages are created by different vendors each using its own proprietary data handling systems. Achieving seamless interoperability between inherently different technologies often compromises the security of the systems and introduces interoperability vulnerabilities. Threats from insiders are often the most difficult to detect and prevent, as humans can't be monitored and controlled as easily as machines. Some may argue that such threats should not exist amongst uniformed patriotic personnel who are willing to lay down their lives for their country, yet even if there exists one person who is willing to be compromised; it is enough to compromise the security of the entire system.

Given the almost identical nature of the backbone structure (hardware, software and communication technologies) of the public internet and the private Network Centric Warfare framework, there is a clear and present danger of a crippling attack on specific parts of the NCW framework. Experts believe that the absence of any major attack till date may be attributed to the lack of political will rather than a lack of technical capability.[24] While cyberattacks against websites can be treated as proxy war or cold war tactics primarily causing nuisance or only business losses, any specific attack against a Network Centric Warfare framework is bound to be treated by the target country as an act of war and is bound to generate a response against the perpetrator that would include conventional warfare strategies. This has been the primary deterrent that has prevented the occurrence of any high-profile incident targeting the Network Centric Warfare framework.

This brings in the aspect of 'Deterrence' in the cyber domain. Is it possible to deter a conflict between two nations based on the theory of cyber deterrence, like in the case of nuclear deterrence? Can the risk to India's CII be reduced if India develops credible cyber deterrence? Let us examine such issues in greater detail.

Cyber Deterrence

Deterrence is a strategy for combining two competing goals: countering an enemy and avoiding war. Academics have explored countless variations on that theme, but the basic concept is quite simple: an enemy will not strike if it knows the defender can defeat the attack or can inflict unacceptable damage in retaliation.[25] The theory of deterrence has always existed. However, it acquired a new dimension when the term 'Nuclear' started to prefix deterrence.

---

24 Cyber War's Final Frontier: Network Centric Warfare Framework by Amit Grover as available at http://www.scribd.com/doc/161370499/Cyber-War#scribd

25 The Lost Logic of Deterrence by Richard K. Betts, Foreign Affairs MARCH/APRIL 2013 Issue

There are different methods by which a nation can prevent its adversaries from taking undesirable actions. The two most common forms of deterrence which are talked about are:

> **Deterrence by Punishment**: The strategy of deterrence by punishment is one of the most studied. Deterrence by punishment has been best defined by George and Smoke, whereby deterrence is the ability to persuade a potential enemy that the price it will pay as the result of carrying out the undesirable action will outweigh any possible profit.[26] This is the most commonly used form of deterrence. The first essential condition for successful deterrence by punishment is that the defender be able to fix a price from the challenger. For example the presence of nuclear weapons with a state clearly lays down the price its adversary will have to pay if these weapons were to be used against them. Of course the threat has to be credible for high value price. This brings in the factors of capability and intentions. The challenger must be aware of the defender's capabilities and its willingness to use them, only then will the deterrence is credible. Even if one of the two elements is missing, deterrence by punishment loses its standing.
>
> **Deterrence by Denial**: Deterrence by Denial is based on the attempt to persuade potential aggressors that they must avoid taking action because they will fail to attain their goals. This concept of deterrence is based on strength of own defences and making the enemy believe that it will never be able to breach them. For example, China's rise as a major anti-access/ area denial (A2/AD) military power could give it unprecedented capacity to deny sanctuary and communications to the US forces, and thereby challenge the type of military operations for which the US has equipped and prepared.[27]

The concept of deterrence differs from the concept of compellence, which is based on the use of threats in order to make an enemy undertake an action, whereas the aim of deterrence is to make the enemy avoid taking undesirable action. The aim of cyber deterrence is to prevent an enemy

---

26 Alexander George and Richard Smoke, Deterrence in American Foreign Policy: Theory and Practice (New York: Columbia University Press, 1974), p. 11.

27 Deterrence by Denial: How to Prevent China From Using Force, December 16, 2013 by Andrew S. Erickson as available at http://nationalinterest.org/commentary/war-china-two-can-play-the-area-denial-game-9564

from conducting future attacks by changing their minds, by attacking their technology, or by more palpable means.

History has shown that nuclear deterrence has been able to successfully deter a full-fledged war between the two superpowers of the world, the USA and the erstwhile Soviet Union. Of course, post the collapse of USSR, nuclear deterrence lost some of its relevance as one of the powers dwindled in its offensive capabilities. Yet even today, nuclear deterrence does play an important role in war prevention. So if presence of a strong nuclear arsenal and the second strike capability can deter a war, can similar parallels be drawn in the cyber domain also? Is there something called as credible cyber deterrence?

The ambiguities of cyber deterrence contrast starkly with the clarities of nuclear deterrence. As Martin C Libicki explains in his Rand report, in the Cold War nuclear realm, attack attribution was not a problem; the prospect of battle damage was clear; the 1,000th bomb could be as powerful as the first one; counterforce was possible; there were no third parties to worry about; private firms were not expected to defend themselves; any hostile nuclear use crossed an acknowledged threshold; no higher levels of war existed; and both sides always had a lot to lose.[28]

Libicki in his above report has brought in the aspect of private firms being subjected to cyberattacks. While in the theory of deterrence, nowhere else does one find mention of private firms; this important component appears only while discussing cyber deterrence. These are the people who own the CII of the nation. In the cyber domain, the threat of the enemy targeting our CII is much more than that of enemy attacking and putting down our battlefield systems. In the battlefield, targets have to be accessible and have vulnerabilities. These vulnerabilities have to be exploited in ways the attacker finds useful to impact his overall operational plan. Hence, the CII is much more vulnerable than battlefield systems. This brings in the aspect of how much CII the government is willing to protect both during peace as well as during a conflict situation. There may be a case that while a nation though possesses credible offensive cyber capabilities, its adversary on the other hand may be willing to accept some of its CII going down for a finite duration of time on outbreak of hostilities to the enemy's cyberattacks. That is to say that the adversary may be resilient in

28 Cyberdeterrence and Cyberwar, Rand Corporation monograph by Martin C. Libicki, Published 2009 by the RAND Corporation

the cyber domain, and have the ability to withstand attacks and failures, as well as to mitigate harm more than in other domains. This is because cyberattacks may not be able to cause any physical damage to systems and also the capability to bounce back after a cyberattack.

One of the aspects on which the concept of Deterrence by Punishment is based is the factor of 'Capability and Intentions'. Applying this to cyber deterrence, it implies that for developing credible cyber deterrence, a nation must hold a stockpile of cyber weapons and make its intention clear for using them. When intending to use a conventional weapon or nuclear weapon for deterrence, the choice of targets available is in abundance. You destroy one city of mine and I will destroy five of yours. But this is not the case when using cyber weapons as deterrent. While USA may boast of owning the most devastating cyber weapons developed till day, the adversary may not be networked enough to present a viable target to these weapons. Take for example the ISIS or the Taliban fighting the US in Afghanistan. Both these radical groups do not rely upon technology and networks for their operations and hence may not get deterred by the cyber might of the Americans. On the other hand, they certainly do get cautious of conventional strikes may it be using airpower, drones or ground forces. Thus, for the concept of cyber deterrence to be credible, the opposing nations have to be sound cyber power themselves.

Lastly, there is the issue of attribution, which distinguishes cyber warfare from warfare in other domains. Attribution in the cyber domain is hard because it lacks the obviousness of a kinetic attack and leaves no physical evidence. Also, extensive cyber forensic is required to establish the source of attack. Attacks can be masked or routed through the networks of another country. Even if one knows for sure that the attack came from a computer in a certain country, one cannot be sure that the government is behind it as non-state actors play a very important role in this domain. It is hard to deter without being able to punish, and one cannot punish without knowing who is behind the attack. Moreover, hitting back on a wrong target weakens the logic of deterrence and also creates a new enemy.

The above clearly indicates that the concept of credible cyber deterrence is not as effective as in the case of nuclear deterrence. Actually, in the cyber domain low cost of aggression and low probability of detection make the task of deterrence difficult. That is the reason we often hear of cases of nations like Iran and North Korea taking on the might of a powerful nation like the USA by attacking its infrastructure through the cyber domain. Admiral Mike Rogers, Director, National Security Agency and Commander of the Cyber Command of US Armed Forces, in Feb 2015 admitted that "Nations such as China and Russia have enough offensive cyber capabilities to one day carry out a "cyber Pearl Harbor" attack".[29] As per him, a cyber Pearl Harbor could include an attack on critical infrastructure or the financial sector. Considering the fact the Americans were able to deter a war with these two adversaries using the nuclear and conventional deterrence card, are today unable to deter the same two nations from implementing a Cyber Pearl Harbor. This raises serious concerns about the efficacy of Cyber deterrence.

Whether the theory of cyber deterrence works or not, time will tell. But if the presence of cyber weapons in a country's arsenal is able to make an adversary think twice about the consequences it may face, the aim would have been achieved. Hence we as a nation must consider the option of developing offensive cyber capabilities to contribute towards deterrence. For a meaningful cyber deterrence strategy to be effective, we must have network penetration tools, tools for carrying out DDoS attacks, parallel scanning, reconnaissance, surveillance, cyber espionage and other capabilities. Most importantly, we must be able to assess cyber-attack attribution rapidly, and with certainty.

Cyber deterrence is a challenging problem at all levels, that is strategic, operational and technical. It is a relatively unexplored domain with huge uncertainties. The non-existence of any legal framework for cyberwar makes it even more complex. Only time will tell how effectively will nations be able to deter a war using cyber threat as a tool of deterrence.

Pillars of Cyberwar

Richard Stiennon in his book "Surviving Cyberwar" talks of the four pillars of cyberwar, namely intelligence, technology, logistics and command.[30] He suggests that the four pillars of cyberwar must be mastered to engage an enemy effectively. Let us examine what is the role of the above factors in waging a successful cyberwar.

29 NSA Chief: China, Russia Capable of Carrying Out 'Cyber Pearl Harbor' Attack by Yasmin Tadjdeh as available at http://www.nationaldefensemagazine.org/blog/Lists/Posts/Post.aspx?List=7c996cd7-cbb4-4018-baf8-8825eada7aa2&ID=1757

30 Surviving Cyberwar by Richard Stiennon, The Scarecrow Press, P 115

Intelligence. Intelligence gathering and its significance as part of cyber espionage has already been discussed in detail in this chapter earlier. Cyber intelligence gathering is systematic collecting of information about target's cyber assets. The target could be military DNS servers, web servers, email servers, routers, firewalls and database. They could also be similar assets of governmental organisations, state organisations or even private companies who operate CII. Also, intelligence gathering in the cyberspace, like other domains is a continuous process. This is because servers, database and networks are updated on a daily basis. It should not happen that we plan an attack based on vulnerabilities of say X version of a system firewall , while the adversary has already upgraded to a Y version of firewall. Lack of this knowledge will result in complete failure of an attack at a critical time. Cyber reconnaissance therefore is essential for tracking all such changes that the adversary may have brought about as well as discovery of new assets that are brought online and finding out about any changes in the network architecture. Regular cyber reconnaissance could yield valuable information such as operational plans, weapon design and deployment and a host of such data. While a lot of information may be gathered through the cyber domain, its assessment, collation and interpretation is also a very important task. The speed and quantum with which data is gathered may even lead to information overload.

Technology. There is a constant arms race taking place in the cyberspace. While the attacker devices newer methods of intelligence gathering and cyberattacks, the defender shores up his defences by blocking ports, patching systems and developing better defences for his network. The speed with which technology changes in the cyberspace is astounding. Newer versions of operating systems, better encryption protocols, stronger firewalls, steadier anti-malware software are constantly being flooded in the market. In such a scenario, the attacker has to constantly keep honing his attack skills while defender has to constantly update technology. There is never a situation when defences of a network are completely prepared and impregnable.

Logistics. Cyber logistics is not about resupply and replenishment. Cyber logistics deals with networks and the ability to deliver an attack while also defending those network paths the attack could come from[31]. It could also include effective management of cyber assets such as undersea fiber links, control and defence of routers, management of DNS servers and so on. Hardening of country's CII could also form part of cyber logistics. Management of cyber arsenal too would come under the gamut of cyber logistics.

Command and Control. As brought out earlier, command and control plays a key role in network centric operations. Destruction or degradation of command and control, can render the enemy paralysed in the battlefield. The focus of cyber operations is to target enemy's command and control structure. While defending, it is essential to develop capability to prevent own command and control structure and channels from adversaries cyberattacks. The importance of command and control in the cyber domain can be determined by the fact that during a symposium organised by AFCEA on Defensive Cyber Operations in Jun 2015 at Baltimore, USA, Lt. Gen. James McLaughlin, USAF, Deputy Commander, U.S. Cyber Command spoke at length on Commanding and Controlling the Cyber Domain and highlighted the importance of command and control in defending cyberspace. I had the good fortune of listening to the general officer.

A Cyberwar Scenario

The Western world is already talking about Hybrid Warfare, a military strategy that blends conventional warfare, irregular warfare and cyberwarfare. Hezbollah fighters supposedly were blamed for using such a model of warfare in the 2006 Lebanon War. During this conflict, Hezbollah fought the Israeli military to a standstill by engaging them from either concealed, fixed positions and underground tunnel complexes (emulating the Viet Cong) or by conventional infantry combat maneuvers in Lebanese villages. The outcome of these tactics was that the Israel Defense Forces failed to conquer a single village along the Israel–Lebanon border, in the time of its two-week ground assault on Hezbollah. Israel's greatest

31 Ibid P 128.

strengths, namely, having a modern and capable armoured corps and air force, were nullified by Hezbollah fighters utilising hardened bunkers and modern Russian ATGMs, capable of destroying any known type of armoured vehicle. This was combined by Hezbollah succeeding in hacking into Israeli communication and Israeli soldiers' mobile phones to receive first-hand knowledge about enemy troop movements, communications and casualties.

Can India too face such a scenario of being engaged in hybrid war? The Indian Armed Forces have been involved in a number of small scale operations including Operation Vijay in 1999. The line of control with Pakistan and Siachen glacier are two of the most militarily active areas in the world. In the recent past, there have been a number of intrusions by the Chinese on the Northern as well as on the Eastern boarders. Coupled with this is the fact that we have a neighbor on our Eastern and Northern frontiers capable of integrating cyberwarfare with conventional and irregular warfare.

With this as a background, let us try and paint a picture of a possible cyberwar mixed with conventional/ irregular warfare scenario in the Indian context. Chinese troops have been regularly intruding into Indian territory both in the Ladakh sector as well as Arunachal Pradesh. One such intrusion attempt by the Chinese in Chaglagam in Eastern Arunachal's Anjaw district in August 2013 is represented in the map below.[32] The face-off lasted three weeks before Indian and Chinese soldiers withdrew from their positions following a flag meeting

32 The Telegraph, 22 August 2013 as available at http://www.telegraphindia.com/1130822/jsp/frontpage/story_17258566.jsp#.VTCPRSGeDGc

Map 1: Recent Areas of Intrusion by PLA in the Eastern Sector
(Map courtesy *The Telegraph*)

Let us now presume that a similar intrusion takes place in last week of August 2015 where in over 1000 strong Chinese force intrudes into the Walong sector and establish a temporary camp. Despite a flag meeting, the Chinese do not withdraw. India too decides to beef up the defences in Walong sector and additional troops are ordered to move into the area on 01 Sep 2015 to counter the Chinese threat.

On the night of 01 Sep 2015 the following events are reported:

(a) A group of people with dozers and JCB are reported digging along national highway 31C in the Kokrajar area. As the result of the digging, all OFC routes laid along the highway are disrupted.

(b) Another group of people with similar equipment is reported digging along the railway track Siliguri – Guwahati and have completely damaged the OFC routes laid along the railway track.

OFC connectivity to the eastern states of India passes through the

Siliguri corridor as shown in the map below.[33] Complete cable is either laid along the existing roads or along the railway tracks. Any damage caused to the network can result in a complete breakdown of telecom services in these states.

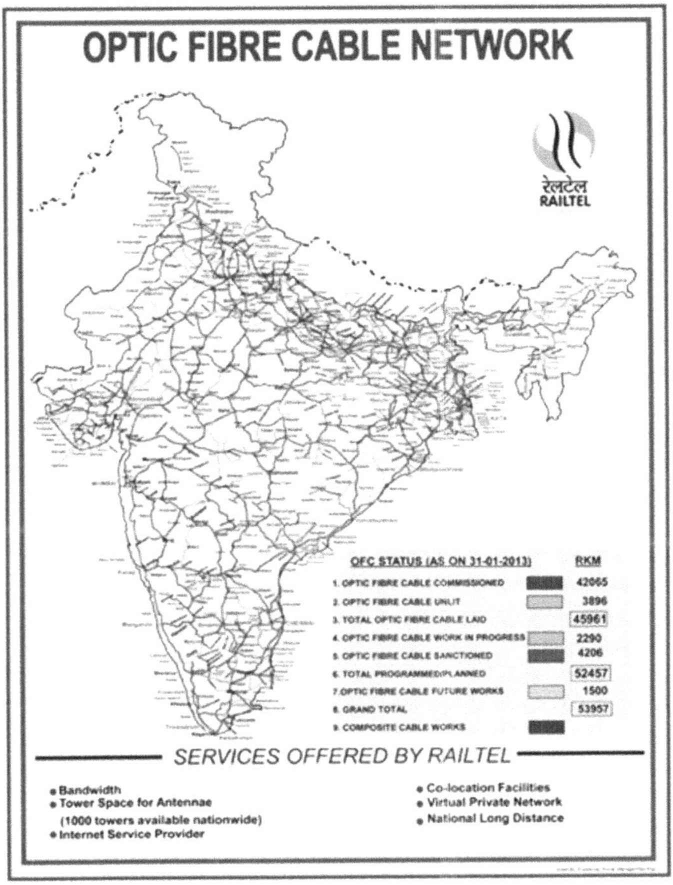

Map 2: Optic Fibre Cable Network

(Map courtesy Railtel)

On the same night, the following was also reported:

(a) A cyberattack on the eastern power grid causes major disruption of power and the entire North-Eastern part of the country is plunged into darkness.

33 RailTel OFC Communication Network to boost National Telecom Policy 2012 as available at http://www.railnews.co.in/15097/

(b) Another cyberattack on the INSAT 3E causes the satellite to malfunction. The satellite was providing transponders for voice and data connectivity to Assam and other North-Eastern states.

(c) Posts start appearing on Twitter and Facebook indicating that major ethnic violence has broken out in parts of Assam in which large number of Bodos have lost their lives. Large number of photographs of bloodshed is posted on the social media. Citizens from the North-Eastern states working in rest of the country try to call back their homes but are unable to contact their near and dear ones as the communication links have been severed. By mid day of 02 Sep 2015, the situation results in major exodus of these people heading back home.

(d) Army wireless communications start getting jammed in the areas of intrusion. It is reported that large number of Chinese UAV's flying over the area of intrusion are responsible for it.

The above is an example of an operation which uses physical sabotage, electronic warfare and cyberattacks in consonance to disrupt and create confusion in a peace time scenario. Imagine the chaotic situation that is likely to prevail in the North-Eastern states in such circumstances. With no power, no telecom connectivity and army's communication getting jammed, an intrusion to handle and an exodus happening from all major cities towards these states. The government will be faced with multiple challenges to handle simultaneously. A much more complex situation can be created during war using the same methodology.

Conclusion

For any future conflict, cyberwar involves a broadening of the dimensions of warfare. It would be surprising if a nation intent on attacking another nation failed in the future to carry out preparatory or simultaneous attacks of the target's infrastructure and defence capabilities through the cyberspace. That is the reason that a large number of nations are in the process of developing cyber weapons.

By itself cyberwar can achieve neither conquest nor in most cases coercion. Yet when used as a tool of warfare in conjunction with conventional warfare, it can be a force multiplier. Though there have not been many cases reported where cyberattacks have put down secure networks which form backbone of NCW, yet as is evident from the analysis above, that this may happen in any future conflict. The time therefore has come for us to take stock of the situation and develop capabilities not only to defend ourselves in the cyber domain but also respond to any misadventure being undertaken by our adversaries.

6 Cyberwar : The Way Ahead

"Is it not possible for us to create a foolproof mechanism against cyber threats so that the world can sleep well?"

– Prime Minister Nerendra Modi while speaking to IT Players at NASCOM

The continued rapid development of ICT, globalisation, tremendous increase in data volumes in all types of organisations and the growing number of varied types of devices connected to data networks have an impact on daily life, the economy of the country and general growth of our nation. High level of ICT development in a nation contributes to improved availability and usability of public services, enhances transparency in public dealings and encourages citizens participation in governance of the nation. While the Internet is becoming increasingly accessible and the number of users in India continues to grow at a very rapid rate, with new technological solutions and services such as the Internet of things and cloud computing, the number of potential vectors for attacks, along with the complexity of attacks, is also growing.

The world is still getting to understand how to counter the threats from the cyberspace, especially those arising from cyber warfare. The ambiguities of cyber warfare worry international law experts, diplomats, and military commanders alike. What qualifies as an act of war *versus* a cyberattack to degrade the performance of a commercial system *versus* cyber espionage? Does the law of "proportionality", (Under international humanitarian law governing the legal use of force in an armed conflict, proportionality and distinction are important factors in assessing military necessity) that collateral damage to civilians in battle must not be disproportionate to the military target attacked, apply to cyberwar, especially since the line between civilian and military networks computer systems is not so clear? Should a cyberattack by a lone hacker be treated differently than that engineered by a nation state or non-state actors acting on behalf of the nation state? A large number of such questions were addressed in the previous chapters. What clearly emerged was that our dependence on the cyberspace is here to stay for a long time. We therefore need to see what effort at international and national level can be made to bring down the challenges thrown up by it.

As worldwide concerns on cyber security grow, preventing war and regulating conflict in the cyberspace through a treaty have come to the top of the international agenda. Similarly, at the national level, concerns have started to grow on how to deal with cyber warfare so that it does not threaten our national security. We need to tackle this aspect at three different levels, namely:

- **International efforts required to be made to prevent a cyber war**: To include International cooperation and treaties to prevent cyberwar.
- **Efforts required at national level**: Efforts and preparedness required at the national level including the national strategy, organisation and legal protection.
- **Efforts at the level of armed forces**: Preparing the armed forces of the country to undertake cyberwar, both offensive and defensive.

International Cooperation and Treaties on Cyberwar

Compiling or estimating the numbers of deaths caused during wars and other violent conflicts is a controversial subject. Historians often put forward many different estimates of the numbers killed during various wars. As per estimates, the total number of military personal who died during World War II varies between 22,000,000 to 30,000,000.[1] Besides this, there were civilian deaths due to military activities and war related famine and diseases. It is estimated that a total of 60,000,000 to 85,000,000 people lost their lives during the Second World War. This was about 3.5 percent of the world's population in 1939. It was only after losing over 60 million people that the world came together to form United Nations in

1 World War II casualties as available at http://en.wikipedia.org/wiki/World_War_II_casualties

1945 so that any future war crimes could be prevented.

As analysed in previous chapters, we are in the midst of a cyberwar. Though it may not be a full-fledged war and is taking place in sporadic forms, yet it is destabilising and it tends to threaten the very fabric of the cyberspace. More and more countries are engaging in offensive actions in the cyberspace with tools like Stuxnet and Flame. Before the situation goes out of hands, now is the best time to react and draw a framework under which we can govern and cause conflict resolution in the cyberspace. Let us analyse the pros and cons of an international treaty on cyberwar. Are we waiting for such a disaster to happen again, this time through the cyberspace though, before the world wakes up and draws out an international treaty to prevent cyberwar?

A number of studies have been undertaken to address the function, role, and activities of international organisations in the cyberspace and cyberwar. Most international organisations active in the cyber domain today are intergovernmental bodies, founded by governments based on multilateral treaties. Yet, as on date there are no international treaties or agreements to prevent a cyberwar or cyberattacks on CII. In fact there are no international treaties to deal with either cybercrime or cyber espionage and surveillance. The only treaty which has some legal international standing in parts of the globe is the **Convention on Cybercrime, CETS Number 185** by the Council of Europe popularly known as the Budapest Convention. The Convention on Cybercrime is a treaty that seeks to harmonise national laws on cybercrime, improve national capabilities for investigating such crimes, and increase cooperation on investigations. As on date, 45 nations have signed and ratified the Convention while eight nations have signed but not ratified the Convention.[2] The Convention came into force on 01 July 2004. Though initially only European nations ratified it, as on date there are 20 nations who are non-members of the Council of Europe, who too have signed/ ratified the Convention. This includes the USA (it played an important role in drafting the treaty) and Israel, both of whom have signed the treaty. Russia and China till date have not signed it. Even India is not a signatory to it. The Convention obliges ratifying states to create laws allowing law enforcement to search and seize computers and "computer data," engage in wiretapping, and to obtain real

2 Convention on Cybercrime, CETS No.: 185 as available at http://conventions.coe.int/Treaty/Commun/ChercheSig.asp?NT=185&CL=ENG

time and stored communications data, whether or not the crime under investigation is a cybercrime.[3] One of the pillars of strength on which the Convention relies is international cooperation. It mandates the signatory nations to assist each other in investigating cybercrimes and other crimes involving electronic evidence. It requires nations to provide mutual assistance to each other in the real-time collection of traffic data associated with specified communications in their territory transmitted by means of computer systems.

Russia has been opposed to the section of the provision allowing unilateral trans-border access by law enforcement agencies to computers or data with the consent of the computer or data-owner, seeing this as a violation of national sovereignty.[4] This is one of the reasons that the treaty despite being around for over ten years, has not been able to solve major cases of cyber crimes as most seem to have originated from Russian soil. Yet, the Convention on Cybercrime has perhaps been the only success story where a large international community has come together and pledged to fight cybercrime across the boundaries of their nations.

Efforts by the United Nations

The United Nations General Assembly has approved a number of resolutions relevant to ICTs and cyber security that have served to draw the attention of United Nations Member States to future cyber challenges. The most important and the relevant one is UN Resolution 64/211 dealing with protection of CII.

UN Resolution 64/211: Creation of a global culture of cyber security and taking stock of national efforts to protect critical information infrastructures. When the Law of Armed Conflict was first codified into the Geneva Conventions, Internet may as well have been the subject of a science fiction. Now the world is faced with questions of how to apply nearly a century-old charter to a technology that allows the aggressor to hide behind a veil of anonymity. It is time for the United Nations to address this new international security challenge. Resolution 64/211 was the first step towards this. It is an attempt by the UN to provide a loose framework

3 Convention on Cybercrime, Articles 18-21

4 U.S. Talks to Russia on Internet Security by J. Markoff and A. Kramer, N.Y. Times December 12, 2009, as available at http://www.nytimes.com/2009/12/13/science/13cyber.html

for the international community for protection of CII. The resolution is just the beginning and there is still large ground that needs to be covered. Adopted on 21 Dec 2009, the Convention is an attempt to protect CII from cyberattacks. The resolution recognises that national efforts to protect CII benefit from a periodic assessment of their progress.[5]

1. Invites Member States to use, if and when they deem appropriate, the annexed voluntary self-assessment tool for national efforts to protect critical information infrastructures in order to assist in assessing their efforts in this regard to strengthen their cyber security, so as to highlight areas for further action, with the goal of increasing the global culture of cyber security;

2. Encourages Member States and relevant regional and international organisations that have developed strategies to deal with cyber security and the protection of critical information infrastructures to share their best practices and measures that could assist other Member States in their efforts to facilitate the achievement of cyber security by providing such information to the Secretary General for compilation and dissemination to Member States.

Annexure of Resolution 64/211 lays down self-assessment tool for national efforts to protect CII. However, the resolution as mentioned earlier is just the first step towards global cyber security. In no way can it prevent cyberattacks on CII, nor does it lay down any punitive action that can be taken against rogue nations who indulge in cyberattack against CII. The UN needs to assert its role in these fields too.

In 2012, UN Secretary-General Ban Ki-moon appointed the group of 15 experts from the five permanent members of the UN Security Council plus Argentina, Australia (the chair), Belarus, Canada, Egypt, Estonia, Germany, India, Indonesia, and Japan to carry out a mandate from the UN General Assembly to "study possible cooperative measures in addressing existing and potential threats" related to the use of ICTs.[6] The mandate of the group was to determine the need to elaborate confidence-building measures and "norms, rules or principles of responsible behaviour of States.

5 Resolution adopted by the General Assembly on 21 December 2009 as available at https://ccdcoe.org/sites/default/files/documents/UN-091221-CultureOfCSandCI.pdf

6 UN General Assembly, A/RES/66/24, 13 December 2011 as available at http://www.un.org/ga/search/view_doc.asp?symbol=A/RES/66/24

At the end of the study, for the first time at the UN level, a group of governmental experts was able to agree to an important set of recommendations on norms, rules, and principles of responsible behaviour by states in cyberspace. Governmental experts from the five permanent members of the UN Security Council and 10 leading cyberpowers from all regions of the world have recognised that international law; including the principles of the law of state responsibility, fully apply to state behaviour in cyberspace. This recognition represents a landmark step towards universal acceptance of the legal framework. The report recommends the following confidence-building measures :-[7]

- Exchanging views and information on national policies, best practices, decision-making processes, and national organisations and structures with regard to cyber security. As an example, the US in 2012 and Germany in 2013 exchanged White Papers on cyber defence with Russia.

- Creating bilateral or multilateral consultative frameworks for confidence-building measures, for example, within the Arab League, the African Union, the Association of Southeast Asian Nations (ASEAN) Regional Forum, the Organisation for Security and Co-operation in Europe (OSCE), and the Organisation of American States. These frameworks could include workshops and exercises on how to prevent and manage disruptive cyber security incidents.

- Enhancing the sharing of information and crisis communication among states on cyber security incidents at three levels: between national CERTs bilaterally and within already existing multilateral CERT communities to exchange technical information about malware or other malicious indicators; through previously existing or newly created channels for crisis management and early warning to receive, collect, analyse, and share such information to help mitigate vulnerabilities and risks; and through channels for dialogue at political and policy levels.

- Increasing cooperation to address incidents that affect critical

7 The UN Takes a Big Step Forward on Cyber security by Detlev Wolter as available at https://www.armscontrol.org/act/2013_09/The-UN-Takes-a-Big-Step-Forward-on-Cybersecurity

infrastructure systems, particularly those that rely on ICT-enabled industrial control systems.

- Enhancing mechanisms for law enforcement cooperation to reduce incidents that could be misunderstood as hostile state actions and that affect international security.

The experts' group report gave the UN and its member states a unique opportunity to advance toward a more predictable, secure, and peaceful international cyberspace. The report recommended that the UN pursue regular, ongoing institutional dialogue "with broad participation" to enhance common understandings and intensify practical cooperation on global cyber security.[8] The report though is just a small initial step. The UN needs to play a much bigger role in prevention of cyberwar and ensuring that cyberspace remains a peaceful domain.

As per Tim Maurer, the emergence process at the UN regarding cyber security can be divided into two main streams of negotiations: focusing on politico military issues and economic issues.[9] The politico-military stream will look after how information technologies and means can potentially be used for purposes that are inconsistent with the objectives of maintaining international stability and security and may adversely affect the security of States i.e. cyber warfare. The economic stream is about the criminal misuse of information technologies i.e. cyber crime. A third possible norm could be for governance of the internet, a task that is presently being done by The Internet Corporation for Assigned Names and Numbers (ICANN) and Internet Governance Forum (IGF).

United Nations Institute for Disarmament Research (UNIDIR) in Geneva is one of the first UN bureaucracies to be involved in cyber-security. At present, Germany funds ongoing research titled "Perspectives on Cyber War: Legal Frameworks and Transparency and Confidence Building". This project raised awareness among diplomats and policy-makers about the spectrum of cyberwar and to begin multilateral discussions about how

8 UN experts group cyber security report, Para 29

9 Cyber Norm Emergence at the United Nations by Tim Maurer as available at http://belfercenter.ksg.harvard.edu/files/maurer-cyber-norm-dp-2011-11-final.pdf

to prevent and restrain such conflicts.[10] UNIDIR's partner is Hamburg University's Institute for Peace Research and Security Policy.

Though some effort is being made at the level of the UN, it is still insignificant. All that UN has done is to bring awareness that a grave threat that can emanate from the cyberspace in the form of disruptive activities and crime. It is important for UN member states especially the P5 to work closely to defend nations against these emerging cyber threats. The UN needs to mandate itself with the following tasks:

- **Cyber Conflict Prevention**. Coordinate effort at the highest level to prevent a cyberwar between nations. This of course would be a very tough job for obvious reasons. Yet an attempt has to be made to ensure that critical infrastructure of nations is not damaged/ destroyed by cyberattacks both during war and peace.

- **Cyber Conflict Resolution**. Develop an organisation to investigate cyberattacks especially against CII of a nation. Once the identity of the attacker is established with certain degree of certainty, the UN Security Council should be empowered to initiate action against rogue nation/ elements including armed action.

- The UN must coordinate international efforts not only in sharing knowledge, but also training human resource, especially from developing countries.

Tallinn Manual on the International Law Applicable to Cyber warfare

In 2009, the NATO CCD COE, an international military organisation based in Tallinn, Estonia, invited an independent group of experts to produce a manual on laws governing cyber warfare. NATO CCD COE was born post the massive cyberattacks on Estonia and today is accredited by NATO as a 'Centre of Excellence'. The project brought together distinguished international law practitioners and scholars in the field of cyber security in an attempt to examine how legal norms can be applied to this new form of

10 Perspectives on Cyber War: Legal Frameworks and Transparency and Confidence-Building as available at http://www.unidir.org/programmes/emerging-security-threats/perspectives-on-cyber-war-legal-frameworks-and-transparency-and-confidence-building

warfare. The Tallinn Manual's focus is on cyber operations. Though Tallinn Manual is not an official document, yet it is the first ever attempt by an international body to determine what kind of laws would be applicable to cyber warfare. The manual makes the following recommendations:-[11]

(a) A cyber operation, or threatened cyber operation, constitutes an unlawful threat of force when the threatened action, if carried out, would be an unlawful use of force (Rule 12).

(b) A state that is the target of a cyber operation that rises to the level of armed attack may exercise its inherent right of self defence (Rule 13).

(c) A use of force involving cyber operations undertaken by a state in the exercise of its right of self defence must be necessary and proportionate (Rule 14).

(d) The right of self defence against a cyber operation amounting to an armed attack (Rule 16).

The manual recommends the United Nations Security Council determines that an act from the cyberspace constitutes a threat to peace, breach of peace or act of aggression. Based on its findings, the Security Council may decide upon forceful measures against the defaulter, including cyber measures.

As can be seen from the above recommendations, even the Tallinn Manual recommends the UN play a pivotal role in cyber conflict prevention and cyber conflict resolution. Yet as on date there exists no international laws promulgated by the UN which can govern the use of cyberspace for waging a war. It is therefore time to bring in international consensus on this issue under the ambit of the UN. If a world body like the UN does nothing to acknowledge the threats emanating from cyberspace which can result in a conflict or a conflict like situation between two nations, the world will soon be embroiled in a bitter cyber conflict with no one to prevent it from spiraling into a major conflict.

11 Tallinn Manual on the International Law Applicable to Cyber warfare, as available at http://www.knowledgecommons.in/wp-content/uploads/2014/03/Tallinn-Manual-on-the-International-Law-Applicable-to-Cyber-Warfare-Draft-.pdf

ASEAN Regional Forum

The ASEAN Regional Forum is a multilateral dialogue organisation, consisting of 27 participating States, founded in 1994 to foster constructive dialogue, consultations, and cooperation primarily in the field of political relations and security in the Asia–Pacific region. In 2006, the participating states issued the ARF Statement on Cooperation in Fighting Cyber Attack and Terrorist Misuse of Cyber Space.[12] The focus of the forum was criminal and terrorist misuse of cyberspace and not cyberwar. Yet it was a beginning made in this part of the world.

Arms Control Convention/ Treaty for Cyber Weapons

As discussed in the previous chapter, the concept of cyber weapons has evolved. Today a large number of nations boast of possessing cyber weapon capabilities. If so, then isn't there a need to bring in a cyber weapons control treaty? A number of arms control treaties have been around for a long time. Any arms control treaty aims to establish an international legal regime. There are various categories of arms control and disarmament treaties that can broadly be grouped into treaties that:

(a) Limit the level of armaments - for example 1972 Strategic Arms Limitation Talks I (SALT I), 1972 Anti-Ballistic Missile Systems Treaty and 1979 SALT II.

(b) Prohibit or restrict the use of specific weapons – for example 1925 Geneva Protocol for the Prohibition of the Use in War of Asphyxiating, Poisonous or Other Gases and of Bacteriological Methods of Warfare.

(c) Prohibit the testing and deployment and attacks on the environment - for example 1963 Partial Test Ban Treaty, 1974 Threshold Test Ban Treaty and 1996 Comprehensive Nuclear Test Ban Treaty.

(d) Prohibit development and acquisition of specific weapons – for example 1968 Non-Proliferation Treaty, 1972 Biological Weapons Convention, 1993 Chemical Weapons Convention and 1997 Ottawa Convention on Anti-Personnel Mines.

---

12 Statement on Cooperation in Fighting Cyber Attack and Terrorist Misuse of Cyber Space as available at http://www.mofa.go.jp/region/asia-paci/asean/conference/arf/state0607-3.html

If one has to draw parallels between existing arms control treaties and a cyber arms control treaty then, any cyber arms control treaty would be very similar to the Chemical Weapons Convention (CWC). As in the case of chemical weapons, a chemical which is used to make a weapon is also used by the industry to make for example, pesticides. Similarly, a code of software written with malicious intent could possibly have been designed to be used in the field of cyber security. Like a chemical weapon can be hidden very easily, so can a cyber weapon. But the similarities finish there. While the chemical weapons can be classified based on the level of harm they can cause on the target, it is not possible that cyber weapons can always be linked to the level of harm that could potentially be caused by the malware. Also the speed with which technology is developing, a cyber weapon can be created with each new technology, whereas chemical weapons by and large have stabilised in their shape and form. Yet despite the differences, if the UN ever decides to develop a Cyber Arms Control Treaty, then the CWC will certainly be a guideline.

What could be the aim of such a treaty/ convention? The primary aim would be to ensure that nations do not develop cyber weapons which could be employed both against CII as well as military targets. The first concern in any attempt to ban cyber weapons would be the verification problems. Being a dual use technology or perhaps primarily peaceful use technology, it would be difficult to identify the real intent behind developing a malware. Even the most intrusive and disruptive monitoring procedures would be inadequate to the task especially because the weapon in question is not even 'Physical' in form. Another purpose that such a convention/ treaty could serve would be "Prevention of disruptive cyber technologies". Growth of North Korea as a rogue cyber state is an example of this aspect. If China had not assisted North Korea with technology and expertise required to carry out cyberattacks, North Korea on its own could have never achieved what it has been able to. If a convention/ treaty of such a nature will ever take shape, only time will tell.

Bilateral Cyberwar Treaties

As rational actors, nation-states ratify bilateral treaties when the anticipated net transaction benefits are positive for both ratifying parties at the time of signing. Bilateral treaties involve transaction costs for administration, communications, enforcement, and monitoring; all of which can hamper treaty formation and adherence. Monitoring can be extremely difficult and costly in such treaties especially if the two countries signing the treaty have been at war on a number of occasions. Yet each party must monitor the other in order to guard against treaty violations. Even after detecting a violation, the cost of enforcement is generally high and often uncertain and could even lead to another conflict. Yet bilateral treaties are a good method of conflict prevention or use of certain weapon systems in the eventuality of a conflict.

On 31 Dec 1988, India and Pakistan signed a Non-Attack Agreement which came into force from 01 Jan 1991. As per the agreement, both India and Pakistan pledged that "Works or installations containing dangerous forces, namely dams, dykes and nuclear electrical generating stations, shall not be made the object of attack, even where these objects are military objectives, if such attack may cause the release of dangerous forces and consequent severe losses among the civilian population".[13] Similar agreements exist between a numbers of other nations too. Both the nations since then have respected the treaty and have abided by it. Despite the state of present relationship between India and Pakistan, it is expected that both nations in future too will abide by the treaty. If two nations who have gone to war four times can work out modalities for not physically attacking each other's critical nuclear infrastructure, why cannot such treaties be worked out for the cyberspace too?

In the absence of an international law governing use of cyberspace for waging a war, nations need to work on bilateral treaties to prevent cyberspace from threatening national security. National governments often cooperate with each other informally by exchanging information, investigating attacks or crimes, preventing or stopping harmful conduct, providing evidence, and even arranging for the rendition of individuals to a requesting state. However, there are still no formal agreements between any two nations which would prevent them from attacking each other's CII using the cyberspace.

Though cyberspace is global and a cyberattack knows no boundaries, yet more often than not, it is a long-established adversary who is likely to target your assets through the cyber domain, especially the CII. In the eventuality of a war, the probability of such attacks from the enemy is even

13 India-Pakistan Non-Attack Agreement as available at http://www.nti.org/treaties-and-regimes/india-pakistan-non-attack-agreement/

higher. In such circumstances, a mutual "Cyber Non Attack Agreement" will be advantageous. Let us examine this in a little detail.

A Cyber Non Attack Agreement could be specifically aimed to prevent CII of the nation from coming under cyberattacks. Any CII whose disruption or destruction could result in damage or loss of public property or life needs to be covered under such a treaty. Though the number of operators in cyberspace who pose a threat to the CII is large, yet such an agreement between two nation states would be beneficial. The treaty may not be able to prevent non-state actors and cyber terrorists from targeting CII, yet a major threat to CII which emanates from the nation state itself, especially in an eventuality of war will be eliminated.

What could be the framework of such an agreement? Any Cyber Non Attack Agreement between two countries should include the following:

(a) A commitment that the two nations agree not to use cyberspace to attack each other's CII. Both the nations would need to exchange a list of such CII. The list will need to be updated every time any new infrastructure is added.

(b) In case one of the two nations resorts to such an act, the matter would be investigated though joint working group consisting of members of both the nations. If proved that the attack on CII was initiated by the opposing nation or originated from its soil, the act could be then considered as use of force. The other nation will be at liberty to retaliate with force. This will provide the aspect of deterrence to the treaty.

(c) Both countries will give a commitment that they will not resort to a proxy cyberwar on each other by employing non-state actors or using a third state as a proxy.

(d) A commitment that both the nations will not resort to cyber espionage against each other's CII.

(e) Hold routine dialogue with each other to ensure maintenance of a free cyberspace.

There may still exist the issues of attribution of a cyberattack to its perpetrator and how to determine whether the damage caused by the attack was proportionate to the retaliatory action taken by the other nation. Hence, before finalising any such bilateral treaty, the two nations will need to work out the details of determining the attribution. Also, developing the trust that the other signatory will abide by the treaty is not easy to come by. Yet, a bilateral Cyber Non Attack Agreement in the present circumstances appears to be a good solution to ensure safety of CII from attacks through the cyberspace.

For a nation like the USA, such bilateral treaty though may not be the best solution. Being amongst the most networked States, USA faces a threat to its CII from a host of sources. China, Russia, North Korea, Al-Qaeda and ISIS, everyone seems to be targeting CII of USA. In such circumstances, a Cyber Non Attack Agreement for the US could imply that a powerful nation like the US signs such an agreement with a number of small nations or even rogue elements. This may neither be acceptable to the US nor beneficial. But for a nation like India, which is still on its way to networking and automation, such a bilateral treaty with countries like Pakistan and China may be advantageous.

A first ever bilateral treaty on non-aggression pledge in cyber warfare has been signed between Russia and China as reported by the media in May 2015.[14] The foundation for this treaty was laid in November 2014 when the Russian President was in Beijing to attend the APEC Summit. The details of the agreement are still not known. Similarly in 2013, Russia and the US created a new working group, under the auspices of the Bilateral Presidential Commission, dedicated to assessing emerging ICT threats and proposing concrete joint measures to address them.[15] The aim of the working group is to increase transparency and reduce the possibility that a misunderstood cyber incident could create instability or a crisis. Under the provision of the pact, White House and the Kremlin have authorised a direct secure voice communications line between the US Cyber security Coordinator and the Russian Deputy Secretary of the Security Council, should there be a need to directly manage a crisis situation arising from an ICT security incident.

14 China and Russia Grow Even Closer, The Atlantic 10 May 2015 as available at http://www.theatlantic.com/international/archive/2015/05/china-and-russia-grow-even-closer/392882/

15 US and Russia Sign Cyber Security Pact, 18 June 2013, as available at http://www.atlanticcouncil.org/blogs/natosource/us-and-russia-sign-cyber-security-pact

If the Russians, the Americans and the Chinese can work out a methodology to manage cyber security, why cannot India too create such bilateral agreement? It will only result in a more safe and secure cyberspace in the region.

Efforts at the National Level

India is ranked amongst the top ten powerful nations of the world. As per the National Power Index ranking of 2012, India is the eight most powerful nation, ahead of Canada and Israel.[16] Be it economic power or conventional military power, India in the last decade has grown by leaps and bounds. The BJP led Government in the Center is taking big initiatives to usher in the digital era in all spheres of governance in the Country. The Modi Mantra of IT + IT = IT (Information Technology plus India's Talent = India's Tomorrow) is creating a new wave of progress using IT as a basic infrastructure for national development. It is therefore essential that the correct environment is created in the Country where in the cyberspace is shielded from any kind of threat both during peace as well as war.

For ensuring the above, the efforts at the national level need to be focused on the following two aspects:

(a) Formulation of a National Strategy on cyber warfare. This will include a strategy on cyber security to make our systems secure and a cyber warfare doctrine which will lay down the offensive and defensive cyber capabilities that the nation needs to build.

(b) Based on the national strategy and the doctrine, creation of organisations at the national level as well as for the armed forces to undertake cyber warfare,

While formulation of the strategy may be a simple task, its implementation will need budget not only to create such a force but also to maintain and train it. Allocation of funds for the task of cyber warfare may therefore prove to be a limiting factor in India. Let us delve into each of these aspects in a little greater detail.

16 Top Ten Most Powerful Countries in the World as available at http://www.mapsofworld.com/world-top-ten/world-top-ten-powerful-countries-map.html

Formulation of a National Strategy on Cyber Warfare

The starting point of a strategy has to be a threat. Without a threat – real or perceived, there is no need for a strategy. In the previous chapters we have analysed the threat in great amount of detail. It is time now to see what should be our national strategy to negate this threat. The national strategy on cyber warfare should ideally provide a framework which is essential to protect our critical infrastructure and other national and military assets and lay down a response policy in the eventuality of the above being attacked by an adversary. To a large extent, framework for protection of the CII has been created by the National Cyber Security Policy (NCSP) 2013. Let us therefore first see what are the strategies recommended by the NCSP–2103 to counter the security threats from the cyberspace:- [17]

#1: Creating a Secure Cyber Ecosystem. This aspect has been dealt with in great detail in Chapter 4. By creating a secure cyber ecosystem in the Country, we will provide inherent security to our networks and systems dependent on cyberspace.

#2: Creating an Assurance Framework. An assurance framework provides organisations with a simple but comprehensive method for the effective and focused management of the principal risks to meeting their objectives. NCSP–2103 recommends adoption of global best practices, implementation of global security best practices in formal risk assessment and risk management and creation of a process of verification of compliance to best practices, standards and guidelines.

#3: Encouraging Open Standards. Open standards are required to be adopted to facilitate interoperability and exchange of data among different products and services. However, only tested and certified IT products based on open standards should be encouraged.

#4: Strengthening the Regulatory Framework. As there exists no international treaty to regulate cyberattacks, a nation has to therefore deal with them under domestic criminal laws. The commitment of a nation to ensure a secure cyber ecosystem can be gauged by the legal framework that the country has in place. The legal framework must be reviewed from time to time to cater

17 National Cyber Security policy – 2013, section IV, Strategies

to advancement in technologies and must mandate periodic audits for the CII providers. The IT act 2000 in India was last reviewed in 2008. Despite the review, the Act still has a number of shortcomings. Firstly, it deals more with e-commerce and less with cyber crime. Secondly, it is completely silent about cyber warfare. It is time to once again have a relook at the IT act.

#5: **Creating Mechanism for Security Threat Early Warning, Vulnerability Management and Response to Security Threats.** Timely detection of a cyber threat is very essential for its mitigation. Early detection will also ensure that the extent of damage is curtailed. Hence, India needs to develop a national level system, processes, structures and mechanisms to generate timely situational awareness of cyber threats. Once the situation has been assessed, it can then be handed over to the concerned CERT to neutralise the threat. India must implement a cyber crisis management plan for dealing with cyber related incidents impacting critical national processes or endangering public safety and security of the nation by way of well coordinated multi disciplinary approach at the national, sectoral as well as entity levels. A very essential part of this would be conducting regular cyber security drill and mock exercises at various levels, none of which is being done as on date.

#6: **Securing E-Governance Services.** To reduce the risk of disruptions and to improve the overall security posture of various e-governance services, it is essential to implement global best practices. For trusted communication and transactions within the government, NCSP recommends wider usage of Public Key Infrastructure (PKI) which is an asymmetric form of encryption. PKI supports the distribution and identification of public encryption keys, enabling users and computers to both securely exchange data over networks such as the Internet and verify the identity of the other party.

#7: **Protection and Resilience of CII.** This is perhaps the most important strategy amongst the 12 strategies spelt out by the NCSP 2013 and was discussed at length in Chapter 4.

#8: **Promotion of Research and Development in Cyber Security.** Unless there is adequate amount of R&D which is carried out in the country itself, we will never be self sufficient in securing our cyberspace. The R&D has to address all aspects of development aimed at short term, midterm and long term goals. Some of the problem areas which need detailed R&D in the field of cyber security are as under:-[18]

(a) **Scalable Trustworthy Systems:** Scalability is the ability to satisfy given requirements as systems, networks, and system of systems expand in functionality, capacity, complexity, and scope of trustworthiness requirements security, reliability, survivability, and improved real-time performance. Critical systems and their operating environments must be trustworthy despite a very wide range of adversities and adversaries. Large organisations in all sectors, for example, government, military, commercial, financial, and energy, suffer the consequences of using large-scale computing systems whose trustworthiness either is not assured or is potentially compromised because of costs that outweigh the perceived benefits. Hence this is the most important area for R&D.

(b) **System Evaluation Life Cycle:** Systematic, realistic, easy-to-use and standardised evaluation methods are needed to objectively quantify performance of any security artifacts and the security of environments where these artifacts are to be deployed, before and after deployment, as well as the performance of proposed solutions. Through R&D one needs to develop cost-effective methods to specify security features for succeeding life cycle phases, develop adversarial assessment techniques that identify and test for abnormal or unintended operating conditions that may cause exploitable vulnerabilities and perform speedy reevaluations of successive versions resulting from changes in requirements, designs, implementation, and experience gained from uses of system applications.

(c) **Combating Insider Threats**: Cyber security measures are often focused on threats from outside an organisation, rather than threats posed by untrustworthy individuals inside an organisation. R&D in this field will help in collection and

18 A Roadmap for Cybersecurity Research https://www.dhs.gov/sites/default/files/publications/CSD-DHS-Cybersecurity-Roadmap.pdf

analysis of data relating to insider behaviour and insider misuse. Models are needed to represent both normal and abnormal insider activities and methodologies are needed for measuring and comparing techniques and tools meant to handle insider threats. Anti-tamper technologies are needed for situations where insiders have physical access to systems and mechanisms are needed that exhaustively describe and enforce the privileges that a user is actually granted. The two aspects of the threat are Detect and Protect. Through effective R&D, organisations need to develop applications of cryptography that might limit insider threats and also develop insider prediction techniques for users, agents, and actions. Combating insider threats perhaps would be the toughest area of R&D for cyber security.

(d) **Combating Malware and Botnets**: Considerable R&D is happening around the world in malware detection, capture, analysis, and defence, both by the private sector as well as the public sector undertakings. Current research initiatives however do not adequately address the increasing sophistication and stealth of malware, including the encryption and packing of the malicious code itself, as well as encrypted command and control channels and fast-flux DNS for botnets. Broadly speaking, any R&D should understand the agility and polymorphism of malware. Automatic detection of the command and control structure of a malware sample is a significant challenge. The focus of the R&D should be on techniques to capture and analyse malware and propagate defences faster in order to contain epidemics.

(e) **Global Scale Identity Management**: Global-scale identity management concerns identifying and authenticating entities such as people, hardware devices, distributed sensors and actuators, and software applications when accessing critical IT systems from anywhere. Two categories need R&D identity and attribute management, namely:

(i) Mechanisms e.g., for authentication, attribution, accountability, revocation, federation, usable user interfaces, user-accessible conceptual models, presentation, and evaluations thereof.

(ii) Policy-related research e.g., privacy, administration, revocation policies, international implications, economic, social and cultural mores, and policies relating to the effective use of the above mechanisms.

(f) **Survivability of Time-Critical Systems**: Time-critical systems are systems that require response on nonhuman timescales to maintain survivability under relevant adversities. With respect to survivability, a time-critical system is a system for which faster-than-human reaction is required to avoid adverse mission consequences and/or system instability in the presence of attacks, failures, or accidents. Military command and control systems and electric grid systems for smart grids are the most time critical systems. Through R&D we need to develop architectures with scalable and composable components that can satisfy critical trustworthiness requirements for real-time system behaviour. Also, we need to have sophisticated and reliable detection methods with self-healing systems to restore time-critical system properties.

(g) **Situational Understanding and Attack Attribution**: Attack attribution is determining the identity or location of an attacker or an attacker's intermediary. Accurate attribution supports improved situational understanding and is therefore a key element of research. Though with the present architecture of the internet, it may not be possible to correctly attribute an attack, yet through R&D we can ensure better situational understanding thereby resulting in better handling of the situation.

(h) Research in attack detection has continued along the path of faster signature development and propagation, seeking to reduce the time window in which zero day attacks have an impact. Egress filtering is increasingly used to identify internal assets that may be currently compromised. Scalable information processing, data mining, statistical analysis, and other similar techniques are applied to situational understanding. There remain significant gaps in the intrusion detection field, and currently deployed intrusion detection systems (IDS) fall short of needs. Extensive continued research would be needed to ensure accurate situational awareness and methodology for attack attribution.

As part of the strategy, the Government proposes to set up centres of excellence in areas of strategic importance of the cyberspace.

#9: Reducing Supply Chain Risks. Many networks have been compromised because of the supply chain vulnerabilities. NCSP 2013 talks about creation of testing infrastructure and facilities where supply chain risks can be detected. It also focuses on building trusted relationships with product/ system vendors and service providers for improving end to end supply chain security visibility. Another important aspect of supply chain risks is creation of awareness of threats. For most of us, cyber security means network and data protection, intrusion detection, firewalls, secure network design, secure and trained workforce, social engineering, and other security activities. We never even consider that the hardware we use could be compromised. Supply chain flaws can be difficult to detect since they are usually masked by the proper functioning of the device.

#10: Human Resource Development. If human resource doesn't get involved in strategies to combat cyber security, any initiative of the nation/ organisation will not work properly. The nation has to develop and maintain a large pool of manpower who can be employed in various fields of cyber security. To achieve this goal, we need to start educational and training programs both in formal and informal sectors, establish cyber security training infrastructure across the country by way of public–private partnership and establish cyber security concept labs for awareness and skill development in key areas. NCSP talks of 500,000 strong professional workforce which will form the core of the cyber security tasks in the Country.

#11: Creating Cyber Security Awareness. It is people, not high technology software solutions that are at the heart of the success of any cyber security programme. The nation has to be made aware that the risk of a cyberwar is real and not science fiction. India needs to launch a comprehensive national awareness programme on security of cyberspace by using electronic media. Adequate number of awareness workshops, seminars and certification courses need to be conducted both by governmental and non-governmental organisations to create awareness in the general public.

Cyber security awareness in India is still at the infancy stage and this aspect has still not been taken up seriously by the government. There is no formal organised effort by any government agency to create awareness amongst general public. In the US, a National Cyber Security Awareness Month is observed every year which is designed to engage and educate public and private sector partners through events and initiatives with the goal of raising awareness about cyber security and increasing the resiliency of the nation in the event of a cyber incident.[19] National Cyber Security Awareness Month takes place in October every year and is sponsored by the Department of Homeland Security in cooperation with the National Cyber Security Alliance and the Multi-State Information Sharing and Analysis Center. India too needs to start a programme like this so that public awareness can be slowly created. Government agencies and private players need to take up this issue as a social responsibility.

#12: Developing Effective Public-Private Partnership. The best way to combat cyberattacks is by joint public-private partnership between government and business. Enough studies have been carried around the world to determine what methods of public-private sector collaboration have been more successful than the traditional models of governance, and what roles can, and should, different parts of the government agencies play in a comprehensive cyber security strategy? NCSP – 2103 talks of the government facilitating collaboration and cooperation among stakeholder entities including private sector, in the area of cyber security in general and CII in particular for actions related to cyber threats, vulnerabilities, breaches, potential protective measures and adoption of best practices. The policy also mentions about creating

19 National Cyber Security Awareness Month as available at http://www.dhs.gov/national-cyber-security-awareness-month

a think tank for cyber security policy inputs, discussions and deliberations.

#13: Information Sharing and Cooperation. The aspect of information sharing and cooperation has already been discussed in detail in the previous chapters. The importance of cooperation and sharing of information can be gauged by the fact the President of the USA, Mr. Barak Obama while addressing the CEOs of financial services in Feb 2015 admitted that the US Government alone cannot ensure cyber security. Nor can the private sector do it alone.[20] The President stressed that the private sector needs to share more information more quickly both with each other and with his administration. If a nation like the USA lays so much of emphasis on information sharing, we too must take a cue from it and organise the government and the private sector for better information sharing.

The above thirteen strategies pave the path for ensuring cyber security at the national level and protection of critical infrastructure. What now needs to be done by the government is to implement the policy and make it fully operational at all levels, i.e. national, sectoral, state, ministry, department and enterprise as may be appropriate to address the challenges of cyber security. The key to success of this policy lies in its effective implementation. Though a number of academicians have pointed out certain flaws in the NCSP, yet it needs to be implemented. Whatever flaws that come to light post its implementation can then be taken care of by tweaking the strategies.

Creating a Cyber Warfare Doctrine

Despite having laid down strategy at the national level for ensuring cyber security and having put it into action, cyberattacks will still continue to occur. They will still target the CII and financial institutions of our nation during peace and all possible kinds of military and non-military targets in case of a war. Hence there is a need to lay down a cyberwar doctrine which will guide our response to such attacks both during peace and war. It should cover all aspects of cyber warfare like cyber deterrence, defensive cyber operation capabilities and certainly the offensive capabilities that

20 Obama at Stanford: Industry, government must cooperate on cybersecurity as available at http://news.stanford.edu/news/2015/february/summit-main-obama-021315.html

India needs to develop to retaliate to a massive cyber offensive by our adversaries.

A military doctrine is the expression of how military forces contribute to campaigns, major operations, battles, and engagements. It is a guide to action, rather than hard and fast rules. Doctrine provides a common frame of reference across the military. It helps standardise operations, facilitating readiness by establishing common ways of accomplishing military tasks. In October 2004, Indian Army for the first time ever came out with a doctrine paper. Though the Indian Army never itself put into practice the said doctrine and post Operation Parakram, the so called 'Cold Start Strategy' is often now termed as the unofficial doctrine for the Indian armed forces, yet the doctrine of 2004 continues to be the official doctrine of the India Army. Lessons learnt from Operation Parakram may perhaps get included in the next edition of the doctrine. The illustration below, taken from the Indian Army Doctrine, depicts the inputs that traditionally contribute to the formulation of a military doctrine and outputs that flow from its enunciation:[21]

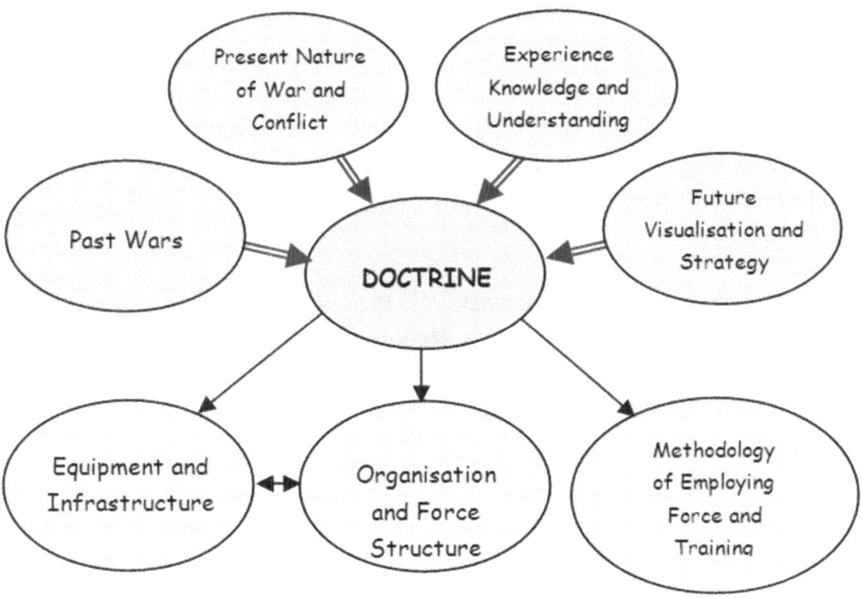

Figure 27: Indian Army Doctrine

21 Indian Army Doctrine, First edition, October 2004, P4

The very nature of conflict has changed over the last century and war has evolved as more violent and more destructive in the past few years. Asymmetric warfare capabilities have emerged as forms of war fighting for nations who are not able to match-up to the might of the powerful countries. This form of warfare therefore needs to be taken into account while planning any future war strategy. The figure above too takes into account future visualisation of war and strategy. If that be so, cyber warfare too will form part of any conflict that our nation is pulled into in the future. Any doctrine of the Indian Army for future war will have to include cyber warfare capabilities. But cyberattacks do not take place only during war. The CII of the nation is being attacked all the time and the country needs to respond to these attacks even when we are not in a state of war. Therefore there may be a need to lay down a doctrine which is not just a pure cyberwar doctrine for the military but a cyberwar doctrine for the nation.

If one analyses how cyberattacks have been handled by nations, it would emerge that there were no fixed responses to the way a nation reacted. The way Georgia negated the impact of massive DDoS attacks in 2008 was very different from the way Estonia handled a similar situation in 2007. What stands out clearly is that most modern nations lack a grand strategy for handling cyberattacks, one that gathers and coordinates their national resources for shared security and prosperity. In such circumstances it is essential that India develops a Cyber Warfare Doctrine (CWD) that includes all stakeholders, brings about a decisive conclusion when such attacks occur, and serves to deter future conflicts through a unified national security policy.

Developing a comprehensive CWD though is a complex task requiring much preparation. It will require both civilian and military establishments to come together towards securing their national infrastructure and preparing for war in the cyber realm. Unfortunately, these efforts in India are happening in a piecemeal manner. The planning components of both civilian and military interests are separate and disjointed, regardless of provisions that both sides believe will create synergistic outcomes. This is because handling conflicts originating in cyberspace needs a true systems approach to cross many jurisdictional boundaries and interests.

Establishing a CWD is the first step in determining how a country needs to respond when attacked via cyberspace. A CWD in principle represents a set of rules and standards for governing a war involving cyberspace. The term war here is not to be confused with a military conflict. As analysed in earlier chapters, a nation can be in a constant state of cyberwar. It is just that the intensity of the war varies. So how does a nation go about drafting a Cyberwar Doctrine? In their article 'Establishing Cyber Warfare Doctrine', Andrew Colarik and Lech Janczewski state that to form a CWD, the dominant doctrines governing people's lives must be examined[22]. According to them, there are three dominant doctrines that will govern the framework of a nation's CWD, namely:

(a) Political Doctrine.

(b) Legal Doctrine.

(c) Military Doctrine

As on date India does not have a political and a legal doctrine. Its military doctrine too is of 2004 era and needs to be reviewed as the security scenario in this part of the world has changed immensely. Does this mean that in absence of the above three factors, India cannot possess a cyberwar doctrine? We can. Like we have a nuclear doctrine which we promulgated in 2003, similarly we need to work out a cyberwar doctrine which will lay down the framework of how we conduct defensive and offensive cyber operations in future. Some of the aspects which the CWD needs to cover in great detail are as under:

Defining Cyberwar: The starting point of the doctrine has to be what India considers as cyberwar. A large number of countries and organisations have defined cyber warfare in different manner. India still has not defined what she considers as cyberwar. Unless we clearly specify what actions of our adversaries will we be considered as waging a war through the cyberspace, we will never be able to lay down the CWD.

Threshold of Cyberwar: Merely defining cyberwar is not enough. The doctrine needs to clearly lay down what action of the adversaries will be considered as an act of cyberwar and what action will be below the threshold of war. Will an attack on Mumbai stock exchange by Pakistan based hackers be an act of cyberwar or will tripping of national power grid by hackers based in China be an act of cyberwar? Different countries may

22 Establishing Cyber Warfare Doctrine by Andrew M. Colarik and Lech Janczewski D.Eng as available at http://scholarcommons.usf.edu/cgi/viewcontent.cgi?article=1123&context=jss

have different level of tolerance and therefore what each nation considers as an act of cyberwar will also be different. The threshold of tolerance and resilience of our networks will decide the acts in cyber domain which we will term as part of war time activities.

No First Use: A posture of "No First Use" forms part of our nuclear doctrine. Similarly the doctrine can postulate cyber weapons only be used in retaliation against a cyberattack on Indian territory or on Indian forces anywhere. This will ensure that India does not get branded as a rogue cyber nation, ever willing to undertake attacks through the cyberspace.

Cyber Retaliation: Having decided upon the threshold of cyber war and 'no first use' of cyber weapons, the next most important aspect which the doctrine needs to lay down is the retaliation to a first strike. Any response to a first use of cyber weapons against the nation has to be massive and designed to inflict unacceptable damage. It is only when such retaliation will inflict unacceptable damage on the adversary, will the adversary be deterred from undertaking a first strike.

Offensive Cyber Capabilities: Whenever we discuss cyberwar, we talk only of cyber defence and protection of our CII. Very seldom does any nation talk of its offensive cyber warfare capabilities. But unless we build and maintain an offensive cyber force how will we as a nation retaliate to cyberattacks? Full transparency about the nation's capability for obvious reasons will remain impossible, yet the nation must develop offensive cyber capabilities for a response which is proportional and within the laws of war.

Deterrence: The aspect of cyber deterrence has been discussed at length in Chapter 5. Though cyber deterrence may not always be credible, yet it may be able to prevent an all out cyberwar. Hence, the doctrine needs to lay down the kind of cyber deterrence capabilities that the nation needs to develop.

Continued Commitment to Fighting Cyber Crime and Cyber Terrorism. Though this aspect will form part of the national cyber strategy, yet the doctrine needs to lay down clearly the intent of the nation in its continued commitment to fighting cyber crime and cyber terrorism. Within the country, what measures need to be taken to safeguard cyberspace and ensure that cyber weapons do not fall into the hands of such elements that can then hold the nation to ransom.

Creation of an Organisation for Cyber Warfare

Implementation of the National Cyber Security Policy along with the National Policy on Electronics 2012, the National Telecom Policy 2012 and formulation of a National Cyber Doctrine are some of the steps which reflect on the will of the nation for ensuring safe cyberspace. Once all the policies are put in place, the next logical step is to create organisations in the country that would be responsible for ensuring security of cyberspace and countering the threat of a cyberwar.

A well structured organisation with clearly laid out mandate and well defined role and tasks is like a well-oiled machine. It works at optimum efficiency all the time and is capable of rising to peak efficiency during hours of emergency. Before recommending such a task force at the national level, let us first examine which all agencies exist as on date with their mandates and how are they organised to fulfill their tasks. Some of these organisations that are responsible for intelligence gathering, development of cyber infrastructure and cyber security in the country are as under:

Organisations at the National Level

National Intelligence Board (NIB):[23] The NIB was constituted in August 2002 for national level policy formulation on information warfare and information security as well as for the creation of the required institutions and structures for implementation of the policies developed. It is chaired by the NSA with a number of members.

Strategic Security Technology Coordination Group (SSTCG):[24] Set up in 2012, the task of the SSTCG is to look into all security related areas including counter-terrorism, border and internal security, aviation and ports security, intelligence network, and coordinate with various departments and agencies concerned. The 10-member group is headed by Joint Secretary in the Ministry of Home Affairs and the group was given freedom to co-opt any other expert based on his/her special knowledge of the subject.

23 Press release after CCS meeting, 11 May 2001

24 High-level group to boost security preparedness, *The Hindu* 17 July 2012

Multi Agency Centre (MAC):[25] Based on the recommendations of Kargil Review Committee and Group of Ministers (GoM) to review the National Security Apparatus, a MAC was set up at Delhi in 2002 and Subsidiary Multi Agency Centres (SMACs) in various states comprising representatives from various security agencies, for streamlining intelligence efforts. MAC is a multi-agency centre for Counter Terrorism whose mandate is to share terrorism related inputs on a day-to-day basis including cyber terrorism.

Joint Cipher Bureau:[26] The inter-services Joint Cipher Bureau has primary responsibility for cryptology and SIGINT, providing coordination and direction to the other military service organisations with similar mission.

Telecom Security Regulatory Authority of India: In 2011, the Government had proposed for the establishment of Telecom Security Regulatory Authority of India (TSRAI). Has the organisation been created or not is not known.

Telecom Security Council of India:[27] DoT had in 2011 suggested the creation of the Telecoms Security Council of India (TSCI) that would look into security related aspects of hardware and network equipments. This was a good step as India's dependence upon foreign players for its cyber security and telecom security is not conducive for telecom growth in India.

The National Intelligence Grid (NATGRID):[28] NATGRID, an attached office of the Ministry of Home Affairs, has been conceived to develop a cutting edge framework to enhance India's counter-terror capabilities. It commenced its operations in 2014. As per the CEO of NATGRID, 21 data sources of various intelligence and enforcement agencies have been brought on board to put together a better picture of an incident.

Crime and Criminal Tracking Network System (CCTNS):[29] The goals of the system are to facilitate collection, storage, retrieval, analysis, transfer

25 Multi Agency Centre as available at http://cbi.nic.in/mac/mac.php

26 Joint Cipher Bureau as available at http://www.globalsecurity.org/intell/world/india/jcb.htm

27 Telecom Security Council of India, as available at http://cjnewsind.blogspot.in/2011/03/telecom-security-council-of-india.html

28 About NATGRID as available at http://nisg.org/natgrid-vacancies

29 Crime and Criminal Tracking Network System as available at http://ncrb.gov.in/cctns.htm

and sharing of data and information at the police stations and between the police stations, the State Headquarters and the Central Police Organisations.

The National Counterterrorism Center (NCTC):[30] NCTC is a center for joint operational planning and joint intelligence, staffed by personnel from the various agencies.

Telecom Testing and Security Certification Centre (TTSCC):[31] The task of TTSCC is to create a security testing framework to ensure that telecom service providers only induct 'safe to network' elements, as part of the telecom Security Policy.

Indian Computer Emergency Response Team (CERT-In):[32] CERT-In is mandated to enhance the security of India's communications and information infrastructure through proactive actions and effective collaboration.

National Informatics Centre (NIC):[33] Established in 1976, NIC is responsible for setting up of ICT Infrastructure, implementation of national and state level e-governance projects and research and development.

National Technical Research Organisation (NTRO):[34] The NTRO is a highly specialised technical intelligence gathering agency under the R&AW. The organisation does hi-tech surveillance jobs, including satellite monitoring, terrestrial monitoring and internet monitoring considered vital for the national security apparatus.

Cyber Regulations Advisory Committee:[35] Established under the IT Act 2000, the Cyber Regulations Advisory Committee is responsible to advice

30 The National Counterterrorism Center as available at http://www.nctc.gov/overview.html

31 CCS nod for Telecom Testing and Security Certification Centre as available at http://www.business-standard.com/article/economy-policy/ccs-nod-for-telecom-testing-and-security-certification-centre-113021101330_1.html

32 As available at http://india.gov.in/official-website-indian-computer-emergency-response-team

33 As available at http://www.nic.in/about-us

34 NTRO as available at http://en.wikipedia.org/wiki/National_Technical_Research_Organisation

35 Cyber Regulations Advisory Committee as available at http://www.naavi.org/cl_editorial/ edit_18aug00_1.html

the Central Government either generally with regards to any rules or for any other purpose connected with this Act.

National Cyber Coordination Centre (NCCC):[36] NCCC is a proposed cyber security and e-surveillance agency in India. It is intended to screen communication metadata and co-ordinate the intelligence gathering activities of other agencies. It received an in-principle approval from the cabinet committee of security in May 2013.

Central Monitoring System[37]: It is a clandestine mass electronic surveillance data mining program installed by the Centre for Development of Telematics (C-DOT) and operated by Telecom Enforcement Resource and Monitoring (TERM) Cells. It has the ability to listen-in on and record mobile, landline satellite calls and VoIP calls, and read private emails, SMS and MMS and geolocate people via their cell phones all in real time.

National Critical Information Infrastructure Protection Centre: Has been dealt with in detail in Chapter 4.

Listed above are seventeen organisations which are amongst many other governmental bodies responsible for either information gathering and sharing or security of the cyberspace. Besides these, there are organisations at the level of defence forces, public-private partnership organisations and state level organisations, sectoral CERT who carry out similar tasks in their areas of responsibilities. Some of the noteworthy ones are Data Security Council of India (DSCI), Information Sharing and Analysis Centre and state level Cyber Defence Research Centres. As per a rough estimate, there are over fifty organisations in India at various levels dealing with this subject. With so many players in the field, the overall organisation tree would look something like this:

36 As available at http://www.hindustantimes.com/india-news/cyber-protection-body-pushes-ahead/article1-1174753.aspx

37 CMS as available at http://en.wikipedia.org/wiki/Central_Monitoring_System

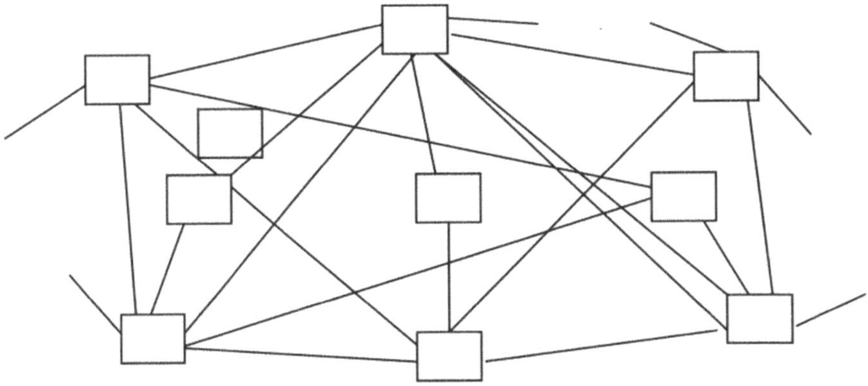

Figure 28: Cyber Organisation Structure at the National Level

National Cyber Command (NCC): It is not that with a structure like above, ensuring secure cyberspace in the nation is not possible. It is, but it becomes a complex task to coordinate between so many agencies. So what would be an ideal organisation for ensuring that the strategies mentioned above are smoothly implemented and the nation gets a safe, secure and incidence free cyberspace? Perhaps a national cyber command could do this job of coordinating all the agencies and ensure a safe and secure cyberspace. Functioning under the PMO directly or even Department of Electronics and Information Technology under Ministry of Communication and Information Technology, the task of the NCC will be to fuse India's full spectrum of cyberspace operations. It will plan, coordinate, integrate, synchronise, and conduct activities for day-to-day defence and protection of India's information networks and coordinate cyberspace operations at the national level. The organisation of the NCC would be something like this:

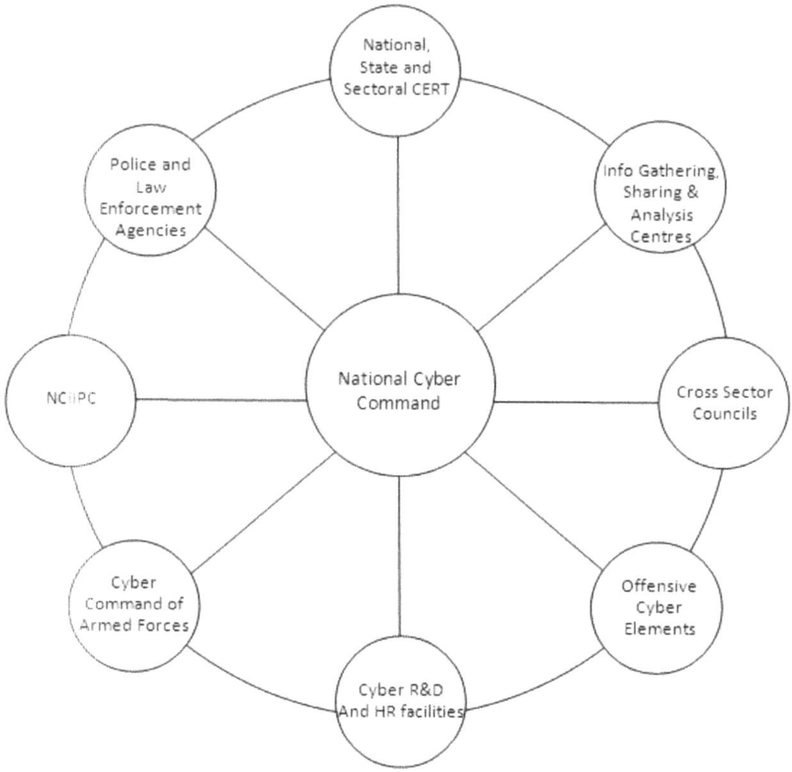

Figure 29: Proposed Cyber Organisation Structure at the National Level

While it may not be possible to put all the above elements under direct control of the NCC, yet it must be able to exercise its jurisdiction over these elements. The National Cyber Command can then be entrusted with the following tasks:

(a) Coordination of all cyber operations at the national level in India. This will include all types of operations i.e. intelligence gathering, defensive cyber mechanism, cyber forensic and offensive cyber operations.

(b) Ensure protection of national assets in the cyberspace. This would include both CII and other assets. While for protecting the public assets, it will exercise direct jurisdiction, for protection of private infrastructure and assets, cross sector councils will play an important role. This aspect was discussed in Chapter 4.

(c) Prepare a national level response to cyber incidents and ensure its implementation when approved by the Government. This will include launching coordinated cyberattacks in response to the cyber misadventure carried out by the adversary.

(d) Policy making. All policies on cyberspace issues should be formulated by one single agency which should be the NCC. It would work out the short, medium and long term policies for cyber security and cyber warfare and ensure their implementation.

(e) Coordinate with critical infrastructure owners/operators and sector specific agencies to reduce risk to the CII from the cyberspace.

(f) Collaborate with state governments and other independent bodies by establishing Information Sharing and Analysis Centers to ensure that all actionable intelligence reaches the place where it is required the most.

(g) Enhance cross-sector cyber security efforts and collaboration by coordinating with all cyber security and communications partners in the Country.

(h) Identify the national resources and capabilities and recommend to the Government of India the steps required to be undertaken to build capacity and enhance the cyber warfare resources.

(i) Cooperating with international partners to share information and respond to incidents.

(j) Disseminating cyber threat and vulnerability analysis information to all concerned.

(k) Assist the stakeholders in recovery and restoration process.

(l) Facilitation of various training and operations exercises to build the collective knowledge base of its partners and test integrated operational processes. By conducting regular exercises, it will ensure the preparedness and response goals established in the National Strategy to secure cyberspace. The exercises will be at international, national, state and sector level.

In effect, NCC will have four distinct tasks, namely: coordination of gathering of intelligence and its dissemination; ensure defence preparedness of cyber assets of the nations from various threats; cyber risk assessment, incidence response & forensic and finally conduct of offensive cyber operations in retaliation to cyberattacks launched against India.

National Budget and Cyber Warfare

Once the national goals and policies are clearly defined, the organisational structure has been decided upon, all that is thereafter needed is the money to convert the dream into a reality. But when it comes to budget allocation in India, unfortunately, cyber security takes a back seat. May it be governmental organisations or private companies; cyber related aspects do not get adequate budget allocations. Here is a comparison:

USA: President Barack Obama's budget proposal for the 2016 fiscal year seeks USD 14 billion (approx 90000 crores Indian rupees) for cyber security efforts across the US Government to better protect federal and private networks from hacking threats.[38] The additional budget was asked for to cater for deployment of more intrusion detection and prevention capabilities, greater sharing of data with the private sector and other countries and more funding to beef up the Government's ability to respond to attacks.

UK: The British Government has allocated a budget of budget of 860 million Pounds for the financial year ending March 2016 and expects to spend the complete money in nation's four pronged national cyber security programme.[39]

South Korea: In light of the numerous cyberattacks launched against the country's systems, South Korea has started taking cyber security seriously. The Government has decided to double its cyber security budget. The South Korean Ministry of Science and Technology says that the Government is prepared to spend 10 trillion Won ($ 8.77 billion) through 2017 on cyber security. For a year, the Government's budget is approximately USD 3

38 Obama seeks $14 billion to boost U.S. cybersecurity defenses as available at http://www.reuters.com/article/2015/02/02/us-usa-budget-cybersecurity-idUSKBN0L61WQ20150202

39 Update on the National Cyber Security Programme as available at http://www.nao.org.uk/wp-content/uploads/2015/09/Update-on-the-National-Cyber-Security-Programme.pdf

billion.

What is the Indian government spending on cyber security? India too has doubled its cyber security budget in the financial year 2014- 15 from the previous year. In 2014-15, the Department of IT had set aside Rs 116 Crore for cyber security.[40] When compared to spending by other countries, this allocation is woefully inadequate. How can a country with the size of India prepare to take on the challenges of the cyberspace with so little money allocated for the task? Rs 116 Crore is not sufficient for taking care of the cyber security needs of the nation. Nothing out of this can be spent on developing offensive cyber capabilities or towards much required R&D for the cyberspace. How will the Country effectively protect its CII from cyber threats is anyone's guess.

There have been some talks in the Country of setting up a National Cyber Coordination Centre (NCCC) with a separate budget of Rs 1,000 Crore, but till date it has not become a reality on ground. The Government is said to have prepared a 250 page note for final approval from the Cabinet Committee on Security (CCS).[41] A news report of 10 April 2015 indicated that the Finance Ministry has approved a budget of Rupees 800 Crore for it and the Prime Minster has asked the Communications and IT Ministry to fast track the establishment of NCCC. [42] CERT-In will be the main agency handling the establishment of NCCC. NCCC is expected to coordinate between intelligence agencies, specifically during network intrusions and cyberattacks. Its mandate may also include cyber intelligence sharing among agencies.

To effectively protect the national assets from cyberattack and to develop a minimum credible offensive cyber capability, the Government of India needs to allocate more funds than the present allocation. The rough division of this budget under various heads should be as under:

---

40 India's cyber-security budget 'woefully inadequate' as available at http://articles.economictimes.indiatimes.com/2015-01-28/news/58546771_1_cyber-security-cert-in-national-cyber-coordination-centre

41 India to spend Rs 950 Cr to guard against Cyber Attacks as available at http://www.ifsecglobal.com/india-spend-rs-950-guard-cyber-attacks/

42 Government clears setting up of National Cyber Coordination Centre as available at http://www.igovernment.in/news/1002950/govt-clears-setting-up-of-national-cyber-coordination-centre

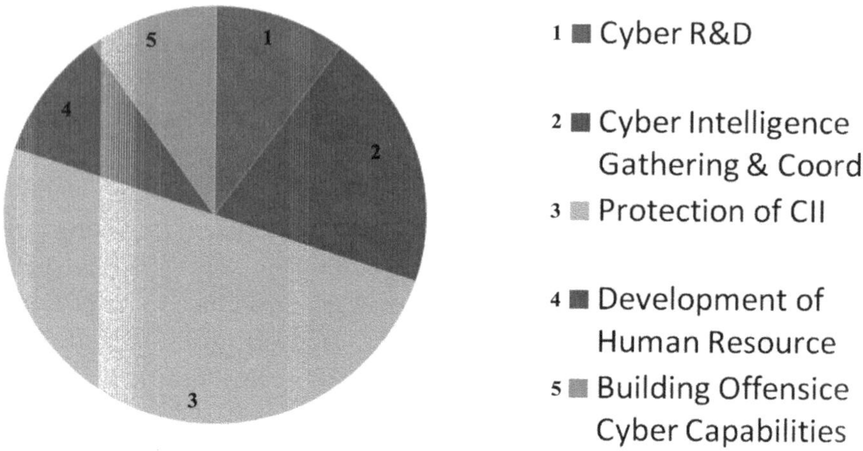

Figure 30: Proposed Division of national Cyber Budget

Protection of CII will include all aspects such as capacity building, risk management and cyber forensic. In other words, all defensive cyber activities would be covered under this head. Though the exact allocation of the budget cannot be spelt out, it needs to be in comparison with what other nations are spending in cyber capacity building and offensive cyber capabilities. The above does not include building up of cyber capabilities of the Armed Forces. That will form part of the defence budget of the Country.

Cyber Warfare and Armed Forces

The Indian Army doctrine under the section "Types of War" had a chapter on Information Warfare. This Chapter also described Cyber Warfare besides other forms of information warfare. The Indian Army way back in 2004 had identified cyber warfare as a means of waging an unconventional war. Despite this, not much effort has gone into developing the capabilities for cyber warfare either by the army or by the other two services.

Strategic cyber warfare targets CII of a nation while operational cyber warfare aims to target battlefield targets. While the former would be undertaken by a strategic force after a clear national mandate has been established and a go ahead has been given by the Government of India, the latter will be undertaken by field force commanders and will form part of any future conflict. It is therefore essential that Armed Forces equip themselves with the knowledge of this form of warfare and also organise themselves for it so that enemy's cyber capabilities do not take us by surprise.

Armed Forces of certain developed nations such as the USA, Russia, NATO, China and Israel are well organised for undertaking cyber warfare both offensive and defensive operations. We may follow any of their models for organising our Armed Forces. Let us therefore study one such organisation, the US cyber command to understand the capabilities of such a force.

The United States Cyber Command (USCYBERCOM) is an armed force subordinate to United States Strategic Command (USSTRATCOM) that is one of the nine Unified Combatant Commands of the US Department of Defense. The mandate of the USCYBERCOM is to fuse the Department's full spectrum of cyberspace operations and plan, coordinate, integrate, synchronise, and conduct activities to: lead day-to-day defense and protection of Department of Defense (DoD) information networks; coordinate DoD operations providing support to military missions; direct the operations and defense of specified DoD information networks and; prepare to, and when directed, conduct full spectrum military cyberspace operations.[43] The command is charged with pulling together existing cyberspace resources, creating synergy that does not currently exist and synchronising war-fighting effects to defend the information security environment. It is said that there are over 6000 personnel both uniformed and civilians who are working under the USCYBERCOM. A large number of them have undergone training at the United States Army Cyber School, Fort Gordon, Georgia. The organisation of the USCYBERCOM is as under:[44]

43 US Army Cyber Command as available at http://www.arcyber.army.mil/org-uscc.html

44 As given out in the article China vs US, cyber superpowers compared as available at http://resources.infosecinstitute.com/china-vs-us-cyber-superpowers-compared/

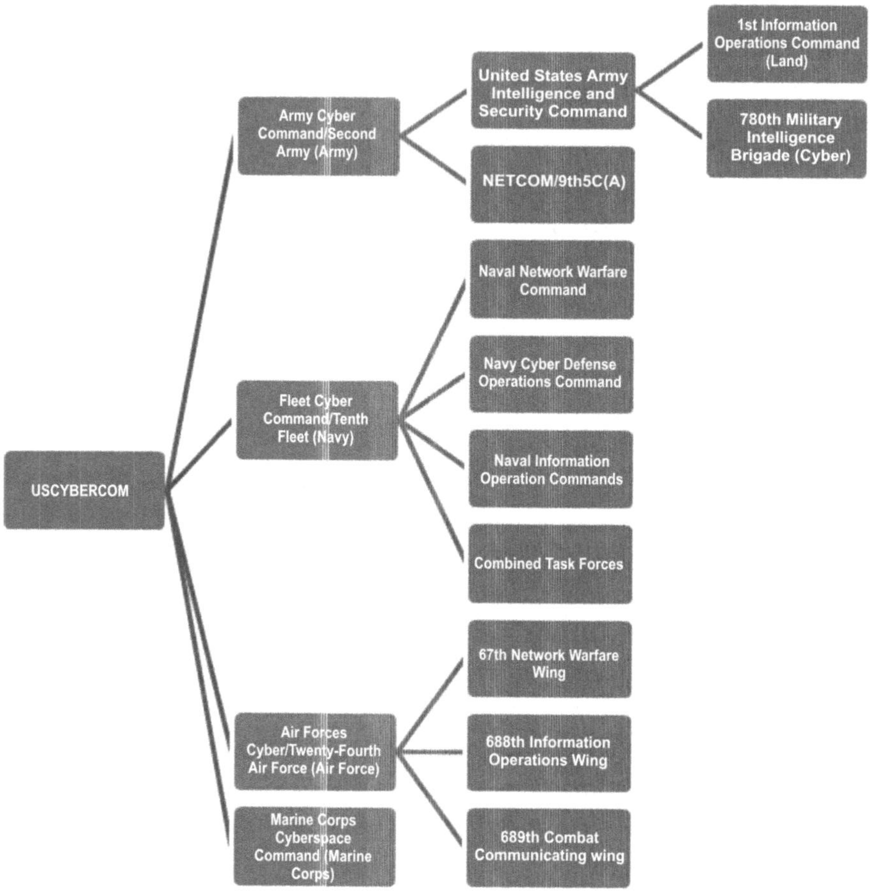

Figure 31: Organisation of the USCYBERCOM

An analysis of the above organisation reveals the following:

(a) Each service of the US Armed Forces including the Marine Corps has a cyber command/ element associated with it.

(b) Intelligence/ information elements too are under each of the service cyber command.

(c) The army cyber command consists of intelligence & security command and the NETCOM/ 9th Army Signal Command. Under the US Army intelligence and security command is the 1st Information Operations Command (Land) which provides multi-disciplinary Information Operations (IO) support to the component and major commands of the United States Army.[45] The 780th Military Intelligence Brigade conducts expeditionary and remote cyber attack, cyber exploitation, and cyber defense operations of US Army and Defense information networks.[46]

(d) The 9th Army Signal Command is the operational executive agent for Army-wide network operations and security. It is the single point of contact for Army network development and protection, providing C4 information management of common-user services in support of the combatant commanders and Army service component commanders. It is the numbered command for the Network Enterprise Technology Command.[47]

In short, the cyber command of each service is responsible for intelligence gathering, coordinating network operations and offensive cyber operations.

The Armed Forces Cyber Command (AFCC)

The structure of the cyber command proposed for the Indian Armed Forces needs to be developed on similar grounds. A suggested organisation is as under:

45 http://en.wikipedia.org/wiki/1st_Information_Operations_Command_(Land)

46 http://en.wikipedia.org/wiki/780th_Military_Intelligence_Brigade_(United_States)

47 http://en.wikipedia.org/wiki/9th_Army_Signal_Command_%28United_States%29

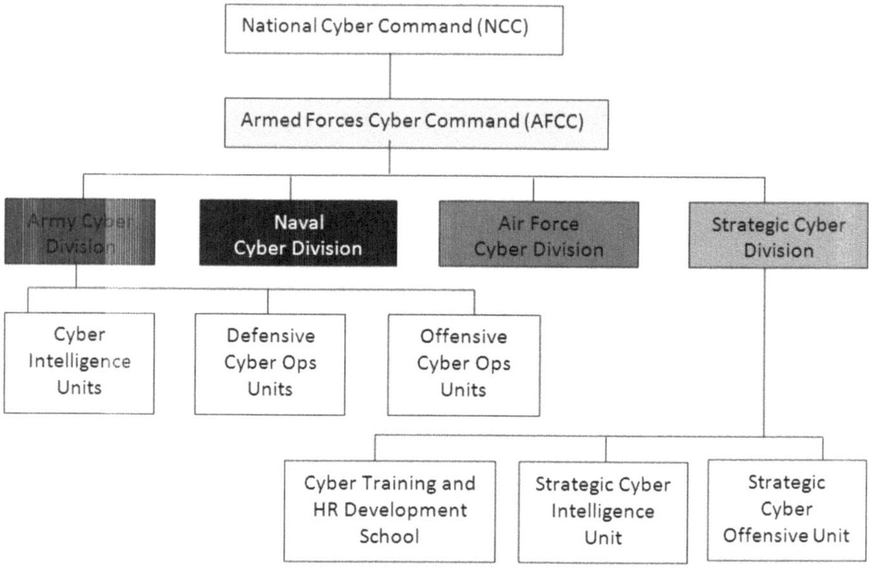

Figure 32: Proposed Organisation of Armed Forces Cyber Command

The Armed Forces Cyber Command (AFCC) will be a tri-services organisation that would function under the National Cyber Command or an equivalent organisation which the government needs to create. AFCC will be responsible for defending the Armed Forces from attack, which may perpetuate through the cyberspace. It will also be the highest coordinating agency for the Armed Forces of the Country for all matters pertaining to cyberspace and its use by the Armed Forces.

Under the AFCC, each of the three services will have an organisation of its own namely Army Cyber Division (ACD), Naval Cyber Division (NCD) and Airforce Cyber Division (AFCD). Besides this, a Strategic Cyber Division (SCD) has been recommended to undertake strategic cyber warfare and training. Coordination between the four elements will be carried out by the AFCC.

The aim of raising the AFCC would be:

(a) Build and maintain a tri-services force with the capabilities to conduct cyberspace operations for the Armed Forces. Such a force will have a mix of regular armed forces personal and professional experts drawn from the civil street. Even the USCYBERCOM follows the same model as this has large number of advantages vis-a-vis a purely uniformed force.

(b) Defend the Armed Forces voice and data networks both during peace and war. Besides protection, it will also be responsible to secure the Armed Forces data, and mitigate risks to its missions.

(c) Offensive Cyber Operations: AFCC should be the only organisation in the Country with offensive cyberwarfare capabilities. This option of offensive cyberwar would be used to control conflict escalation and to shape the conflict environment at all stages. This can happen only when the Armed Forces fully integrate the cyber offensive options with the operational plans. Great amount of synchronisation will be required to achieve this in the battlefield.

(d) Assist other organisations working under the NCC against disruptive or destructive cyberattacks. As has earlier emerged, cyber operations cannot be conducted in isolation. Great amount of coordination and strong partnerships are required to be established to ensure overall security of the cyberspace in the nation. The AFCC will do this task at the highest level.

Army Cyber Division (ASD): The ACD would be responsible for planning, coordination, integration, synchronisation and conduct of all cyber operations for the Army including defensive cyber operations, offensive cyber operation and intelligence gathering and analysis. Based on this, ACD will consist of cyber intelligence units, defensive cyber operation units and offensive cyber operation units. As the names suggest, each unit will be responsible for specific type of cyber operations. Defensive cyber units will be responsible for securing networks, cyber risk assessment and management, cyber forensic and emergency response. Offensive cyber unit would be the offensive arm of the organisation capable of undertaking organised cyberattacks on enemy's military network and degrade them.

A unit each of cyber intelligence, defensive cyber operation and offensive cyber operation could be combined into one composite cyber warfare unit and be authorised to a command or a strike corps. Independent defensive cyber operation unit could also form part of logistic echelons where only the networks need to be protected and no offensive actions are envisaged.

The Navy and Airforce will also have similar organisations as is recommended for the Army.

Strategic Cyber Division: Besides the three services cyber commands, a strategic cyber command is also recommended to be raised for performing the following tasks:

(a) Provide support to the three services by generating integrated cyberspace effects in support of operational plans.

(b) Protection of CII of the Armed Forces such as tri services and strategic forces networks, defence production organisations, networks in the hinterland etc.

(c) Undertake strategic cyber warfare which would include degrading adversary's cyber assets both as a pre-emptive strike as well as in conjunction with the three services during the war.

(d) Training of human resource for all the three services in cyber warfare. At present the three services in India do not have a pool of talent which can be employed for various tasks such as cyber intelligence gathering and cyberattacks. Hence, the aspect of creation of a pool of trained manpower is very essential and will be the key to success of any cyber operations. Even in a nation like the USA, despite having a large pool of trained manpower on cyber jobs, the US Armed Forces are still facing acute shortage of the required talent which could be employed as part of the cyber command.[48]

Before the cyber organisation is raised and its functioning is integrated completely into that of the Armed Forces, a joint doctrine for conducting cyberspace operations is required to be evolved. The joint cyber doctrine for the Armed Forces will flow out of the national cyber warfare doctrine.

Once the AFCC has been created and made fully functional, the existing organisations such as Defence Information Assurance and Research Agency (DIARA) which looks after the cyber security of defence forces and agencies which do not come under the jurisdiction of CERT-In

48 US Cyber Command Has Just Half the Staff It Needs as available at http://www.defenseone.com/threats/2015/02/us-cyber-command-has-just-half-staff-it-needs/104847/

and NTRO and Defence Information Warfare Agency (DIWA) established to handle all aspects of information warfare including psychological ops and cyber war can then be merged within the AFCC. Similarly all intelligence gathering agencies of the Armed Forces which are presently tasked to gather cyber intelligence would also come under the jurisdiction of AFCC. Unless this is done, synchronisation of full spectrum of cyber operations can never happen.

Conclusion

India can find herself at cyberwar in many ways. It could be through deliberate provocation or through escalation. It could be with a nation state, non-state actors acting on behalf of nation state or even cyber terrorist. Whatever is the case, we as a Nation need to organise and equip ourselves for this form of warfare. Our Armed Forces need to be prepared to take on an onslaught of cyberattacks in any future war. Our infrastructure operators need to incorporate cyber security as an embedded layer when creating national assets. Our Government when creating smart cities needs to be aware that these cities could be held hostage to cyberattacks if adequate cyber security measures have not been put into place. A clear national strategy therefore needs to evolve and organisations created to ensure that our cyber frontiers remain safe at all times. It is time we started treating cyberspace as a national asset. An asset which when threatened will threaten our national security.

Conclusion

We have never ever, outside of the defence industry, seen commercial industrial companies come under that level of sophisticated attack. It's totally changing the threat model

– Dmitri Alperovitch, vice president of threat research for McAfee.

The cyberattacks on Estonia in 2007 ushered in a new era in the history of cyberspace. It was for the first time that a full fledged war was waged in the cyberspace. It was a war in which the foot soldiers were called script kiddies — relatively unsophisticated troublemakers who copied programs line for line off hacker Web sites. Their primary weapon was a simple ping attack, a request for a response from a Web server, repeated hundreds of times per second. When deployed by masses of attackers, the pings could overwhelm a server. The attack originated from unsuspecting computers called Botnets all across the globe without the knowledge of their owners. The cyberattacks took the Estonian government and public by complete surprise. The financial systems of the nation which relied heavily on the internet were rendered useless for a long period of time. Even when the banking networks recommenced work, it was not business as usual because a major percentage of the population which used these networks had lost trust in it. It was a kind of situation that the world had neither experienced nor predicted.

Since 2007, cyberwar has been seen in many forms. It accompanied kinetic attacks in Georgia in 2008, sabotaged the nuclear facilities in Iran in 2010 and assisted the Russian troops during the Ukraine crisis in 2015. Today we have reached a stage where our CII and smart cities lie vulnerable to cyber warfare. Public safety can be jeopardised by launching cyberattacks on targets on which we rely very heavily for our day to day functioning. Nations are equipping themselves with cyber weapons to threaten the CII of their adversaries. It is therefore time that we in India also acknowledge its existence and prepare ourselves not only to counter the threat of cyberwar but also to undertake cyberwar if the need arises.

The Chinese Government decided long ago to make control of information a central plank of the country's policy. At the 10th National People's Congress, in 2003, the Chinese army announced the creation of 'information warfare units'. Similarly, Pakistan with active assistance from China is growing its cyberwarfare capabilities. The next war will not be just a kinetic war, it will be a war which will be fought in all the domains, including the cyberspace. It will be a war where, computer networks and standalone systems will collapse, commercial factories and chemical plants will explode, satellites will spin out of control and the financial and power grids will fail.

The connotation of national security is changing. National security today encompasses military security, political security, economic security, environmental security, security of energy and natural resources and cyber security. As is evident from above, the military aspect of security is an important facet of national security, but not the sole component of national security. To be truly secure, a nation needs other forms of security. Only when we as a nation are able to secure all of the above domains, will our people be secure.

India is faced with a large number of challenges in the cyberspace. These range from protection of the CII to countering the threat of supply chain vulnerabilities to our systems to lack of policy and legal framework in the country. We also need to concentrate on development of the human resource and bring in awareness against the threats from cyberspace. While the government needs to play an important part in ensuring the security of cyberspace, the private sector too plays an equally important role in this domain. Hence to be effective, our cyber security framework must be based on a public –private partnership model.

Dependence on cyberspace has today become the defining feature of a modern, interconnected and knowledge based society and economy. Being a high tech country in a volatile environment, India faces a different reality than most of the developed world. A large part of our nation is coping with problems of terrorism, left wing extremism and communal violence. If radical elements take the cyber route to spread terror, they could cause high degree of damage to the delicate framework of the country which could impact our national security.

The challenges in the cyberspace are innumerable. There is no avoiding the security implications emerging at the intersection of cyber space and critical infrastructure. India therefore needs to quickly workout an action plan on how to counter these threats and ensure its implementation. Unless we do this on top priority, our systems will continue to remain vulnerable to cyber threats and our national security will continue to be threatened from the cyberspace.

Bibliography

Books

1. Cyber War by Richard A Clarke
2. Cyber war will not take place by Thomas Rid
3. Cyber infrastructure protection edited by Tarek Saadwi and Louis Jordan Jr
4. Cyber warfare and the Laws of war by Heather Harrison Dinniss
5. Inside Cyber Warfare by Jeffery Carr
6. Cyber Warfare: Techniques, Tactics and Tools for Security Practitioners by Jason Andress and Steve Winterfeld
7. Surviving Cyberwar by Richard Stienno
8. Cyber Warfare: power of the unseen by M K Sharma
9. Characterizing Cyberspace: Past, Present and Future by David Clark
10. On Cyberwarfare by Fred Schreier
11. Comprehensive National Power A Model For India, P K Singh, Y K Gera and Sandeep Dewan

Policy Documents, Reports and White Papers

12. National Cyber Security Policy - 2013
13. Guidelines for Protection of National Critical Information Infrastructure, Version 1.0 (June 2013), issued by National Critical Information Infrastructure Protection Centre

14. Indian Army Doctrine, First edition, October 2004

15. Cyber Deterrence and Cyberwar, Rand Corporation monograph by Martin C. Libicki

16. UN Convention on Cybercrime, CETS No.: 185

17. Tallinn Manual on the International Law Applicable to Cyber warfare

18. National Security Threats in Cyberspace, Post-Workshop Report by Paul Rosenzweig

19. India's National Security – Challenges and Priorities, Talk by by Shri P Chidambaram, 06 Feb 6, 2013

20. Revamping India's National Security Architecture for Optimum Synergy in the Use of its Instruments of National Power, The 18th Pyara Lal Memorial Lecture, 2014 by Shri Shyam Saran, IFS (Retd)

21. National Cyber Security Framework Manual, Edited by Alexander Klimburg

Articles

22. From Cyberspace to Cyberpower, Defining the Problem, Dr Dan Kuehl

23. NASSCOM-DSCI Cyber Security Advisory Group Report

24. Cyber Operations: The New Balance by Col Stephen W. Korns

25. Cyber-weapons: legal and strategic aspects by Stefano Mele

26. Cyber war is coming! by John Arquilla and David Ronfeldt

27. Thresholds for Cyberwar by James A. Lewis

28. Understanding Cyber Weapons by Colonel Sanjeev Relia, USI Journal Dec 13

29. Living with Cyber Espionage by Colonel Sanjeev Relia, USI Journal Jun 14

Index

D

E

F

G

H

I

J

L